2004

SHAKESPEARE, LAW, AND MARRIAGE

This interdisciplinary study combines legal, historical and literary approaches to the practice and theory of marriage in Shakespeare's time. It uses the history of English law and the history of the contexts of law to study a wide range of Shakespeare's plays and poems. The authors approach the legal history of marriage as part of cultural history. The household was viewed as the basic unit of Elizabethan society, but many aspects of marriage were controversial, and the law relating to marriage was uncertain and confusing, leading to bitter disagreements over the proper modes for marriage choice and conduct. The authors point out numerous instances within Shakespeare's plays of the conflict over status, gender relations, property, religious belief, and individual autonomy versus community control. By achieving a better understanding of these issues, the book illuminates both Shakespeare's work and his age.

B. J. SOKOL is Professor of English at Goldsmiths College, University of London. Mary Sokol is Honorary Research Fellow at University College London and is also a lawyer. They have collaborated previously on a number of articles and are joint authors of *Shakespeare's Legal Language* (2000), a comprehensive reference work on the vast number of legal terms and phrases used throughout Shakespeare's plays and sonnets.

SHAKESPEARE, LAW, AND MARRIAGE

B. J. SOKOL AND MARY SOKOL

CAMBRIDGE
UNIVERSITY PRESS

PUBLISHED BY THE PRESS SYNDICATE OF THE UNIVERSITY OF CAMBRIDGE
The Pitt Building, Trumpington Street, Cambridge, United Kingdom

CAMBRIDGE UNIVERSITY PRESS
The Edinburgh Building, Cambridge, CB2 2RU, UK
40 West 20th Street, New York, NY 10011–4211, USA
477 Williamstown Road, Port Melbourne, VIC 3207, Australia
Ruiz de Alarcón 13, 28014 Madrid, Spain
Dock House, The Waterfront, Cape Town 8001, South Africa

http://www.cambridge.org

© B. J. Sokol and Mary Sokol 2003

First published 2003

Printed in the United Kingdom at the University Press, Cambridge

Typeface Adobe Garamond 11/12.5 pt.   *System* LaTeX 2_ε [TB]

A catalogue record for this book is available from the British Library

Library of Congress Cataloguing in Publication data
Sokol, B. J.
Shakespeare, law, and marriage / B. J. Sokol and Mary Sokol.
p.   cm.
Includes bibliographical references (p.) and index.
ISBN 0 521 82263 7
1. Shakespeare, William, 1564–1616 – Knowledge – Manners and customs.   2. Marriage in
literature.   3. Shakespeare, William, 1564–1616 – Knowledge – Law.   4. Marriage – England –
History – 16th century.   5. Marriage – England – History – 17th century.   6. Law and
literature – History – 16th century.   7. Law and literature – History – 17th century.
8. Law in literature.   I. Sokol, Mary, 1945–   II. Title.
PR3069.M32.S65   2003
822.3′3 – dc21   2003048481

ISBN 0 521 82263 7 hardback

For our sisters Nancy Sokol and Lee Langley

Contents

Acknowledgments

As our bibliography indicates, our understanding is vastly in debt to many scholars. In addition we have gained a great deal from discussions with our students of legal history at the University of Sussex, and of Shakespeare at Goldsmiths College, the University of London. A great deal has been gained also from papers and discussions we have attended at the London Legal History Seminar and at successive Stratford-upon-Avon International Shakespeare Conferences. Among many others who have helped and inspired us we wish to thank especially Andrew Lewis, Stanley Wells, David Crankshaw, Theresa Sutton, Inga-Stina Ewbank, and Fr Robert Hanson. We also wish to thank Sarah Stanton at Cambridge University Press, and an anonymous reader for the Press, for many valuable suggestions.

Goldsmiths College and its English Department provided study leave and other forms of valuable support, and we wish to thank especially Helen Carr for making this possible. The Public Record Office, the British Library in London and at Boston Spa, and the University of London Libraries at the Senate House, the Institute for Historical Research, and the Institute for Advanced Legal Studies have provided the vital sources of this study. Long may such citadels of learning survive and thrive.

Abbreviations: Shakespeare titles

Unless otherwise noted we cite all Shakespeare texts from the electronic version of the Oxford Shakespeare, edited by Wells and Taylor, 1989. This edition supplies the title abbreviations used in the notes, and the lineation used in the notes and running text. We append a table of the Oxford edition Shakespeare title abbreviations.

1H4	*Henry IV, part 1*
1H6	*Henry VI, part 1*
2H4	*Henry IV, part 2*
ADO	*Much Ado About Nothing*
AIT	*All Is True (Henry VIII)*
ANT	*Antony and Cleopatra*
AWW	*All's Well That Ends Well*
AYL	*As You Like It*
COR	*Coriolanus*
CYL	*The First Part of the Contention (Henry VI, part 2)*
CYM	*Cymbeline*
ERR	*The Comedy of Errors*
H5	*Henry V*
HAM	*Hamlet*
JC	*Julius Caesar*
JN	*King John*
LC	*A Lover's Complaint*
LLL	*Love's Labour's Lost*
LRF	*The Tragedy of King Lear* (Folio)
LRQ	*The History of King Lear* (Quarto)
LUC	*The Rape of Lucrece*
MAC	*Macbeth*
MM	*Measure for Measure*
MND	*A Midsummer Night's Dream*

MV	The Merchant of Venice
OTH	Othello
PER	Pericles, Prince of Tyre
R2	Richard II
R3	Richard III
RDY	Richard, Duke of York (Henry VI, part 3)
ROM	Romeo and Juliet
SHR	The Taming of the Shrew
SON	Sonnets
STM	Sir Thomas More
TGV	The Two Gentlemen of Verona
TIM	Timon of Athens
TIT	Titus Andronicus
TMP	The Tempest
TN	Twelfth Night, or What You Will
TNK	The Two Noble Kinsmen
TRO	Troilus and Cressida
VEN	Venus and Adonis
WIV	The Merry Wives of Windsor
WT	The Winter's Tale

Introduction

Shakespeare, in common with many of his fellow dramatists and with his society in general, was fascinated by law. His and other Elizabethan drama also focused a great deal of attention on complex, often legal, issues surrounding contemporary marriage. So the subject of the present study – Shakespeare, law, and marriage – is a large one.

Before turning to matters having specific bearing on that subject, this Introduction will outline some of the historical reasons for the great importance of the law of marriage, and indeed law in general, in everyday Elizabethan life. Observations of the litigiousness of Shakespeare's age will lead to descriptions of some of the more important jurisdictions active in the period. We will then offer examples (chosen because reflected by Shakespeare) of some of the innovations made by Elizabethan jurisdictions, and some of the dynamically changing relations between them. The impression we hope to convey is that of a legal situation that was not static, but which rather expressed the pressing social desires and needs of the age.

OUR PURPOSES

There are now new possibilities and a new need for a study of Shakespeare, law, and marriage. Shakespeare scholars are increasingly interested in the insights that can be gained by studying the laws and legal institutions of Shakespeare's world. We welcome this development, and indeed hope to contribute to it and to demonstrate its advantages in practical ways. At the same time, new studies have advanced the investigation of early modern English law and its essential contexts. Some of the legal–historical materials often used by Shakespeare scholars have become distinctly dated, and so we will update older discussions of the Elizabethan laws of marriage by reference to new, or to very new, work. Also, other older but still very valuable legal–historical studies will be re-addressed here in relation to their applications in Shakespeare studies. This is because certain confusions have crept into the use of these, and in some cases these confusions have become entrenched and have produced misleading orthodoxies. For instance, insufficient distinctions have sometimes been made by Shakespearians between legal debates, legal proposals, enacted laws, and laws enacted but not enforced.

However, our aims go beyond contributing to, updating, or offering corrective revisions for an advancing interdisciplinary field of study. We also hope that this book will produce an impression of how profoundly influenced Shakespeare and his audiences were by the contemporary legal and allied social, political, and intellectual backgrounds. The value of obtaining such an impression is not merely the satisfaction of antiquarian curiosity. For we believe that in many ways Shakespeare may become more our 'contemporary' (in the true sense that he speaks to our vital concerns and interests) as he becomes more his own contemporary (in our understanding). This paradox is explained by the fact that if we can better appreciate the considerable differences and also similarities between Shakespeare's time and ours, then we can better empathise with the ways in which his remarkable art embodied, measured, and responded to a complex and disagreement-riven society, no less dynamic and unpredictable than our own.

We propose, therefore, that we can better enjoy and learn from such art the more we can grasp its contexts.

KNOWLEDGE OF LAW, AND LITIGIOUSNESS

These contexts, especially in relation to Elizabethan marriage, may seem extremely alien today. Indeed, today many people are unfamiliar with even our contemporary laws of marriage. Every year a new group of law students respond with astonishment and disbelief when they learn of the fate of Valerie Burns who, despite living with her partner for seventeen years and bringing up their children, found that when they separated she had no rights in the family home in English law. A wife would have done.[1] These students, together with many people, erroneously believe that there is such a thing as a 'common law marriage' that makes cohabitation equivalent to marriage, unaware that to date marriage still confers a distinct new legal status on the wife and husband.

In Shakespeare's England, a similar unawareness was most unlikely. Rather, there was then a widespread lively appreciation of the legal significance of marriage. As we will see, this greater awareness of the law of marriage accorded with several important social factors. Marriage then had far more serious legal consequences (especially for women). Many people then used pre-marital financial legal agreements. There were heated religious and political controversies over the laws governing formation of valid marriages. Moreover, there was much greater awareness then in all ranks of society of the language and institutions of law.

It will be helpful to note how often Shakespeare's contemporaries would have come into contact with law. As premature mortality in families was common, and people of all sorts attempted to make some provision for widows and children, many of them would have encountered the customary or testamentary procedures governing the disposition of property after death. In the countryside and towns, landowners from the smallest to the greatest were familiar with the complexities of the land law, often personally dealing with freeholds, leases, taxes, tithes, and conveyancing. Even without land, merchants, masters and their apprentices, and servants, also needed to understand a wide range of legal arrangements.

Many in Shakespeare's audiences would have negotiated commercial agreements, marriage settlements, employment, and other contractual matters. Therefore, without having anything extraordinary happening in their lives to account for it, they would have been familiar with the sorts of private agreements called in his plays 'specialties' (*LLL* 2.1.164, *SHR* 2.1.126). These could have included indentures, recognisances, bonds, statutes merchant, deeds of gift (each of these are mentioned by Shakespeare), and other sealed or unsealed contractual instruments. Such private legal documents were 'drawn between' parties, as Petruchio of *The Taming of the Shrow* puts it, for good order and to avoid future litigation.

That good intent to avoid dispute, however, was far from always successful. Partly in consequence, a late Elizabethan population of about four million persons were involved in over one million legal actions every year![2] Some of these court actions were collusive, using fictitious disagreements to get on record previously agreed matters, as for example debts, land ownership, or agreed customary rights.[3] Many other actions were genuinely contentious, as in numerous disputes over debt, inheritance, property, or commerce. Some litigants sought private redress or damages for alleged wrongs by bringing 'instance' litigation to the church courts, or 'informations' alleging riot to Star Chamber, or private criminal prosecutions by 'appeal' to the common law courts. In addition, many crimes were prosecuted by the church, local, or royal courts in a restless society in which, it was complained, 'sin of all sorts swarmeth'.[4]

THE COURT JURISDICTIONS, THEIR RELATIONS
AND INNOVATIONS

Such enormous volumes of litigation were heard in a large range of some-times overlapping, sometimes competitive, sometimes co-operative, some-times waning, sometimes burgeoning, sometimes conservative, and sometimes innovatory jurisdictions.

Repeated attempts were made to distinguish jurisdictional boundaries, as in the writs *Circumspecte agatis* (1285) and *Articuli cleri* (1315) which re-served to the church courts and away from common law courts matters of marriage, bastardy, inheritance of personal property (but not land), and the punishment of fornication, adultery, etc.[5] These courts, which had jurisdiction over English marriage until the nineteenth century, are often discussed later, especially in chapter 1, but we offer an overview here. The post-Reformation English church courts included the archdeaconry courts, the consistory courts presided over by the bishops, and the two provincial courts at Canterbury and at York which could hear appeals from consis-tory courts. Because the most severe punishment the church courts could order was excommunication, some early Jacobean members of Parliament attempted to remove some of their moral jurisdiction and increase the powers of the royal courts. For a variety of reasons, these attempts failed.[6] What could have happened had they succeeded, and Parliament had, for instance, made fornication a capital felony (as it was to be under the Commonwealth), may well have inspired the structure of Shakespeare's *Measure for Measure*.[7]

Shakespeare named or alluded to a number of the contemporary juris-dictions, but these were by no means all of, or even the most prominent of, the law courts known to his audiences. For instance, Falstaff is threat-ened with a Star Chamber action for riot in *The Merry Wives of Windsor* 1.1.1–31. Although allegations of riot were often made by Elizabethan landowners as fictional devices to get cases heard in Star Chamber to 'an-noy one's neighbour'[8] or to gain tactical advantages in litigation in other jurisdictions,[9] in Falstaff's case it seems that he actually did violently break into a park to steal deer (1.1.102–9). This factuality might have brought a smile to the faces of the legally knowing in Shakespeare's audience, as it made literal an often-alleged fictional action.[10]

The prerogative court of Star Chamber was a good example of an innova-tory jurisdiction. By Shakespeare's time (from the 1560s) Star Chamber had ceded to the central common law court of Common Pleas all questions over the title to land, but it had become more important than ever before because it was developing a body of new law relating to serious misdemeanours. These included inchoate criminal offences such as conspiracy and attempt, and libel, forgery, fraud, perjury, corruption of jurors, extortion, vexatious litigation, maintenance, and fraudulent Parliamentary elections.[11] (Falstaff indulged happily in almost all of these practices.) Because it did not use grand juries or juries, in accord with Magna Carta the Star Chamber could not try felonies punishable by death, but it did impose lesser corporal punishments. It is apparently mythical that the Star Chamber used torture, and its criminal procedure did allow the accused to give evidence in their own defence, unlike that of the common law courts.[12]

In another instance of innovation, incremental developments in the common law courts of 'actions on the case' were leading in Shakespeare's time towards the development of a new civil law of tort. Such actions on the case circumvented the narrow restrictions of the required formulaic writs for trespass *vi et armis* used in medieval times for access to the courts of King's Bench and Common Pleas. They therefore theoretically made possible new ways of enforcing contractual undertakings. Yet, despite allegations by a number of Shakespeare scholars, the possibilities of such contractual actions were not yet widely exploited in Shakespeare's time, and so these did not indicate a great paradigm shift in society.[13]

Shakespeare mentions actions on the case in a punning way in *The Comedy of Errors* 4.2.41–51, and in an obscenely punning way when Mistress Quickly in *Henry IV, part 2* 2.1.30–1 says her 'exion is entered, and my case so openly known to the world'. The implications of Quickly's lawsuit are interesting because although she is seen appointing officers to arrest Falstaff for debt, the special sort of an action on the case called *assumpsit* was just about to become available for complaints of breach of a promise to marry. Quickly hilariously muddles her complaints to the bemused Chief Justice about both the money Falstaff owes her and his unmet promises to marry her (*2H4* 2.1.87–105).

Again we see that developments of legal technicalities are treated in a wickedly knowing manner by Shakespeare. Here and elsewhere Shakespeare also alludes to legal matters that are unstated but were undoubtedly well understood by the legally sophisticated in his audiences. The use of *assumpsit* in debt collection was a ploy to use the cheaper jurisdiction of Queen's Bench, where otherwise an action on a writ of debt would be required in the more expensive court of Common Pleas.[14] Prohibitions issued by Common Pleas disallowing this were first upheld, and then overturned, in case law of Shakespeare's time;[15] this was just one instance of the ways in which the more conservative courts were losing business and

fees to the more innovative ones.[16] The contemporary decline of the jurisdictions of the summary Courts Merchant, the civilian law jurisdiction of
Admiralty, the Courts Staple, and local Leet courts, did not prevent Shakespeare from mentioning or alluding to these;[17] it is possible that the relative
safety of mentioning declining or near-defunct jurisdictions, which lacked
the powerful sway to do him harm, rather than anachronism, led prudent
Shakespeare to his choice of allusions. For example, he never directly mentioned the central common law courts at Westminster Hall in London:
Common Pleas, Queen's Bench, Chancery, and Exchequer Chamber.[18]

JURISDICTIONAL CONFLICTS, AND THE QUESTION
OF SHAKESPEARE AND EQUITY

When the jurisdictions of Shakespeare's time overlapped they did not necessarily coincide. Several examples come readily to hand. For instance, Star
Chamber and the common law courts each treated and defined slander
differently from one another, and from the church courts.[19] In certain circumstances the church courts would disagree with the common law courts
concerning findings of illegitimacy.[20] Numerous litigants began Chancery
cross-pleadings to block common law actions, while some opponents of
particularly the newer prerogative courts played on jurisdictional differences for political reasons.

It was even possible for very serious charges of *praemunire* to be brought
against litigants seeking to exploit inter-jurisdictional prohibitions or injunctions; such a threat arose when attacks, particularly on the prerogative
courts of Chancery and High Commission, came to a head in the spec-
tacular events of 1616 that included the dismissal of the Chief Justice, Sir
Edward Coke.

Beyond the personal enmity of Coke and Lord Chancellor Egerton, the
constitutional and philosophical background of this crisis was very complex,
and has often been over-simplified. It is salutary to remember that 'progressive' pro-Parliamentary, pro-common-law, and anti-royal-prerogative
propaganda found equity the villain in the case. For alleged differences
between equity and law have frequently been treated by Shakespeare critics
as differences in which law has the complexion of the villain. In an attempt
to clarify often-confused matters, we have recently presented a detailed
historical study of this tradition in Shakespeare criticism, and of the actual
events and attitudes of the times in which Shakespeare lived.[21]

In briefest outline, we have found that Shakespeare (perhaps) alludes to
the equity jurisdiction of Chancery once only, in a passage of *The History of*

King Lear (Quarto) that was perhaps significantly expurgated in *The Tragedy of King Lear* (Folio). The Lord Chancellor (a role assigned by Lear to his Fool) is probably indicated in mad Lear's invitation to the 'commission' to try Goneril: 'Thou robed man of justice, take thy place; / And thou, his yokefellow of equity, / Bench by his side' (*LRQ* s.13.32–4). State trials, such as that of Mary Queen of Scots, involved a panel of judges including the Lord Chancellor and the Chief Justice. This fact and much other historical evidence indicate that equity and law were far from at loggerheads, but in fact co-operative and increasingly so throughout most of Shakespeare's career. In many matters brought before him, as for instance mercantile disputes, Lord Chancellor Egerton refused to hear the case and reserved it to the common law courts. The common law and equity judges knew one another well and routinely consulted one another.[22] Common law judges sat on Chancery cases and by a long-held tradition important civil cases were referred to 'all the judges of England' who would sit together to hear argument.[23]

The reasons for including this precis of our detailed arguments elsewhere are two. For one, the notion that equity, as opposed to common law, was unbounded by rules and therefore was more just or merciful than the inflexible or tyrannous strictures of law, is a misleading commonplace that has repeatedly been applied in analyses of various Shakespearian plays.[24] It thereby serves as a paradigm for some of the dangers, when legal matters are related to Shakespeare's works, of accepting critical notions based originally on reading old propaganda as historical fact, in the place of attending to the complexities of history.[25]

There is also a second reason that makes condign here some consideration of the equity jurisdictions of Shakespeare's time. This is because treatments of early modern law and marriage must consider equity because the court of Chancery was then developing a way for married women to overcome some of the extreme legal disabilities imposed on them by the doctrine of coverture. In particular Chancery upheld trusts or uses for the benefit of married women which operated to preserve some of their own property from the otherwise unlimited rights of their husbands to control or even dispose of it (those rights are very explicitly described by Portia in *The Merchant of Venice* 3.2.150–71). These matters will be gone into in detail in chapter 7. Here it is worth mentioning some important peripheral circumstances. For one, the equity courts were not performing an *ad hoc* function guided by the Chancellor's conscience when the devices making possible married women's separate estates were upheld. Rather, they were following, or developing further, the principles upon which equity had long protected trusts or uses. However, the advantages accruing to women from these developments were often offset by the possibilities that trusts could be used against women's interests. For although the inexpensive equity court of Requests did protect some poor widows,[26] for the most part the costs and complexities of using equity to protect married women's property were great. This meant that in practice separate estates were often protected for the benefit of the wealthy families of married women and not for the benefit of the women themselves. The aims of these families were to protect wealth in a way that was more likely to limit than to enhance the women's independence.[27]

A further point to be made about Elizabethan married women's equitable estates is that Shakespeare never mentions them. He does, however, portray a great many independently minded single, widowed, or even married women. Such women are often found flourishing in quite fantastic circumstances, such as in forests or (wholly chaste) in a brothel of Mytilene. However, in the much more real-seeming world of the earlier acts of *The Merry Wives*, married Englishwomen (not to mention the unmarried daughter of one of them, Anne Page, with her own estate), seem to follow the pattern described recently by Tim Stretton, who claims that 'many married women went about their daily lives as if the concept [of coverture] did not exist'.[28]

SHAKESPEARIAN MODES

In what modes did Shakespeare's drama express these alleged social realities, or behind them such influential legal realities as wives' separate equitable estate? We find three modes characteristic of Shakespeare's deployment of legal materials and ideas. In one mode Shakespeare creates a dramatic 'mirrorland' in which (within margins of verisimilitude allowing dramatic shorthand or other artistic licence) his drama more or less realistically represents actual and well-known practices of English law. In a second mode Shakespeare creates a legal 'fableland' where folkloric, biblical, or stereotypical images hold sway in tales of, say, wicked power, justice abused, but truth at last triumphant. In a third mode a Shakespeare play presents a 'fantastical mooting' where impossibly complex contrived legal situations are premised. Fantastical moots may merely amuse with challenging riddles, or they may lead to instructive intellectual dead ends, *aporia*, intended to test received ideas or methods in a kind of poetic stress laboratory. These modes may also interact; Shakespeare produces fascinating generic and dramatic effects, for example in *Measure for Measure*, by allowing slippage between fantastical mooting, dramatic mirroring, and legal fables. Despite such intricacies we may generalise on one point: in nearly all cases where legal matters come into question, Shakespeare's dramatic articulation alludes to actual English legal problems, ambiguities, or enigmas.

OUR STRUCTURE

In order to unravel a subject matter which is in textual and social terms tentacular, and in intellectual and historical ones labyrinthine, this book is organised around a deliberately simple framework. Its chapters follow, in mainly serial order, the chronological stages of a marriage, from courtship, through valid formation, then through events in its duration, until its end in either separation, divorce, or death. Each of these stages will be discussed in relation to their frequent Shakespearian representations, as well as being furnished with in-depth legal–historical discussions.

In our view such discussions must not be narrow. For we believe that law cannot be seen only as an agency of state power, or else as a set of professional technical rules, but rather that law and legal debates reflect far wider social and cultural contexts. For example, in chapter 3 we will discuss the legal institution of wardship in relation to early modern arranged marriages. In this case, a historical perspective based only on a narrow view of the political and legislative agitation in King James's first Parliament concerning the abuses of wardship would distort the issues involved. We must consider also the widely accepted social practice of sending adolescent children away from home to live in other households for education or training. So, in one Shakespearian instance, the wardship of young Count Bertram is not first introduced in *All's Well That Ends Well* in the familiar terms of the contemporary politicised debates concerning cruel, greedy, or negligent guardians. His forced marriage is in fact supported by his widowed mother, just the opposite of the pattern typically alleged as an abuse of wardship. The questions of his possible disparagement, and the validity of his consent to marry, are problematised rather than propagandised by Shakespeare.

Moreover, wider questions surrounding Bertram's marriage to Helena, and other resonant questions about marriage implicit in *All's Well*, are treated elsewhere in our book under a range of different heads, as well as within discussions of wardship and arranged marriage. This is typical of our method, in which a single play or important Shakespearian marriage may be discussed in several different chapters under the headings of varied and often multiple issues.

We believe that such an issue-based approach, sometimes bringing to bear more than one legal viewpoint on a particular text or passage, does not unnecessarily over-complicate Shakespeare's dramatic microcosms. Rather, it can reveal true intricacy, for Shakespeare's fictions and problems often reflected how complexly contemporary marriage expressed a web of social, sexual, religious, ethical, jurisprudential, political, and even constitutional issues.

OUR CHAPTERS

Finally, it may be useful to indicate some of the contents of and connections between our nine chapters.

In chapter 1 we begin, as we think a book on law and marriage must, with topics surrounding the logically prior question of what exactly made a legally valid marriage in Shakespeare's England. A simple rule, that the formation of a contract by the present mutual consent of bride and groom (as long as they were eligible to marry) made an indissoluble marriage, certainly applied. But that very simplicity brought in almost innumerable quandaries. The question of what constituted present consent (since no particular words, ceremonies, or gestures were specified) gave rise to many contentions. So, for instance, portions of *As You Like It* and *Measure for Measure* focus (lightheartedly and enigmatically respectively) on almost parodic exaggerations of such difficulties. Indeed an extraordinary range of legal and social problems, many having Shakespearian reflections, arose in various ways from the 'consensual model' underlying the legal definition of marriage for Shakespeare's England. Thus the principles discussed in our first chapter may be said to be foundational, and will be seen to permeate nearly all that follows.

Indeed all the chapters of this book are interactive in various ways, and some in a schematically reciprocal fashion. For example, chapter 4 on the provision of dowries concerns privately made legal arrangements. And yet the private and public domains of law interacted when dowries funded widows' jointures (as they often did). For then the public law deriving from Henry VIII's momentous Statute of Uses linked pre-marital economic arrangements (often based on dowries) with the legal rights of English widows to support from their late husbands' estates. Thus the dowries treated in chapter 4 were very often vitally linked with the issues taken up in our final chapter concerning widows and the aftermath of marriages.[29]

Other sorts of interaction or reciprocity will be seen between the matters discussed in chapter 2, which concerns family pressures on marriage choices, and chapter 3, which concerns the legal imposition of certain kinds of marriage, and between both of these chapters and the financial matters surrounding marriage formation discussed in chapter 4. All of these complex connections will be seen to be reflected in Shakespeare's plays.

The extraordinary degree of autonomy theoretically available under the consensual model to eligible Elizabethan or Jacobean marriage partners (much greater than is available today) was of course a main issue of the times. The financial and other familial pressures that could be used to direct marriage choices were obsessive themes, treated *pro* or *con*, of the Shakespearian stage. In addition to such practices, there were proposed and actual legal attempts made to restrict this autonomy. The first and crucial point to grasp is that no such attempts made in Shakespeare's England ever succeeded in making invalid a marriage formed by consent alone. However, they did make such marriages illicit, and forming them was a (usually mildly) punishable offence. The complexities over this are discussed, with their many Shakespearian reflections, in chapters 5 and 6. These chapters are strictly reciprocal. Chapter 5 discusses the highly contentious requirement imposed by the Elizabethan Act of Uniformity that marriages must be solemnised according to the words and rubrics of the Book of Common Prayer. Chapter 6 discusses the converse matter of unsolemnised or 'clandestine' marriages, and then goes on to discuss irregular marriage formation in elopement, abduction, or ravishment. There are many subtle Shakespeare references to the contemporary religio-politico-legal Prayer Book controversies. We especially discuss some important formerly unnoted ones in *Much Ado About Nothing*, *The Tempest*, and particularly *The Shrew* and *All's Well*. Shakespeare's treatments of unsolemnised, clandestine, or runaway marriages are widely varied; we show that the mixed treatments in various of his plays of clandestine marriage reflect contemporary highly inconsistent social and legal attitudes and practices.

Chapter 7 deals with the legal status of married people and the resulting theory and practice of relations between husbands and wives. Although both the legally required Prayer Book ceremony and the reigning ideology taught a 'companionate' style of marriage (which was not necessarily a uniquely Protestant innovation), lack of mutual affection and/or abuses of household patriarchal power sometimes could lead to violence, as discussed in this chapter, or to marriage breakdown as discussed in chapter 8. That chapter, concerning separation or divorce, and the following chapter 9, considering widowhood and orphans, treat the ending of marriages, a topic that was perhaps surprisingly no less interesting to Shakespeare than the romantic formation or sometimes difficult continuation of marriages.

Marriage and family were the central institutions of private life for Shakespeare's contemporaries. They were also the basis of the household, which was seen as the basic building block of society.[30] The issues that marriage threw up are therefore not surprisingly among the most prevalent ones reflected in the plots and structures, and also the textures and motivations, of the plays of Shakespeare's age. It is our contention that the greatest dramatist of those times gave such matters their greatest treatment.[31]

CHAPTER I

Making a valid marriage: the consensual model

SPOUSALS

> I have heard lawyers say a contract in a chamber
> *Per verba de presenti* is absolute marriage:–
> Bless heaven, this sacred Gordian, which let violence
> Never untwine.

Today it is almost unbelievable that a valid marriage could have been created as informally as it was seen to be in John Webster's play *The Duchess of Malfi*. Yet the above few words, spoken by Webster's Duchess,[1] quite properly describe the simple process that allowed willing couples to be married in Shakespeare's age.[2]

The Duchess's remark makes an explicit (if perhaps defensive) reference to legality, and also refers to an indissoluble Gordian knot. In so doing, she correctly claims that the secret union she is about to form with her steward Antonio will be 'absolute marriage'. She then marries privately, without any written licence or other form of permission from Church or state. She is not married in a church. There are no clergy present, and no religious rites. Her family play no part and there is no more publicity than the witnessing presence of a waiting woman. No particular formal words or ritual words are spoken. Rather, she and Antonio express, using highly figurative language, their agreement to be married. Because they are not prohibited from giving such consent (by 'impediments' of incest, bigamy, or incapacity to express consent), they are then immediately and irrevocably married.

In this scene Webster portrays the creation of a valid and binding marriage by what was known as spousals. Through the Duchess Webster foregrounds a legal opinion that was relevant to such a case. Shakespeare also repeatedly portrayed marriage by spousals, but with much less bluntness, and frequently (as we shall see) with more ambiguity. This accords with a general difference between Shakespeare and some of his rivals: Shakespeare continually relied on the recognition of the principles, procedures, oddities, and enigmas of contemporary laws concerning marriage, but his handling of such matters was typically complex, ingrained, and implicit rather than simplified, highlighted, or explicit.[3] We shall see, for example, that Shakespeare dealt with divorce repeatedly and in many different ways, yet did not fill his plays with the technical legal details and legal jargon found, for instance, in Ben Jonson's *Epicoene* concerning the laws of divorce.

In our conclusion we will offer an assessment of Shakespeare's characteristically complex modes of treating issues arising from the law concerning marriage. But first it is necessary to set out and discuss the circumstances and history of that law, and to match matters arising from such discussions with the dramatic instances on which they bear.

The present chapter will begin such an analysis at its natural starting point, by considering in detail the consensual model of marriage that allowed marriage formation by spousals. We will reserve the term 'spousals' here to mean the act that formed the contract constituting a valid marriage.[4] As we have seen, this sort of contract was made by the two consenting parties, and by them alone. Their consent (expressed in the present tense) was all that was required by law to form a valid marriage. The marriage was then indissoluble and, except for arguments over evidence of spousals, incontestable.

That notwithstanding, a marriage by spousals alone, although legally binding and valid, had serious limitations. It was quite possible both to be legally married, and yet to be fined by the church courts for marrying in a 'clandestine' manner, that is, without church solemnisation.[5] Such marriages were disapproved of, but not uncommon. In a notorious example, the church courts summoned the Queen's Attorney General, Sir Edward Coke, to answer charges that in 1598 he had privately married the young widow Lady Elizabeth Hatton without either a church blessing or a public ceremony.

Thanks to the power of spousals to form valid marriages, a remarkable autonomy (almost unimaginable today) was theoretically available to men and women in Shakespeare's England. This autonomy derived from the logic that mutual consent alone was required for marriage. Yet spousals were also the starting point for what may seem an illogicality. This was that they created a wholly legal, yet not a wholly licit, marriage. For although spousals made a marriage that was binding and valid, yet marriage by spousals alone was viewed as an offence by both society and Church law. This contradiction was regarded by many contemporaries as unsatisfactory, and especially by families who deplored the excessive freedom – as they saw it – allowed a bride and groom.

Other difficulties over spousals arose from the definition of consent itself. According to Henry Swinburne's important (if not entirely reliable) *Treatise of Spousals or Matrimonial Contracts*, written c. 1600,[6] consent to marry was legally understood to be an inward state, constituted by a sober and well-considered intention. No particular formula of words or deeds was required to give valid consent; a variety of signs, not all of them even verbal, was accepted as sufficient to indicate the existence of this consenting state. Not surprisingly, there were often difficulties in the interpretation of such signs, as seen in many cases contested in church courts.

Indications of inward states by words or gestures are also fundamental to drama. Law courts, like theatre audiences, may find that this is problematic because communication and verification of 'authentic' inner intent is not an easy matter.[7] For the law of evidence in disputed marriage cases, as for the theatre, the opinions of spectators were crucial. In contested cases over spousals two witnesses at the least were required by the church courts, which caused many problems.[8] As we shall see in chapter 6, witnesses (including lawyers and clergy) could be punished or even excommunicated if they had attended clandestine marriages. Also, witnesses to marriages or marriage negotiations could be biased in favour of one party or the other, or like Shakespeare himself they may have had unreliable memories.[9]

Confusion about spousals was a lively topic which often inspired Elizabethan or Jacobean playwrights. We will see that, regardless of the period or locale of his dramatic settings, Shakespeare's depictions of marriage usually mirrored the laws and practices of contemporary England. Yet, because those laws were so perplexing, Shakespeare's plays also often posited or mooted extremely complex situations concerning spousals. Whether he used mirror-like modes of representation, or fantastically mooted complexities, it does seem that Shakespeare was somewhat spousal obsessed; representations of spousals are found in a wide variety of his dramatic settings, and they serve many differing dramatic purposes.

We may get a sharper sense of the sort of problems created by the contemporary marriage laws by noting briefly the failure of one attempt at reform. The post-Reformation statute 32 Hen. VIII c.38 (1540) set out to remedy an alleged abuse due to the 'usurped Power of the Bishop of Rome'.[10] This abuse was that church courts would invalidate a marriage (as bigamous) whenever either man or wife were shown to have previously made an earlier marriage contract (spousals) with another party. So a longstanding consummated marriage, perhaps with children, could be undone by disclosure of a prior unconsummated contract. But this Act of 1540, far from curing the problem, itself turned out to be the cause of further abuses. The Act is titled 'An Act concerning Pre-contracts of Marriages, and touching Degrees of Consanguinity'.[11] The 'pre-' in the term 'pre-contracts' implies that after a spousal contract some further legal steps were needed to form a binding marriage, which was not true.[12] However, 'pre-' does correctly indicate that spousals were generally understood to be only part of a marriage process to be accompanied by public announcement, church solemnisation, and various celebrations.

To prevent longstanding marriages being overturned, the Act deemed 'lawful good just and indissoluble, notwithstanding any [prior] Pre-contract or Pre-contracts of Matrimony not consummate with bodily Knowledge' any marriage that is made 'within this Church of *England* . . . being contract and solemnised in the Face of the Church, and consummate with bodily Knowledge or Fruit of Children or Child'. The Act removed from the church courts powers to dissolve such a subsequent consummated marriage, claiming to put right a source of notorious abuse. However, only eight years later this Act was repealed by 2 & 3 Edw. VI c.23 (1548), because it had itself resulted in unforeseen 'ungodly' abuses, or 'divers Inconveniences (intolerable in manners to Christian Ears and Eyes)'. Risking offence to ears and eyes, the Act did name the abuses where feigned pre-contracts served lust: 'Women and Men breaking their own Promises and Faiths . . . set upon Sensuality and Pleasure'.[13] The legislators' good intentions had overlooked the human propensity to act on 'bodily Lust'; attempts at legal regulation of 'Faith and Truth' had allowed the pretext of (an invalid) marriage to be used for seduction.

HISTORY

The failure of Henry VIII's 1540 attempted legal reform illustrates how efforts to regulate marriage were fraught with difficulties and paradoxes in Tudor England (indeed they still are today). Such problems had a long European history. Most difficulties over marriage contracts still relevant in Shakespeare's age had their beginning in disagreements between canonists in twelfth-century Europe on the requirements for the formation of a valid marriage.[14] One view, supported by Gratian and the Bolognese school, argued that all that was necessary to make a valid contract of marriage was the consent of both parties to the marriage. Subsequent consummation would then make the marriage indissoluble, but if such a contracted marriage was unconsummated, a second consummated contract would be valid and take precedence over the unconsummated first contract.[15] An alternative view was put forward by Peter Lombard and the Parisian school of canonists, who considered that if the formulation of Gratian was accepted it would raise difficult theological questions about the nature of the marriage between the Virgin Mary and St Joseph. Lombard's argument was that a contract of marriage could be made in two ways: by *verba de praesenti* or *verba de futuro*. The former, words of present consent, immediately created a valid marriage. Nothing more was needed.[16] So an unconsummated contract using words of present consent would take priority over any subsequent marriage, whether or not consummated. However, a contract formed by words of future consent could be dissolved by mutual agreement unless it had been followed by consummation, and if unconsummated would not take priority over a subsequent consummated contract. A contract formed by words of present consent could not be dissolved either unilaterally or by agreement.

A contract *per verba de futuro* could be conditional, with, for example, a condition relating to payment of a marriage portion or the agreement of a parent. In this case the contract did not become a valid marriage until the performance of the condition, unless the marriage was consummated. So, although a marriage *per verba de futuro* could be dissolved by mutual agreement if not consummated, one *per verba de praesenti* could not.

In the late twelfth century Pope Alexander III in a number of decretals accepted the views of Peter Lombard and the Parisian school, in which merely *verba de praesenti* formed a valid marriage.[17] So the consent of parents, or other family, or lords, was not necessary for validity. Nor was endowment at the church door a requirement. Importantly, neither lack of public ceremony nor lack of priestly blessing would invalidate such a marriage. But there were certain circumstances in which no valid contract of marriage could ever be entered into. Here a dirimentary impediment acted to prevent a valid marriage being formed. Impediments included lack of capacity on the part of either party to contract marriage, duress, pre-contract, or prohibitions on marriages between parties related in some way. Evidence of an impediment could prevent a marriage taking place, and could also be produced in a suit for nullity or divorce.[18]

The parties' consent, the sole fact to be established, could be given by words, or by signs such as the giving and receiving of a ring and handfasting,[19] or by the agency of a third party.[20] Handfasting meant the joining of hands accompanied by mutual agreement to be married, either immediately or in the future; giving of a ring could include an exchange of parts of a ring or gifts of other jewellery or even silver coins. Sometimes the consent giving was performed in public, but a private exchange of words or gestures of consent was common and just as binding.

THE CHURCH COURTS AND MARRIAGE FORMATION

Because William I had transferred jurisdiction over matters of spiritual and moral concern from local courts to church courts (although this transfer was not completed until the twelfth century), the enforcement of the law of marriage in later medieval and early modern England was the concern of the Church. So, although the English common law dealt with disputes concerning real property (land) arising from marriage, from the mid-twelfth century until the mid-nineteenth century litigation about formation of marriage took place in the church courts.

By adopting Pope Alexander's consensual model for marriage formation the Western Church also accepted an individualistic view of marriage, in which (in theory) the importance of control by family, feudal lord, king, or church solemnisation was subordinated to individual consent.[21] Perhaps inevitably, this model gave rise to many contentious cases in church courts. In contrast to the present age, in medieval and early modern England there were large numbers of cases concerning the formation of marriage, and few for separation or divorce.[22] The reason for this can be found in two causes: the absence of any Church-required or state-required formalities for making a marriage valid, and the lack of any agreed formula of words to be used by contracting parties.[23]

The jurisdiction of the church courts was divided into non-contentious matters (mostly administrative, such as probate of wills, or grant of marriage licences), and contentious matters, which included disputes over contracts of marriage, divorce, affiliation and custody, support orders, and investigation and punishment of public and private immorality.[24] Contentious cases could be brought as 'instance' cases, or else as *ex officio* ones. Instance cases were the most common. Many of these were brought by one of the parties to an alleged marriage asking for its enforcement, while the other party denied marriage had ever taken place. Alternatively, in multi-party instance cases the court typically considered competing claims by several parties all claiming that the marriage they had entered into was valid, for example where a man had 'married' several women. Often unresolved questions of inheritance of property or legitimacy of children prompted such cases.

Marriage was also often at issue in *ex officio* church court cases, which were usually instigated by an archdeacon, a rural dean, or the bishop himself on the report of suspicious circumstances made to him by a court official, parish officer, or occasionally a third party. These were disciplinary prosecutions for moral and religious offences such as fornication, adultery, wife-beating and neglect, drunkenness, or other breaches of the peace. After Henry VIII forbade the teaching of canon law, the work of the English church courts was undertaken by lawyers trained at university in Roman civil law, referred to by Shakespeare as 'civil doctors'.[25] Although the church courts' records were in Latin, their proceedings were conducted in English so that litigants and witnesses were heard. The large number of prosecutions for marital and sexual offences explains why the church courts were colloquially known as 'bawdy courts', and why their records are of interest to social historians. Long after the Reformation, English church courts continued to play an important role in the public regulation of private morality.

The early modern church courts were often portrayed by later historians as unpopular – at best ineffective (failing to pursue offenders), and at worst corrupt. However, more recently such opinions have been criticised because they were based on evidence provided by the writings of contemporary Puritans who wanted a more strenuous enforcement of public moral discipline, or the pronouncements of common lawyers critical or jealous of the Church's jurisdiction.[26]

SHAKESPEARE AND MAKING A MARRIAGE

The making of a marriage by mutual consent is either described or portrayed in nearly every one of Shakespeare's plays. For instance, Shakespeare often alludes to or portrays marriage formation by handfasting, as in *The Winter's Tale* 1.2.104–7, *Cymbeline* 1.5.78, *All's Well That Ends Well* 2.3.177, *The Winter's Tale* 4.4.381–2, and *The Tempest* 3.1.88–91. Also, in Shakespeare's plays, words of consent to marriage are sometimes replaced by gestures indicating consent.[27] Thus, following Claudio's marriage-contracting words, 'Lady, as you are mine, I am yours. I give away myself for you, and dote upon the exchange', bashful Hero of *Much Ado About Nothing* speaks with no lines audible to the assembled witnesses or the theatre audience. She only whispers in Claudio's ear, and probably also makes her intent outwardly known by taking Beatrice's merry advice to: 'Speak, cousin. Or, if you cannot, stop his mouth with a kiss, and let not him speak, neither' (*ADO* 2.1.288–92).

Indeed, the word 'contract' is almost exclusively reserved in Shakespeare's use for spousal contracts that established marriages.[28] However, the converse is not the case. The making of a marriage contract is variously called by

Shakespeare a spousal, espousal, contract, pre-contract or just marriage. This variety of terms matches the frequency of Shakespearian portrayals of marriage formation. The multiplicity of terms Shakespeare used also alerts us to a nuanced awareness of the practical and theoretical perplexities over marriage contracts in his age.

Some fine distinctions arise where the dramatic portrayal of spousals by Shakespeare is not accompanied by its explicit identification as a marriage. An example lies in the marriage by spousals made between Ferdinand and Miranda in *The Tempest*. There is no basis for the suspicion expressed by one critic that a *per verba de futuro* contract is implied by the wording of their agreement to marry.[29] Rather, they clearly undertake spousals *per verba de praesenti*. For Miranda's 'I am your wife, if you will marry me' (*TMP* 3.1.83) is not in any way a future promise, and if it is conditional the condition is immediately met in Ferdinand's reply to her question 'My husband then?', which is 'Ay, with a heart as willing / As bondage e'er of freedom. Here's my hand.' To this Miranda offers her reply in the form of a traditional handfasting: 'And mine, with my heart in 't' (3.1.88–91). The couple's intention here could not be clearer: it is to express a mutual, immediate, full and unconditional consent to be married, which in turn does make them married. What is odd is that Prospero subsequently makes what he calls the 'gift' of Miranda to Ferdinand, calling this transaction a 'contract' (4.1.8, 4.1.19). For Prospero knows that the pair have already privately expressed their mutual consent. What he has in mind will be discussed in chapter 5, on marriage solemnisation.

Since, if there were no impediments, genuine consent created a marriage, it was typical and correct for contracted parties awaiting (or even in the absence of) church solemnisation of the marriage to be referred to as a 'husband' or 'wife' (as are Kate in *The Taming of the Shrew* 2.1.317 and Antonio in *Measure for Measure* 4.1.70). Yet there was simultaneously a widespread notion that unsolemnised 'betrothal' was different from a solemnised and consummated marriage, and so the language of Shakespeare's plays contains over a dozen references to the betrothed or betrothing, usually referring to eager lovers, and most probably indicating those having undertaken *de futuro* spousals and not yet having solemnised or consummated their union.

Falstaff as a recruiting officer plans to extort money from unwilling 'contracted bachelors, such as had been asked twice on the banns' (*1H4* 4.2.17–18). A gloss on the status of Falstaff's victims as 'contracted bachelors' raises interesting distinctions. 'Bachelors' was mainly used by Shakespeare to specify unmarried men (as in 'Are you a married man or a bachelor?'

JC 3.3.8). But sometimes marriage law made for ambiguity, as in *A Midsummer Night's Dream* 2.2.65 where Hermia calls Lysander a 'virtuous bachelor' in a context in which their marital status following betrothal is at issue. Hermia denies Lysander's wish to sleep by her side, despite his claim that their 'Two bosoms [are] interchained with an oath; / So, then, two bosoms and a single troth' (*MND* 2.2.55–6). So, as far as Hermia was concerned, but not Lysander, betrothal is not full marriage.[30] Both in some sense were right; the Church condemned his wish to consummate a marriage before solemnisation, but it also saw those who were 'interchained with an oath' as fully married.

Claudio's remark, made in response to Hero's father's suggestion that it was he, Claudio, with whom she had had sexual relations before the church ceremony, very probably closely mirrored a typical social attitude (although not Prospero's attitude in *The Tempest*). This attitude is clearly expressed when Romelio in John Webster's *The Devil's Law-Case* holds that 'no scandal' will attach to a pregnancy out of wedlock if a 'precontract' is believed to have been previously 'exactly done'.[31] Claudio says that if he had been Hero's sexual partner, then their status as pre-contracted would 'extenuate the forehand sin' (*ADO* 4.1.50). It is difficult to be certain if the spousals of Claudio and Hero were made *per verba de praesenti*, for, as we have mentioned, Hero's whispered words are not heard by any witness.[32] But even if they had been made *de futuro*, the alleged intercourse would have made the spousals irrevocable.

Thus Claudio alludes to widespread toleration of the 'sin' that legally would turn a *de futuro* marriage contract made sincerely into a full marriage. Such toleration was not extended to those who made insincere promises of marriage for dishonest purposes. Such cases are often treated satirically by Shakespeare. So the scurrilous Lucio is said to have 'promised' Kate Keepdown 'marriage' (*MM* 3.1.458–60), and Falstaff has egregiously broken faith in a long relationship with Mistress Quickly (during 'twenty-nine years come peascod-time', she says in *Henry IV, part 2* 2.4.387).

Proffering a promise of marriage to seduce or for other illicit purposes was an offence. If accepted, such an offer constituted a valid marriage contract, which if unfulfilled could result in fines and an order to do penance in the church courts. This situation is travestied when the Lord Chief Justice is forced to adjudicate when he comes upon a street brawl between Falstaff and the officers attempting to arrest him for his debt to Mistress Quickly. Showing great attention to detail, yet failing to name the two witnesses required by church courts, Quickly claims that Falstaff owes her:

Marry, if thou wert an honest man, thyself, and the money too. Thou didst swear to me upon a parcel-gilt goblet, sitting in my Dolphin chamber, at the round table, by a sea-coal fire, upon Wednesday in Wheeson week, when the Prince broke thy head for liking his father to a singing-man of Windsor – thou didst swear to me then, as I was washing thy wound, to marry me, and make me my lady thy wife. Canst thou deny it? Did not goodwife Keech the butcher's wife come in then, and call me 'Gossip Quickly' – coming in to borrow a mess of vinegar, telling us she had a good dish of prawns, whereby thou didst desire to eat some, whereby I told thee they were ill for a green wound? And didst thou not, when she was gone downstairs, desire me to be no more so familiarity with such poor people, saying that ere long they should call me 'madam'? And didst thou not kiss me, and bid me fetch thee thirty shillings? I put thee now to thy book-oath; deny it if thou canst. (*2H4* 2.1.87–105)

Not minding giving false testimony to the Chief Justice, Sir John does deny it, supplying a marvellous overplus of detail himself:

My lord, this is a poor mad soul, and she says up and down the town that her eldest son is like you. She hath been in good case, and the truth is, poverty hath distracted her. But for these foolish officers, I beseech you I may have redress against them. (*2H4* 2.1.106–10)

The Chief Justice is not impressed, and comes to the point succinctly:

You have, as it appears to me, practised upon the easy-yielding spirit of this woman, and made her serve your uses both in purse and in person . . . Pay her the debt you owe her, and unpay the villainy you have done with her. The one you may do with sterling money, and the other with current repentance. (*2H4* 2.1.116–23)

The Chief Justice has not got sufficient evidence of a marriage contract having been formed, despite the alleged oath on a 'parcel-gilt goblet', and so merely orders a repayment of the debt and repentance for using her sexually. Here the judge either responds to a lack of proven serious consent, which would invalidate spousals according to Swinburne, or possibly his actions reflect a weakness in existing legal means to control 'moral' offences, much complained of by Puritans.[33]

Moving to the opposite end of the social hierarchy, we may note that when Shakespeare dramatised marriages involving important property or political negotiations, the contingent nature of a conditional *de futuro* contract makes the concept of a marital 'pre-contract' unproblematic. Both Princess Margaret in *Henry VI, part 1* and Princess Katherine in *Henry V* agree to marriage with kings of England conditional on their fathers' approval, surely meaning political approval. The former responds with justified caution to Suffolk's proxy wooing (*1H6* 5.5.83), the latter directly to

Henry V, but in broken English: 'Dat is as it shall please de *roi mon père*' (*H5* 5.2.243–5).

Shakespeare mainly reserved the term 'spousal' as a synonym for a marriage made in contexts involving great social or dynastic significance. It seems that for him 'spousal' was an elevated term, mainly useful for bearing political import. Political does not mean honourable, necessarily. For instance, when the odious Saturninus chooses, on very dubious grounds, to marry the barbarian enemy Queen Tamora (*TIT* 1.1.261–2), he exits to the Pantheon saying: 'There shall we consummate our spousal rites' (1.1.334).

Less dishonourably, Henry V cements territorial gains in war by means of his marriage with Katherine of France. Katherine's mother Queen Isabel comments:

> God, the best maker of all marriages,
> Combine your hearts in one, your realms in one.
> As man and wife, being two, are one in love,
> So be there 'twixt your kingdoms such a spousal
> That never may ill office or fell jealousy,
> Which troubles oft the bed of blessed marriage,
> Thrust in between the paction of these kingdoms
> To make divorce of their incorporate league.
>
> (*H5* 5.2.354–61)

Isabel's metaphor of a secure 'spousal' of the kingdoms, with no fear of future divorce, conveys a vain hope, as revealed in the play's final chorus a few lines later. Her use of marriage as a figure for a close bond employs the term 'spousal' because the bond will be between great nations.

Shakespeare sometimes used the related term 'to espouse' in similarly exalted metaphoric contexts (*LUC* 20; *H5* 4.6.26), and once in a parodic context. In this the ludicrously grandiloquent Pistol invites Nym to 'espouse' the diseased Doll Tearsheet (*H5* 2.1.75), a parody usage indicative of the fact that, like 'spousal', 'to espouse' is generally used by Shakespeare to indicate a politically important marriage. So King Richard III has his wife killed for dynastic reasons, and, wooing by proxy, obtains Queen Elizabeth's 'consent' that 'He should espouse Elizabeth her daughter' (*R3* 4.5.18). Fortunately, Richard is killed first. In a happier context, Pericles at Diana's shrine describes himself as 'the King of Tyre, / Who, frighted from my country, did espouse / The fair Thaisa at Pentapolis' (*PER* s.22.22–4), precipitating the play's second recognition scene between the royal husband and wife.

The complications of a politically important espousal are seen in *The First Part of the Contention* where the word 'espouse' is used twice to describe the marriage of King Henry VI and Margaret. We should first note the rule governing marriage by proxy, or by a 'Proctor' (according to Swinburne): 'A general Mandate to contract Marriage is not sufficient unless his [the actual husband's] Ratification do follow.'[34] In the first instance Henry's agreement to marry Margaret, made by his proxy Suffolk before many witnesses, appears to have been made in the present tense, and it is ratified by Henry's gesture of a kiss:

> SUFFOLK As by your high imperial majesty
>   I had in charge at my depart for France,
>   As Procurator to your excellence,
>   To marry Princess Margaret for your grace,
>   So, in the famous ancient city Tours,
>   In presence of the Kings of France and Sicil,
>   The Dukes of Orléans, Calaber, Bretagne, and Alençon,
>   Seven earls, twelve barons, and twenty reverend bishops,
>   I have performed my task and was espoused,
>   And humbly now upon my bended knee,
>   In sight of England and her lordly peers,
>   Deliver up my title in the Queen
>   To your most gracious hands, that are the substance
>   Of that great shadow I did represent –
>   The happiest gift that ever marquis gave,
>   The fairest queen that ever king received.
> KING HENRY Suffolk, arise. Welcome, Queen Margaret.
>   I can express no kinder sign of love
>   Than this kind kiss.   (*CYL* 1.1.1–19)

But in the second instance the future tense is clearly used ('shall . . . ere . . . May . . . next'), as seen in the written 'articles of contracted peace' between France and England:

Imprimis: it is agreed between the French King Charles and William de la Pole, Marquis of Suffolk, ambassador for Henry, King of England, that the said Henry shall espouse the Lady Margaret, daughter unto René, King of Naples, Sicilia, and Jerusalem, and crown her Queen of England, ere the thirtieth of May next ensuing. (*CYL* 1.1.41–7)

The contract also specifies that no dowry will be given for Margaret (1.1.59), a crucial issue to be further discussed in chapter 4. For now we must note the important difference in the tenses of the two sequential agreements, ratified *de praesenti*, and *de futuro*, which raises a question over the status of the marriage.

In *Titus Andronicus* a diversity of tenses of the verb 'espouse' is used by the Emperor Saturninus to express his shifting marriage intentions.

Firstly, clearly in the future tense, Saturninus says he 'will' make Lavinia 'Rome's royal mistress, mistress of my heart, / And in the sacred Pantheon her espouse' (*TIT* 1.1.240–2). After he obtains her father's and Lavinia's agreement to the marriage (1.1.244–52 and 1.1.271–3), his liking almost immediately shifts to the captive Queen Tamora, as noted above. Soon after, using the pretext of Bassianus' claim of a prior promise,[35] Saturninus uses the present tense when he says of Tamora (as we have seen): 'I lead espoused my bride along with me' (1.1.325).[36] Thus we see that the words 'spousal' and 'espouse' are used repeatedly by Shakespeare to describe the marriages of the great and powerful, and we sometimes see the proper forms for the legality of spousal contracts bent by them.

The importance in marriage contracts of the distinction of tenses of a verb led Sir Frederick Maitland to comment wittily that making such a distinction legally crucial 'was no masterpiece of human wisdom' because, 'of all people in the world, lovers are the least likely to distinguish precisely between the present and future tenses'.[37] Similar wit and perhaps more is exposed by Shakespeare in the wildly mooted circumstance of the 'mock' spousals of Orlando and Rosalind/Ganymede in *As You Like It*, a frolic which presents an extraordinary sort of liminal test case for questions over spousals.[38]

In this fantastic and highly contrived mooting, Rosalind in the disguise of the boy Ganymede, and moreover whilst play-acting the role of herself, exchanges definitively *de praesenti* spousal vows with Orlando.[39] In thus portraying the Ganymede character (quadruply played by a boy actor play-ing a girl who is playing a boy who is on request play-acting a girl) the play represents a parody of legal precision concerning spousals. In partic-ular, Ganymede insists on the careful regulation and corrective revision of Orlando's use of grammatical tense in the proceedings. So, when during the mock spousals Celia asks 'Will you, Orlando, have to wife this Rosalind?' (*AYL* 4.1.122–3), and Orlando replies 'I will', suggesting an ambiguously *de futuro* answer, Rosalind objects 'Ay, but when?' Then Rosalind dictates and Orlando repeats the formula *per verba de praesenti*: 'I take thee, Rosalind, for wife.' Rosalind/Ganymede then also replies definitively in the present tense: 'I do take thee, Orlando, for my husband' (4.1.122–31). All is then in order for a valid marriage by spousals, except for the gender of the participants.

Marriage of a man with a boy was of course not legal, but marriage by proxy was. Could Ganymede/Rosalind serve as a proxy for herself? There is no sign here of the outward duress or inward reservation that could invalidate spousals (although a slight halting in line 130 might indicate a brief mental hesitation, many marriages go forward with these). But is the spirit of play-acting or teasing fun here effectively a mental reservation? For Swinburne denies that matrimony is contracted when 'words of the present time are uttered in *Jeast* or *Sport*, for such wanton words are not at all obligatory in so serious a matter', and such an excuse had been used in reality to invalidate Elizabethan spousals.[40] Perhaps the crux of the matter lies in the question of whether or not Rosalind is wholly serious despite her love-jesting, and it may be implicit that this may be not yet fully known to herself.

The greatest perplexities for Shakespearian critics over marriage have arisen in response to Shakespeare's dramatisations of wholly unrealistic 'bed tricks'. Such tricks involve sexual consummation lacking the element of 'pure and perfect' mutual consent essential to establish a marriage insisted on by Swinburne.[41] Swinburne further details the circumstances in which sexual intercourse following a *de futuro* contract was taken to imply the consent forming an immediate marriage – this is only when it is undertaken 'with that affection, which doth become Man and Wife'.[42] In Shakespeare's dramatic bed tricks such sincere affection is impossible, since one of the parties does not know the true identity of the other. Alternatively, in these circumstances, a 'mistake of person' was an impediment rendering the marriage void. The resulting anomalies have often been discussed, pre-eminently in relation to *Measure for Measure*.[43]

In this play Duke Vincentio, disguised as a friar, encourages Mariana to substitute for Isabella and have sexual relations with Angelo, saying:

> Nor, gentle daughter, fear you not at all.
> He is your husband on a pre-contract.
> To bring you thus together 'tis no sin,
> Sith that the justice of your title to him
> Doth flourish the deceit. Come, let us go.
> Our corn's to reap, for yet our tilth's to sow.
>
> (*MM* 4.1.69–74)

The Duke as friar therefore authorises sexual consummation obtained by stealth where there is a marital 'pre-contract'. The problem long noted is that the same disguised Duke formerly condemned Juliet, pregnant following an apparent pre-contract with *her* lover. He even asked her 'Repent you, fair one, of the sin you carry?' (2.3.20), which strangely contrasts with his 'no sin' advice given later in the play.

Indeed Vincentio's disapproval of Juliet is heavily driven home. Having elicited that she loves 'the man that wronged you', and so having determined that the transgression (if any) was mutual, he encourages her to feel extra guilt, promulgating a double standard: 'Then was your sin of heavier kind than his.' He shows satisfaction at her shame, 'I do confess it and repent it, father. / . . . I do repent me as it is an evil, / And take the shame with joy', and then terrorises her with her lover's death (2.3.20–41).

What is the difference between what the Duke encourages Mariana to do and so heavily condemns in Juliet? Juliet's lover Claudio has explained:

> Upon a true contract,
> I got possession of Julietta's bed.
> You know the lady; she is fast my wife,
> Save that we do the denunciation lack
> Of outward order. This we came not to
> Only for propagation of a dower
> Remaining in the coffer of her friends,
> From whom we thought it meet to hide our love
> Till time had made them for us. But it chances
> The stealth of our most mutual entertainment
> With character too gross is writ on Juliet.
>
> (*MM* 1.2.133–43)

We have no reason to disbelieve him.

The play also makes parallel considerations of dowries the cause for the omission of the marriage ceremonies of Juliet and Mariana. Only Juliet's Claudio is more loving than Mariana's Angelo. As the Duke says of the latter:

[Mariana] should this Angelo have married, was affianced to her oath, and the nuptial appointed; between which time of the contract and limit of the solemnity, her brother Frederick was wrecked at sea, having in that perished vessel the dowry of his sister. But mark how heavily this befell to the poor gentlewoman. There she lost a noble and renowned brother, in his love towards her ever most kind and natural; with him, the portion and sinew of her fortune, her marriage dowry; with both, her combinate husband, this well-seeming Angelo. (*MM* 3.1.215–25)

In the play's long resolving final scene, the fact that he spoke of marriage with Mariana is at first half-denied by Angelo, but finally he admits he was 'contracted to' her (5.1.214–21; 5.1.372–3). Then there is no more doubt that Angelo was Mariana's 'combinate husband' than that Juliet 'upon a true contract' was 'fast' Claudio's 'wife'.[44]

One way out of the enigma of how the parallel spousals of Juliet and of Mariana can be treated so differently is to allege that the contracts in question are not of the same sort, one being *de praesenti* and the other *de futuro*. To imagine this possible is to suppose that, unlike Maitland's 'lovers', theatrical audiences were 'likely to distinguish precisely between the present and future tenses'. Against this could be argued the conventions of Shakespearian stage time, which often give more scope for temporal indeterminacy than for accurate time or tense accounting.[45] However, as we have seen, a fine distinction of grammatical tenses during a spousal declaration in *As You Like It* is fit matter for a Shakespearian jest, and so such distinctions were not invisible on stage.

Although there is little if anything in the text to distinguish them, commentators have long offered a variety of more or less considered opinions about the tenses in the spousals or marriage contracts in *Measure for Measure*.[46] In 1960 Schanzer carefully argued that Claudio's is a spousal *per verba de praesenti*, while Angelo's is *per verba de futuro*; the bed trick then converts the second type to the first.[47] However, various critics have argued just the opposite,[48] or that both couples were espoused by *verba de praesenti*,[49] or that the distinction of the cases would make no difference at all.[50]

There might be some help towards resolving this in the Duke's remark that Angelo's contract was set for solemnisation at a future time: 'the nuptial appointed; between which time of the contract and limit of the solemnity, her brother Frederick was wrecked at sea, having in that perished vessel the dowry of his sister' (*MM* 3.1.216–19). The mention of an appointed time here may suggest a *de futuro* contract, and perhaps one conditional on a dowry.[51] But there is reason to doubt that the contract Angelo had entered with Mariana was conditional upon a dowry, for then it would simply have been cancelled with the dowry's loss. On the other hand, if it had been an unconditional *de futuro* contract, since it had been unconsummated it could have been cancelled either by mutual consent (which was clearly absent on Mariana's side), or else under certain specific circumstances. According to Swinburne an 'Innocent Party' would be freed of such a contract if the other commits '*Fornication*', or else if 'there is a Fame or common report, That there is some lawful impediment'.[52] Just such a reason for cancelling the contract had been falsely alleged, according to the Duke, by Angelo, who had 'swallowed his vows whole, pretending in her discoveries of dishonour' (3.1.228–9). At the play's end, some five years later, while unjustly acting as 'judge / Of [his] own cause' (5.1.165–6), Angelo again alleges that he had broken with Mariana partly for lack of dowry, but 'in chief / For that her reputation was disvalued / In levity' (5.1.218–20).

To repeat, for the rules are complicated, if theirs had been an unconsummated conditional *de futuro* contract contingent on a dowry, Angelo would not have had to disparage Mariana's chastity or reputation in order to cancel the marriage contract. Of course he might have done this to save himself from gaining a reputation of being hard-hearted in his dealings. Yet the play may well imply that Angelo-the-rank-liar is newborn during the time of his deputyship; formerly an unkind man, he becomes worse in the pride of his over-powerful strict magistrate's role. But all these possibilities point to certain common conclusions. While Angelo considers his pre-contract void, Mariana and Vincentio do not, and the status of this contract is open to debate. This, unhappily for the age, was not an unusual sort of dilemma; problems like it were often heard in the church courts.

Some astute critics assess *Measure for Measure* as deliberately presenting flawed or disruptive arguments; from this it would follow that providing answers to difficult questions was not part of Shakespeare's design for the play.[53] Even so, the questioning of marriage contracts in the play may still mirror contemporary realities. These would be the realities of a 'marital limbo' in which some unfortunate people actually found themselves,[54] and the destabilising effect this possibility had on the idea of marriage as a firm basis for social order.

Yet some critics are dubious that English social and legal problems had any bearing on the marital concerns of *Measure for Measure*.[55] One offers instead that the play exhibits the legal conditions either of post-Tridentine Catholic Europe,[56] or else of some sort of 'self-enclosed' fairyland. The same critic also denies in the play the 'kind of authenticity to which a Henry Swinburne can attest', for *Measure for Measure* is not even a 'history play'.[57] Problems with these remarks are multiply instructive. Swinburne's book is proposed to be an exemplar for English marriage practices; no theoretical legal treatise bore such a relation with social practice, and certainly not Swinburne's, as we shall see. Moreover, Shakespeare's plays are embedded in a context of distinctly English law, regardless of genre or setting; as we have noted, even in the self-enclosed non-historical Forest of Arden references to the actual problems of English spousals proliferate like 'real toads in imaginary gardens'.

Significant questions over contracts forming marriages arise in at least fourteen Shakespeare plays.[58] Frequent court cases and attempts at legislative reform attest that corresponding issues were of great current socio-legal interest, and would have been easily recognised by many in Shakespeare's audience. So, despite some contrary views, marriage formation is not a topic that Shakespearians can afford to overlook.

CHAPTER 2

Arranging marriages

FAMILIES AND ARRANGED MARRIAGES

A survey of early modern English sermons, conduct books, court records, and literature leaves little doubt that the family or interested 'friends' expected to play some role in the formation of the marriages of children. Indeed, the terms 'friends' and 'family' often overlapped in early modern England, for 'friends' could include parents, while 'family' was understood to include parents, wider kin, and the household. Servants or apprentices were also considered to be members of the household, and their masters could play a role in arranging their marriages.

Family involvement in arranging a marriage was generally considerable, but it varied widely in degree and kind according to factors such as the age of the children, local traditions, and social level. At one extreme a family could choose the bride or groom and finance the new household.[1] At another the child's own marriage choice was merely condoned with a blessing.[2]

The convention among the gentry and aristocracy was for marriages to be arranged by families with a view to securing advantages or alliances, conforming to a patriarchal model.[3] It was expected that aristocratic children would submit willingly to such marriages, happy to comply with parental wishes. Although some children did resist, such arranged marriages were socially acceptable, even when made on a *de futuro* basis between very young children.

Many children and adolescents of the aristocracy as well as those of the middling and lower sorts lived away from home in other people's households in order to be educated. Those of the middling or lower sorts who lived away from home as apprentices, servants, or farm workers often formed their marriage alliances when out of the control of parents. They were allowed to enjoy a relatively greater autonomy in their marriage choice than the children of the aristocracy and gentry.[4] They also typically married later than the aristocracy, for economic reasons.[5] As a result, for non-aristocratic children conflicts with parents over marriage preferences were less frequent.

Nevertheless, child marriages arranged by parents were not just a 'peculiarity of the nobility'.[6] E. J. Carlson finds evidence that the custom of arranging marriages between very young children of the lower or middling classes still existed in England at the end of the sixteenth century, especially in the north. This practice is evident from cases heard in the church courts, and from criticism in conduct books and popular ballads. But such arranged child marriages, which nearly always served the parents' economic ambitions, were dying out by the end of the sixteenth century because of a combination of 'popular sentiment and church hostility'.[7]

Marriage among the very poor was sometimes discouraged by the wider community when there were fears that in the future the new family might become a drain on parish poor relief funds. The parish could act by, for instance, regulating cottage building on waste land, or by applying the Poor Laws to force onward migration of the destitute wandering poor out of the parish.[8]

Parental coercion to marry that amounted to duress was unlawful. Where portrayed in Shakespearian dramatic contexts, strong coercion to marry either conveyed transgression, or the imaginary locale was furnished with exotic laws such as those of the ancient 'Athens' of *A Midsummer Night's Dream*, the one performing a mirror-like function and the other being fabulation.

Indeed, under Church law, duress was held to be a dirimentary impediment to a marriage preventing it from taking place. This means that even if a forced marriage did go ahead it would not have been valid because it was necessary for both parties to have consented freely to form a marriage. Church courts' records thus show litigants seeking annulment on the grounds that the marriage had been forced.[9] The courts appear to have required witnesses who would attest to a high degree of force used, inducing actual injury or at least fear of it; petitioners had to convince the court that they had only gone through with marriage formalities because of fear. The test applied for duress was the 'constant man or woman test': was the force or fear used sufficient to sway a 'constant' person? A high degree of force was necessary, resulting in actual injury, or producing fear of this.[10]

Among notorious examples of parental coercion and duress is a case involving the great common lawyer Sir Edward Coke. After he had been dismissed from office as Chief Justice of the King's Bench by the King in 1616, Coke decided to arrange the marriage of his unwilling daughter Frances to Sir John Villiers, the weak-minded elder brother of King James's favourite

the Duke of Buckingham. Some historians have alleged that Coke's motivation was not his daughter's interests, but was rather his hope of restoration
to royal favour and high office.[11] His behaviour certainly astonishes modern
sensibilities. In 1617, accompanied by armed horsemen, he broke into a kinsman's house where Frances was in hiding with her mother Lady Elizabeth
Hatton, and carried her off. Frances was imprisoned and subjected to violent verbal and physical assault until she agreed to marry Coke's choice of
bridegroom. An often-quoted story, not necessarily reliable, describes poor
Frances 'tied to the Bedposts and whipped' until she finally consented to
the marriage.[12] Not surprisingly the marriage brought unhappiness to all
concerned.

However, cases alleging marriage under duress have not been found in
great numbers. It has been suggested that this was because, even if a marriage
was entered into under compulsion, subsequent consent was held to 'purge
the effect of force and fear' and so ratify the marriage.[13] Such consent could
be implied by apparently willingly entered sexual relations or cohabitation
following the marriage. In addition, difficulties in producing witnesses
to the force used, the typically late age for marriages, and English social
customs in which many young people were in service or training away from
their families, must also go some way to explaining lack of many claims of
duress.[14]

The theoretical, and often actual, autonomy of early modern children
in making marriage choices ran against patriarchal ideology. Despite much
evidence of children taking the initiative in finding their marriage partners, seventeenth-century Puritan conduct books characteristically insist
on children's subordination to parents. They spell out a hierarchical vision of family life in which a father 'must bee acknowledged for the head'
who has been given the authority by God to govern his family, wife, children, and servants in his household.[15] They in turn owe duties of obedience. For William Gouge this meant a duty of obedience to parents
in matters of marriage because of the Fifth Commandment, and because
'Children should fear and love their parents.'[16] Gouge argued that 'children
ought to have their parents consent unto their marriage' because 'God hath
expresse laws concerning this point', and children were morally bound
'from taking wives or husbands, without or against their parents consent'.[17]
On this important point Gouge cited the support of laws of the 'Papists'
(probably the counter-Reformation Tridentine laws), and the laws of
'nature and nation, the civill and canon law, the common and statute law
of our Land', claiming 'all manner of law is agreeable to Gods law on this
point'.[18]

In stressing a child's duty of obedience, seventeenth-century conduct books sometimes appear to ignore completely the contemporary law of marriage. But that law, which did not require parental consent, was undoubtedly well known and understood. The Puritan Lady Margaret Hoby, writing her diary in 1600, mentions discussing with visiting neighbours 'diuers nedful dutes to be knowne [by children]: as of parence Chousinge for their children'.[19] Lady Margaret's own three marriages were promoted and arranged by the Earl and Countess of Huntingdon in whose household she had been placed by her parents when a child. After the death of Thomas Sidney, Margaret's second husband, the Earl brought considerable pressure to bear on the grief-stricken Margaret to accept Sir Thomas Posthumous Hoby as her third husband.[20]

The new Canons proposed for the Church of England of 1603–4 partially addressed this issue. They included Canon 100 which prohibited marriage for those under twenty-one without parental consent, but importantly this Canon failed to declare such marriages void.[21] Because the new Canons had no force to invalidate marriages made with words of consent alone, their chief effect was merely to perpetuate the already existing anomalies in forming a valid marriage.[22]

Even William Gouge shows a reluctant awareness of the freedoms granted by the existing law of marriage when he criticises the 'boldnesse of many children in setting light by their parents consent' by forming unions 'made indissoluble', thinking 'impudently to resolve to beare out as well they can, the storme of their parents displeasure' afterwards. Gouge reports, however, that 'many Churches' find such marriages 'voide', by which he must mean that many Puritan churches would abominate such a marriage.[23] His remarks are therefore admonitions and threats to wayward children, but they also reflect the legal reality that autonomous marriage was valid as Gouge condemns also the ministers who through carelessness, or bribery marry children in the absence of parental consent as accessories to the children's sin.[24]

The surviving records of the Ecclesiastical Commission that was set up in 1561 in York provide another kind of evidence of disapproval of marriage without parental consent. This Commission operated with delegated authority from the Queen as Supreme Governor of the Church in England, and did not derive its authority from the bishops as did the consistory courts. It differed from them also in possessing powers of imprisonment in addition to powers of imposing excommunication, penance, and fines. Although the Commissioners normally refused to review matrimonial cases, E. J. Carlson's studies indicate that they did sometimes act against children who failed to obtain parental approval for their marriages.[25] In such cases, however, they did not use their powers to imprison or impose fines or spiritual penalties, but instead acted as arbitrators in family battles. One couple brought before the Commission for marrying without a mother's consent are recorded as agreeing to ask her forgiveness on their knees.[26]

ENFORCED MARRIAGE IN ELIZABETHAN DRAMA

By elaborating on notorious actual cases of coercion to marry, or inventing imaginary ones, a number of Elizabethan and Jacobean writers centred their works on enforced marriages of sorts that occasioned misery, murder, or suicide.[27] By contrast, Shakespeare treated even wholly selfish familial involvements in courtship less conspicuously or melodramatically. Instead he encompassed such topics within larger considerations of social, family, or political relations, and was in consequence subtle and multifarious in his approach rather than sensationalist.

A disavowal by Shakespeare's young King Henry VI of an agreed arranged marriage – made in the play to forge a peace between England and France – leads to both personal and national disasters. These are respectively Henry's own ill-fated marriage with Margaret, and huge losses for and contention within England. The play presents a progress from a prudent political marriage to the folly of personal choosing, but this pattern is somewhat a-historical. For although Henry did break a contract to marry the Earl of Armagnac's daughter made in 1442, the peace of 1443 was actually *cemented*, not disrupted, by Henry's subsequent marriage to Margaret.[28] But the dramatised sequence in which a broken royal promise to marry leads to debacle is plausible politically and morally. So in the play, if not in history, Suffolk's casuistry when defending Henry's repudiation of his promise (*1H6* 5.7.30–5) lacks all the civic virtue and selflessness of Henry's first response to the Protector's proposal of a political marriage with the Earl of Armagnac's only daughter:

> Marriage, uncle? Alas, my years are young,
> And fitter is my study and my books
> Than wanton dalliance with a paramour.
> Yet call th' ambassadors, and as you please,
> So let them have their answers every one.
> I shall be well content with any choice
> Tends to God's glory and my country's weal.
>
> (*1H6* 5.1.21–7)

A lack of virtue is seen also in the stubbornness and prejudice that motivate fathers' objections to children's marriage choices in both *A Midsummer*

Night's Dream and *Othello*. In the event, both Egeus' and Brabantio's claims for legal redress against eloping daughters are overruled; a royal pardon is given to Hermia and her Lysander, and the Venetian Senate refuses to act against Desdemona and Othello. This may be seen as merciful on the part of Theseus, and expedient on the part of the Senate, but in both cases the complaining patriarch is overruled in favour of youth and love. The stubborn fathers in these cases might even be seen as victims. Egeus, denied his demand 'I beg the law, the law upon his head' (*MND* 4.1.154), is (in the 1600 Quarto text) silenced and (perhaps self-) excluded from the treble weddings.[29] Brabantio, similarly thwarted, simply dies of 'pure grief' (*OTH* 5.2.211–13).

On another occasion Shakespeare portrayed an alarming attempt to arrange a marriage in order to benefit only the family, and not the young persons marrying, but he turned this at the end into comedy. Desiring that she join his family for the sake of her dowry and the seven hundred pounds left her by her grandfather, Justice Shallow of *The Merry Wives of Windsor* hopes that Anne Page will marry his kinsman Abraham Slender. Shallow is fully satisfied with this young blockhead's response to his question 'Can you love the maid?':

I will marry her, sir, at your request. But if there be no great love in the beginning, yet heaven may decrease it upon better acquaintance, when we are married and have more occasion to know one another. I hope upon familiarity will grow more contempt. But if you say 'marry her', I will marry her. That I am freely dissolved, and dissolutely. (*WIV* 1.1.226–33)

This notion that love can arise after an arranged marriage[30] is called by the Welsh parson Sir Hugh Evans a 'fery dicretion answer', and it satisfies Evans's enquiry 'can you affection the 'oman?' (*WIV* 1.1.210, 234). Worse still, Shallow's ludicrous suit is satisfactory to Anne's father, while her mother favours yet another unattractive suitor.[31] The play ends with Anne and her own preferred suitor Fenton (a reformed fortune-hunter) married, and with Fenton's rebuke against the parents:

> You would have married her, most shamefully,
> Where there was no proportion held in love.
> The truth is, she and I, long since contracted,
> Are now so sure that nothing can dissolve us.
> Th' offence is holy that she hath committed,
> And this deceit loses the name of craft,
> Of disobedience, or unduteous title,
> Since therein she doth evitate and shun
> A thousand irreligious cursed hours
> Which forced marriage would have brought upon her.
> (*WIV* 5.5.213–22)

This sees as shameful the parents' and the clergyman's views of a satisfactory way to 'affection' a bride.[32] Here the daughter of a middling rank family must seize the marital autonomy that was in fact typical for those of her standing. Although Anne's parents could have sought legal redress against Fenton, or even sought to disinherit Anne,[33] instead they genially accept the marriage as a *fait accompli*. No family rupture, forced bigamy, suicide, murder, or madness ensues.

In many Shakespearian romantic comedies issues of family coercion of children to marry are by-passed because the parents of the courting couples are absent, far distant, or actually or presumed dead. In fact a pastoral setting within a fabulous (or in Shakespeare's use often a semi-fabulous and semi-gritty) 'natural' or 'green world' locale, a place where civilised laws and parental restrictions are suspended, is much more common to Shakespearian comedy than are the twists of urban intrigue derived from New Comedy conventions wherein 'to beguile the old folks' over matrimony 'the young folks lay their heads together'.[34] However, even in Shakespeare's Forest of Arden, as Suzanne Gossett points out, Rosalind as a daughter of the legitimate Duke refers with deference to her father's 'loving' of Orlando's late father (*AYL* 1.2.224), and arranges for her father's approval of her marriage with Orlando (5.4.6–19).[35]

Where heavy-handed parents are presented as coercing or obstructing free marriage choice in Shakespeare's plays, this is often within circumstances seemingly deliberately contrived to challenge the patriarchal ideologies of his age. For instance, by exaggerating the manner and matter typical of puritanical pronouncements about a father's rights to direct a daughter's marriage choice, King Theseus of *A Midsummer Night's Dream* brings such dicta into question, and may undermine them. William Gouge argued, quite typically, that since children receive their very life from their parents, parents have the right to dispose of them in marriage.[36] In a nearly parallel way, Theseus urges that Hermia marry Demetrius, her father Egeus' choice for her husband:

> What say you, Hermia? Be advised, fair maid.
> To you your father should be as a god,
> One that composed your beauties, yea, and one
> To whom you are but as a form in wax,
> By him imprinted, and within his power
> To leave the figure or disfigure it.
>
> (*MND* 1.1.46–51)

This is in response to Egeus' plea 'I beg the ancient privilege of Athens: / As she is mine, I may dispose of her, / Which shall be either to this gentleman

/ Or to her death, according to our law' (1.1.41–4). Egeus' invocation of a law of Athens that gives fathers Draconian powers over children may seem to press the claims of patriarchal ideologues to the point of *reductio ad absurdum*. But in the play King Theseus at first re-interprets the law to allow Hermia an alternative to the death penalty for disobedience, which is the option of entering a nunnery for life, and eventually overrules the law altogether in favour of Hermia.

Yet a law punishing a child's disobedience of a father with death was not entirely a notion of only a fableland in Shakespeare's time. From about 1606 some thinkers, including Gouge, Perkins, Whately, and Jean Bodin, actually did propose such powers for fathers on the analogy of the family being equivalent to the state,[37] but of course these powers never became lawful in England. There were, however, some partial parallels seen in some regional laws of sixteenth-century France. These French laws allowed parents to force religious vocations on unwilling children (as Egeus would on Hermia), and specified the death penalty for those who married under the age of twenty-five without parental consent.[38]

Even in English law the rebellious disobedience of servants or wives was seen as analogous to treason. This is expressed in Katherina's notorious speech (which we will analyse more closely in chapter 7):

> Such duty as the subject owes the prince,
> Even such a woman oweth to her husband,
> And when she is froward, peevish, sullen, sour,
> And not obedient to his honest will,
> What is she but a foul contending rebel,
> And graceless traitor to her loving lord?
>
> (*SHR* 5.2.160–5)

However (as we shall see in chapter 7), the degree of insubordination required for the English felony of 'petty treason' was the murder of a husband (or master or religious superior.)

Although Bodin's conclusions were not embodied in English law, English thinking certainly accepted a correspondence of the household with the state, making household treason a possibility.[39] Thus Juliet's Nurse declares 'I speak no treason' (*ROM* 3.5.172) when she defends her charge from the blustering wrath of old Capulet, who is enraged because his daughter resists being forced into a sudden arranged marriage. We as audience know that Juliet has never even seen her father's chosen husband for her, County Paris, and know also that she is already secretly married to Romeo. Not knowing nor caring to know about her real reasons for hesitation, Capulet sputters:

> Mistress minion, you,
> Thank me no thankings, nor proud me no prouds,
> But fettle your fine joints 'gainst Thursday next
> To go with Paris to Saint Peter's Church,
> Or I will drag thee on a hurdle thither.
> Out, you green-sickness carrion! Out, you baggage,
> You tallow-face!   (*ROM* 3.5.151–7)

Then, ignoring his wife's disapproving 'Fie, fie, what, are you mad?', Capulet piles on verbal abuse, and hot-headedly threatens: 'My fingers itch' (3.5.164). Would this behaviour attract audience approval; would it have passed the 'constant woman test'? We think not on both points, and the play does show Juliet in effect hounded to death.

Juliet's extreme youth is emphasised in several ways in Shakespeare's play; indeed it makes her much younger than in Shakespeare's source. At first Capulet demurs when Paris proposes a marriage with her:

> My child is yet a stranger in the world;
> She hath not seen the change of fourteen years.
> Let two more summers wither in their pride
> Ere we may think her ripe to be a bride.
>   (*ROM* 1.2.8–11)

He adds, in perfect accord with high-minded principle:

> But woo her, gentle Paris, get her heart;
> My will to her consent is but a part,
> And, she agreed, within her scope of choice
> Lies my consent and fair-according voice.
>   (*ROM* 1.2.14–17)

However, high principle for Capulet, here and characteristically, is mainly a matter of short-term lip service. In another example, his love of festivity is at first subordinated to tactful conduct in his plans for Juliet's wedding: 'We'll keep no great ado – a friend or two. / For hark you, Tybalt being slain so late, / It may be thought we held him carelessly, / Being our kinsman, if we revel much' (3.4.23–6). But we know he is passionate about parties, for we have seen him furious when Tybalt would have spoiled the masked ball with feuding (1.5.53–80). Before long, therefore, the wedding guest list grows, and Capulet finally arranges to hire 'twenty cunning cooks' to prepare for the celebration (4.2.1–2).

Capulet's genial hypocrisy and amusing self-deception over concerns about what 'may be thought' is less innocent when he quickly forgets his own admonitions that Juliet is too young to marry, or that her heart must be won before he will give his permission. Rather, he demands Juliet's obedience to his plan even in advance of any wooing by Paris.[40]

The fact that Lady Capulet herself was married even younger than Juliet (1.3.74–5) would suggest that hers was also an arranged child marriage. At one time there was a widespread notion among scholars that such marriages were common in Tudor England, a view encouraged by a compilation of cases made in 1897 by Frederick Furnivall. This view was overturned by Peter Laslett, who examined Furnivall's type of instances statistically and showed child marriages to be rare.[41] Yet, as we have seen, there was an English tradition of forcing marriages on unwilling young children in order to benefit even non-aristocratic families (especially in the north); by 1600 such practices were dying out but were still remembered with disapproval and distaste. For instance, Lady Margaret Hoby's diary for 1601 remarks, amongst other news of scandals in the north of England, on a marriage taking place between a girl of fourteen and a man of fifty.[42] So, despite the statistical corrections made by Laslett and others, Juliet's plight might still have reflected a current English perception that child marriage was a contemporary abuse.

It is also implied that County Paris is of higher social standing than the plain Capulets, and so Juliet's marriage with him would advantage her family. It is evident that Paris as well as Juliet's father and mother expect her to cohabit immediately following the arranged marriage, having no plans for the young couple to live apart for several years as was common in aristocratic child marriages. Juliet is indeed over the legal minimum age of twelve, and although her father has some fears of it, her mother expects a rapid pregnancy (1.2.12–13 and 1.3.71–3). So in *Romeo and Juliet* implicit censure of certain English social practices combines with the depiction of a particular family pathology to give point to Juliet's powerlessness and unusually early age for (an English) marriage.[43]

In contrast, when marriages were royal it was normal for autonomy in the choices of spouses to be severely constrained (even now an English royal heir cannot marry a Roman Catholic or a divorcee). Although in a comedy the foolish suitor Sir Thurio is chosen by the Duke of Milan to marry his heir Silvia with no visible political end in sight (*TGV* 3.2.22–3), in the dynastic marriages depicted in Shakespeare's history plays, political reasons for unions are pre-eminent: we are in realistic mirrorland. So, as we have already noted, in the marriages of Princess Katherine to Hal in *Henry V*, or Blanche to the Dauphin of France in *King John*, personal concerns are second to questions of the peace of nations and disposition of great territories.[44] As is subtly argued by Suzanne Gossett, even the apparently autonomous and lighthearted romantic frolics of *Love's Labour's Lost* are probably circumscribed by implied considerations of state.[45]

The same mirroring of realities does not wholly apply in the representations of royal marriages in Shakespeare's four last plays, in which fableland contexts and fabulous plots are used to convey primal emotional drives. Thus the king–protagonists of each of these late works are far more volatile and more threatening in their influence on their children's marriage choices than dynastic concerns alone would dictate. In the most complicated of Shakespeare's plots, King Cymbeline would at first knowingly have forced his daughter Imogen into incest and bigamy.[46] By contrast, high-handed Capulet had no idea that Juliet was married when he chose Paris for her husband. Even worse, Cymbeline's choice for Imogen is the odious Cloten, whereas it appears that Capulet actually did take pains to choose in County Paris what the Nurse calls 'a lovely gentleman'.

So in *Cymbeline* we see a royal father perched on the extreme edge of power, verging on tyranny, in dealing with an heir's marriage choice. Before we condemn this plot premise as wholly fantastic and outrageous we should remember the actual arranged marriage of the child King Henry VIII to his brother's mature widow, which required a papal dispensation to overcome incest. Henry's marriage was demanded for dynastic reasons, as is Imogen's with Cloten; in this respect *Cymbeline* is mirror-like despite its outrageousness.

The two royal fathers in *Pericles*, murderous King Antiochus and good King Simonides, at first uncannily resemble one another in their interventions concerning the marriages of their daughters. The tyrant Antiochus is the incestuous possessor of his unnamed daughter, so his aim is the destruction of all her suitors and he has killed many. In a not-quite-parallel way, Simonides expresses in private an interesting mixed reaction to seeing his daughter Thaisa's declaration of her preference for Pericles:

> She tells me here she'll wed the stranger knight,
> Or never more to view nor day nor light.
> I like that well. Nay, how absolute she's in 't,
> Not minding whether I dislike or no!
> (*PER* s.9.14–17)

Simonides himself has clearly favoured Pericles, and urged Thaisa to speak with him despite her modesty, yet her autonomous 'absolute' choice rankles. He tests Pericles' mettle by pretending to be a heavy father, even accusing Pericles of treason, and when the young man passes the test of his honour Simonides thus 'condemns' Thaisa and him:

Therefore hear you, mistress: either frame your will to mine –
And you, sir, hear you: either be ruled by me –
Or I shall make you man and wife.
Nay, come, your hands and lips must seal it too,
And being joined, I'll thus your hopes destroy,
And for your further grief, God give you joy.   (*PER* s.9.103–8)

Before the *volte face* these tones echo the anger of old Capulet, and moreover parody the destructive actions of Antiochus. When Simonides finally is asked his permission for the marriage, 'if 't please your majesty', he replies 'It pleaseth me so well that I will see you wed, / Then with what haste you can, get you to bed' (*PER* s.9.111–13). It seems that here the patriarch is satisfied with the role of ratifying the marriage, leaving the matter of affection to the young people.

The reluctance of King Polixenes to see his heir married to his beloved shepherdess in *The Winter's Tale* may be justified on the basis of restrictions on those of royal rank. But the fury with which Polixenes attacks the young couple, and especially innocent Perdita, is attributable to forces beyond the political. Polixenes has a fallen view of married sexuality, equating it with the 'imposition . . . / Hereditary ours' (*WT* 1.2.76–7), or Original Sin; on the basis of this he would not mind a pretty concubine for his son, but not a low-born wife. As in all the four Shakespearian Romances, in *The Winter's Tale* an over-insistence on paternal power, excessive possessiveness of daughters, and a hint of incestuousness dog the comic resolution in a romance of divided families reunited.

Prospero of *The Tempest* follows the same pattern as Simonides in secretly approving his daughter's choice of a mate, but outwardly showing a temporary strong opposition. But Prospero differs in the greater apparent seriousness and longer duration of this opposition, and moreover (unlike Simonides) he has good political reasons to approve of his heir's wished-for marriage. Prospero's aim in being obstructive, he says, is to cement the relationship of the suddenly-in-love young people 'lest too light winning / Make the prize light' (*TMP* 1.2.454–5); this is consistent with his overall role as a psychological manipulator. Yet Prospero's vehemence against Ferdinand's wooing may well seem excessive, and *The Tempest* may thus dramatise the possibility that the exercise of paternal control over a child's marriage can disguise a father's over-possessive love.[47] Wise fathers (like Prospero, not Antiochus) must overcome and replace this with genuine concern for their children's welfare.

CHAPTER 3

Wardship and marriages enforced by law

MARRIAGES ENFORCED BY LAW

In a few places in Shakespeare's plays a king or ruler orders the marriage of a subject to a particular partner, reflecting legal circumstances unfamiliar to us today. For instance, the marriage of the widow Paulina to Camillo is ordered by Leontes in a sudden turnaround in which Paulina's sixteen years of admonishing Leontes is reversed; this incident begins with the exclamation 'O peace, Paulina!' which at last silences her (*WT* 5.3.136). The disempowering of Paulina may seem retaliatory, comic, anti-feminist, or unduly pre-emptory – and may well have important symbolic and psychological resonances in the play[1] – but in legal terms it corresponds quite closely with the long-disputed rights of kings to marry off the 'royal widows' of their nobles.[2]

However, legal powers over wards and royal widows do not explain the enforced marriage of Lucio to the prostitute Kate Keepdown, meted as a punishment to him by Duke Vincentio in *Measure for Measure* 5.1.506–22. An actual legal correlative with this, up to a point, is found in the church court action of enforcing a marriage following abjuration *sub poena nubendi*.[3] This action could arise because habitually fornicating couples were sometimes compelled by church courts to 'abjure' continuing sexual relations 'under the penalty of marrying'; that is, they were forced to swear that 'the next time they had intercourse they would be *ipso facto* married'.[4] There are records of church court 'instance' litigation in which,[5] after an abjuration had previously been ordered, women who claimed that intercourse had resumed attempted to enforce a marriage on unwilling men.[6] No exact parallel with the punishment of Lucio in *Measure for Measure* is seen here, but Lucio does boast of having previously been tried by the Duke on a charge of 'getting a wench with child', and of falsely 'forswear[ing] it' (4.3.163–7). This boast is part of Lucio's obsessive calumny of the 'very superficial, ignorant, unweighing' Duke (3.1.401), and the calumny is the

cause of his eventual condemnation. But the mitigation of Lucio's punishment from whipping and hanging to unwilling marrying (5.1.517–20) does
partly resemble a disputed *sub poena nubendi* case. Lucio complains that
'Marrying a punk, my lord, is pressing to death, whipping, and hanging'
(5.1.521–2), while one desperate male defendant pleaded, in vain, that he
had not agreed to marry if caught resuming sexual relations with the plain-
tiff, but rather agreed to be 'lashed around the church and the market in
Beverly on six separate days'.[7]

The forced marriage of Lucio to Kate Keepdown carries other quite
different legal overtones (as well as those of a *sub poena nubendi* case). A
legal principle (discussed in chapter 1 above) that might apply to him, as
well as to Angelo in the same play, is that conditional or *de futuro* spousals
followed by sexual intercourse resulted in an immediate, enforceable, and
valid marriage. For Lucio is said by Mistress Overdone to have promised
Kate marriage (3.1.458–60), while Angelo has had a 'pre-contract' with
Mariana (4.1.70).

WARDSHIP

If a child was a ward it was not the parents who arranged the marriage,
but the child's guardian. Not all children under the care of guardians were
wards; wardship would only arise in the quite specific circumstances where
a child's dead father had held land from his lord by either socage or military
tenure. Wardship therefore only arose when the heir's father died, and it
was irrelevant whether or not the mother still lived. Legal infancy and the
duration of the wardship lasted until twenty-one for male heirs, and until
sixteen for female heirs, but this was reduced to fourteen if the female ward
married.

Wardship was a 'feudal incident', that is, one of the lord's rights attached
to the various land tenures.[8] Not long after the Norman Conquest, because
tenants commuted physical performance of feudal duties for monetary
payments, these rights became financially valuable to lords (including the
king) in what is called 'bastard feudalism'. In medieval England feudal
incidents became an occasional means of raising revenue for lords, but
by the sixteenth century feudal theory was employed unashamedly by the
Tudor kings as a regular source of royal revenues needed to finance their
administration of government and wars.

Although wardship arose in the case of land held by socage (agricultural)
tenure or by military tenure (knight service or grand serjeanty), it was most
onerous in military tenure.[9] This was in part because in socage tenure the

child's nearest relative became his or her guardian and when she or he came of age the guardian had to account to the heir (hand over profits made from the land during the wardship). In contrast, in military tenure once wardship began the lord took all the ward's land under his control and was entitled to keep all the profits from the land for the duration of the wardship.[10] In theory the lord was supposed to be liable for any waste, or damage to the heir's land, but in practice few heirs had sufficient cash assets available when they came of age to allow them to pursue an action for waste.

Wardship ended when the ward reached majority, but in military tenure before taking possession of his lands the ward was required to apply formally by means of a procedure known as 'sue his livery' (as noted in *Richard II* 2.1.204–5, 2.3.128, and *Henry IV, part I* 4.3.64) for those who held land from the king as tenant in chief, and otherwise as '*ouster le main*'.[11] Suing livery required a complex, intrusive, lengthy, and costly investigation into the heir's landholding; to avoid it most heirs paid the king a sum of money instead. In addition the lord was entitled to a fine of half a year's profit from the land when the ward reached majority.

The lord also had control of the ward's body during the wardship and so could dictate where and how she or he lived. The lord was supposed to meet the ward's everyday needs and arrange suitable education, training, and marriage.

A most important and very valuable part of wardship in military tenure was a lord's right to arrange the heir's marriage, up to the age of twenty-one for males or sixteen for females. A statute of 1236 and the Statute of Westminster 1275 confirmed that the heirs could refuse the proposed marriage, but if they did so they were punished with heavy financial penalties. If the male heir married without the lord's licence then the lord was entitled to compensation of double the value of the marriage to the lord, and was entitled to continue to take the profit of the land until he received this payment.

If there was no male heir, then all female heirs took in 'coparceny', in which the inheritance was divided equally between them. Unlike a son, a daughter who was already over the age of fourteen when her father died was not subject to wardship, and daughters under the age of fourteen would become wards until they reached the age of sixteen. Between fourteen and sixteen the lord was allowed to arrange a marriage for her. But if she refused the marriage then she was gravely disadvantaged because the lord was entitled to continue to hold her lands until she became twenty-one and even longer if necessary in order to recover his loss on the rejected marriage.[12]

The king was the greatest beneficiary from wardship because over the years from the time of the statute Quia Emptores 1290 lordships had become concentrated in the king's hands.[13] By the time of the Tudors wardship in the hands of lords, compared with the king's, had become of minimal importance.[14] In the process often described as fiscal feudalism, especially Henry VII, Henry VIII, and Elizabeth recognised the considerable potential for raising royal revenues from all the feudal incidents, and in particular wardship. Although medieval kings had appointed royal officials known as escheators to oversee the administration of wardships, the Tudor monarchs set up more effective administrative machinery to extract the maximum royal revenue from wardship.[15] Henry VIII continued his father's work by putting the administration of wardship onto a statutory basis (32 Hen. VIII c.46; 33 Hen. VIII c.22), and setting up the Court of Wards in 1540. In the reign of Elizabeth I the powers of the Court of Wards were enhanced by Lord Burghley and this was continued into the next reign by Robert Cecil.[16]

There were some limited safeguards for wards in the common law. Magna Carta had dealt with the law of waste mentioned above, and also prohibited a lord from 'disparaging' an heir by arranging an unsuitable apprenticeship or marriage. Coke defined various categories of disparagement by marriage: defects of mind (a lunatic); defects of blood (inferior status, for example marriage arranged with a villein, or with the son or daughter of someone attainted with treason); defects of the body (crippled or diseased).[17]

Hurstfield's investigation of the records of the Court of Wards discovered no lawsuits for disparagement, but did reveal the huge sums of money calculated as the value of marriages, sums which would deter all but the most unhappy ward from objecting. In one unusual instance, Burghley's ward (and Shakespeare's patron) the Earl of Southampton paid the enormous sum of five thousand pounds for refusing to marry one of Burghley's granddaughters.[18]

By the end of Elizabeth's reign, royal rights to wardship were the cause of much complaint. Because of its value the wardship of heirs had become commodified; rights of wardship, or subsidiary rights to arrange the marriage of wards, were sold by the Court of Wards on behalf of the Queen. Indeed, wardships or the marriage of wards were often purchased and traded with the aim of immediate profit. Other petitioners to the Court of Wards for wardships aimed to marry the heir to their own son or daughter. Marriage of wards into a guardian's own family was not uncommon even for such a virtuous man as Sir Thomas More. Mothers too petitioned for the wardship of their own children in order to protect them.[19]

A petition for wardship could be general, or could name a particular heir, and could even be made in the belief, but not knowledge, that the child's father had died.[20] In a sinister practice, grants of authority under patent were regularly made to amateur and professional informers (in return for the payment of a fee); these aimed to make money from discovering a wardship under military tenure. The informers investigated landholdings hoping to uncover what were described as 'concealed lands', meaning an unsuspected or hidden military tenure. The right to search could be granted for a specific landholding, or could be a roving commission to search over a wide geographical area.[21]

Tales of ruthless fortune-hunters, stories of young children torn from their mothers' arms by guardians who were total strangers only to be sold on again, and especially criticism of wards' forced marriages, all combined to make wardship a much-hated institution which was widely considered to be an anachronistic feudal relic. Often to the purchaser of a wardship the well-being of an infant ward and the maintenance of their inheritance were of far less importance than the money to be made. Sir Thomas Smith reported the opinion that many guardians were reluctant to spend money on the education of a ward who might well die before the guardian could gain recompense through selling the ward's marriage. When the ward came of age he would find 'his woods decayed, old houses, stock wasted, land ploughed to the bare'.[22] He or she would probably also find they had been married off to the highest bidder.

For fear of the dire consequences that could befall his heir or his lands in the event of an early death, many a landowner made strenuous efforts in his lifetime to purchase the wardship on behalf of a wife or other relative. Even this did not greatly avail Lady Elizabeth Hatton whose first husband Sir Christopher Hatton had before his death purchased for her as step-mother the wardship of his daughter. Lady Hatton's second husband, Sir Edward Coke, arranged a marriage for this young woman to suit his interests without reference to either her own wishes or those of her protesting guardian, Lady Hatton. As we have seen in chapter 2, in the future Coke would behave even more violently in forcing a marriage on his own daughter.

In another sad instance, Bess of Hardwick's early life was blighted by the financial and emotional rigours imposed on her family by the institution of wardship. When her father died in 1528 the wardship of her brother and a quarter interest in the family lands was sold to John Bugby, who was an official in the Court of Wards, and the widow and her children were reduced to financial peril. Bess's first marriage was arranged when she was very young, probably fourteen, to Robert Barley, a boy of thirteen, who died soon afterwards. Robert had been a ward, and in consequence Bess had to fight for her reduced widow's settlement. Robert's brother was now a ward and the Barley family was ruined. Bess's biographer conjectures that her early bitter experiences were the reason why, unlike so many of her contemporaries who made such investments, she never purchased and sold wardships herself during her long financially adventurous life.[23]

Wards could also be purchased for the purpose of arranging marriages to provide an income. Such an investment is specified in the 1576 will of Sir Richard Ryche, which provided for his 'base' (bastard) son Richard as follows:[24]

My executors . . . shall provide or buy one woman ward or some other woman having manors and lands of value of L200 yearly for a marriage to Richard, and shall pay him at marriage L500; and if he refuse to marry her or if no marriage shall be provided they shall pay him L1000 and sell the ward or other woman if any such be provided to any other person to the utmost advantage to the performance of my will.

It is chilling that this marriage was arranged with an unknown woman to be purchased, and valued, only for her monetary worth.

Although wardship could be a severe abuse involving bounty hunters or enforced marriages, and indeed was often portrayed as such, there is evidence that in other ways it fulfilled a function admired in its time. In a balanced view we must recognise that the picture of young children taken away from widowed mothers and placed with strangers needs to be considered in historical context. In Shakespeare's time children of the English gentry or aristocracy were commonly placed in great households for their education and training, whether or not they were wards. For example, although she was not a ward, her parents placed Lady Margaret Hoby in the household of Catherine Countess of Huntingdon to be educated. Here she met the first two of her future husbands, Walter Devereaux and Thomas Sidney (both wards of the Earl of Huntingdon).[25] In another instance, the household of Lord Burghley, Master of the Wards, which included his own wards, was famous 'throughout England as a training ground for young courtiers and statesmen, and admission to it was sought after by the best families in the land'.[26] But this is not to say that Burghley neglected the financial advantages obtainable through the marriage of his wards (see above on Southampton). In fact Burghley's own daughter was married to one of his wards, the Earl of Oxford. Yet, probably most wards were not so fortunate as those who lived in the Huntingdon and Burghley households. Certainly landowners and parents continued to seek reform of wardship.[27]

In fact, during Elizabeth's reign wardship and the Court of Wards grew increasingly unpopular, while the House of Commons objected strenuously to bills introduced by the Master of the Wards to end evasions which depleted the Queen's revenues.[28] The troubled Parliament of 1603–4 began with hopes that the new King would resolve longstanding grievances over wardship.[29] James's own ministers raised proposals to end wardship by having 'wards turned to a certain annual rent to be propounded in parliament',[30] while Robert Cecil, Master of the Court of Wards, circulated tenants in military service throughout the country advising them that they could offer to pay his Majesty a composition in their own lifetime for the wardship and marriage of their minor children after their death.[31] By 1604 a Commons Committee was meeting to consider the abolition of wardship. Francis Bacon, a committee member and spokesman, asked the Lords to join in the Commons' petition to the King. The Lords' initial sympathetic reception appeared to fade rapidly, possibly as the King's attitude was made known to them.[32] It seems that James's first speech to Parliament brought an end to the proposals;[33] the plans put forward to abolish wardship failed in the face of strong opposition from office holders of the Court of Wards and from the Lords, and unabated royal needs to raise revenues from fiscal feudalism. After the failure of the Commons' proposals the Officers of the Court of Wards themselves presented a petition, ostensibly addressed to the King, in which they complained of the insults to them offered by the Commons and estimated that a sum of one hundred and twenty thousand pounds per annum would be needed to compensate the King for loss of revenue if wardship ended.[34] In consequence of Stuart extravagance, the prerogative Court of Wards and Liveries was not abolished until the Civil War.

WARDS AND GUARDIANS IN SHAKESPEARE'S PLAYS

High adult death rates meant that it was very likely that an early modern child would lose one or both parents either before or soon after they left home, and even more likely for this to be the case by the time that they married.[35] The loss of both parents was relatively rare, and the single missing parent was much more likely to be the father.[36] If the child had lost a father, and was an underage heir at the time of the father's death, wardship could ensue.

Because a ward's marriage was a valuable commodity to be bought or sold, considerable pressure was often exerted to force the marriage arranged by the guardian. This practice was often seen as an abuse. Swinburne, for

instance, gives a harrowing account of the hardships of the ward married
forcibly by greedy 'gardiens' in such a way that 'thou couldest wishe him
no greater torment . . . hell excepted'.[37]

Shakespeare's plays for the most part fail to clearly distinguish wardship
from other forms of guardianship. Also, in Shakespeare's accounts of it,
guardianship is not always an evil or a good. Their appointment is seen to
evoke in guardians various mixtures of self-regard, domination, profitable
rights, responsibilities, and duties for care. Correspondingly, in Shakespearian drama being placed with a guardian may be either helpful or dangerous
to a child.

For instance, Leonato is a benign guardian of his niece Beatrice, whom
he helps with her marriage (*ADO* 2.3.160–1). Yet the nurturing function of
guardianship is traduced when Shakespeare's King John arranges the murder of his nephew Arthur (*JN* 3.3.59–66). At first young Arthur's protector,
King Philip of France, claims that guardianship is ordained by God to protect the helpless (2.1.112–17). But then Philip is bought off by John's transfer
of extensive English lands in a dowry favourable to France. The horror in
Arthur's ensuing murder, and King Philip's change from high-mindedness
to veniality, are commented upon by the bastard Robert Faulconbridge in
his famous soliloquy on 'commodity', or rank self-interest. In this Faulconbridge identifies the deal struck as a 'mad composition' driven by 'commodity' (2.1.562–99). Philip's ruthless self-interest is reminiscent, in an
exaggerated way, of often-deplored abuses of guardianship.

A particularly wide spectrum of guardian-and-child relations is seen
in the late Shakespeare plays, where undisguised psychological forces are
highlighted by means of Romance conventions. The good Shepherd is
Perdita's loving guardian in *The Winter's Tale*, while in *Cymbeline* Belarius
becomes a very fond guardian of the two princes he abducts and raises as
his own sons. But in *The Tempest* Prospero excoriates and enslaves Caliban,
a child he had raised, and in *Pericles* the envious and ungrateful Dionyza,
with her complacent husband Cleon, first educate but then attempt to
murder their charge Marina. The one rule clearly in evidence is a rule of
variety.

Great diversity is also seen in Shakespeare's depictions of the educational treatment by guardians of dependants (some of them wards). This
accorded with reality. For instance, Lord Burghley was a particularly good
provider of education to his wards.[38] Yet, as we have seen, Sir Thomas
Smith reported on selfishly stinted provision; there was also a bitter report
by Sir Humphrey Gilbert of wards brought up 'in idleness and lascivious
pastimes . . . obscurely drowned in education for sparing charges'.[39] In

Shakespeare's fictions, Posthumus of *Cymbeline* (probably a royal ward) is accounted to have been excellently raised and educated at King Cymbeline's court (1.1.40–50). Had he not fled from wardship at the court of France, Count Bertram of *All's Well That Ends Well* might have expected similar treatment. But in *As You Like It* Orlando bitterly complains about his poor breeding, amounting to disparagement, at the hands of his elder brother Oliver (1.1.1–23).[40]

Some wards (as well as orphans and incompetents) were cared for by boroughs or local communities,[41] and here again care could be deficient.[42] A poor standard of official care is indicated in Parolles' calumny that Dumaine: 'was a botcher's prentice in Paris, from whence he was whipped for getting the sheriff's fool with child – a dumb innocent that could not say him nay' (*AWW* 4.3.190–3). Salisbury includes in a list of unholy deeds: 'To reave the orphan of his patrimony' (*CYL* 5.1.185). Yet in Elizabethan times not all guardians were rapacious. Legal protection was offered to 'idiots and natural fools in royal custody' by the Court of Wards.[43] It was also offered to children generally, and particularly to orphans, by the court of Chancery.[44] In some urban communities the interests of private wards (not royal ones) and orphans were supervised by borough courts; the City of London had a specialised Court of Orphans.[45]

Nevertheless abuses persisted, as we have said, in the institution of wardship, and were widely condemned. Patrick Murphy even argues that the scandals of wardship form a background to an imaginative work as far from an explicit portrayal of the institution as Shakespeare's *Venus and Adonis*.[46]

Whether or not this is so, the familiar institution of wardship is named or described in a number of Shakespearian contexts, and in works of contemporary dramatists.[47] It is mentioned casually, for instance, in *Romeo and Juliet* when old Capulet reckons the interval since his last dancing at a marriage by hazily recalling that the son of that marriage 'was but a ward two years ago' (1.5.40). The economic plight of a ward is also tangentially mentioned in *King Lear*, showing it a matter of everyday awareness. Thus a mere allusion to the guardian's control of a ward's property stirs old Gloucester to hot wrath when Edmund alleges, 'I have heard [Edgar] oft maintain it to be fit that, sons at perfect age and fathers declined, the father should be as ward to the son, and the son manage his revenue' (*LRF* 1.2.73–6).

Among Shakespeare's plays, wardship is most crucial in *All's Well*. This is not on account of the notorious economic impact of the institution, but because it gives the King his power to demand Bertram's marriage to Helena.

As the play opens Bertram has just become the King's ward. This seems plausible because we learn that Bertram's aristocratic father had been a soldier with the King (*AWW* 1.2.26), and young Count Bertram also inclines to war. So it may be inferred that Bertram's wardship is an incident of military tenure.

It has been speculated that the removal of young persons from their home to another household, a normal pattern in Shakespeare's age, still may have 'carried considerable emotional weight'.[48] Such an impact may lie behind the way *All's Well* begins with expressions of both fears and reassurances about wardship:

> COUNTESS In delivering my son from me I bury a second husband.
> BERTRAM And I in going, madam, weep o'er my father's death anew; but I
> must attend his majesty's command, to whom I am now in ward,
> evermore in subjection.
> LAFEU You shall find of the King a husband, madam; you, sir, a father. He
> that so generally is at all times good must of necessity hold his virtue to
> you, whose worthiness would stir it up where it wanted rather than lack
> it where there is such abundance. (*AWW* 1.1.1–10)

So we are reassured that the French King is one of the 'good' guardians of wards. Nonetheless Bertram's fears of 'subjection' will be justified; the play will concentrate on the forced submission of a ward's 'fancy' to the King's 'eyes', as Bertram will describe it (2.3.169). Despite some critics' doubts, there is no chance that a reference in this to abuses in the forced marriages of royal wards would have been missed by many in Shakespeare's audiences.[49]

Then, as is its tendency, Shakespeare's dramaturgy complicates the issue (and in so doing moves by degrees from mirrorland to fabulation). In contrast with the usual story of a ward abused, in *All's Well* Helena is worthy and virtuous, and the King is not financially greedy. Moreover, to counterbalance any image of a despotic guardian, the orphaned Helena is herself shown lodged in the custody and household of the benign Countess of Rousillon (1.1.36–43), Bertram's mother and Helena's loving and generous guardian.

Thus Helena is shown placed where young persons in Shakespeare's world often met prospective spouses, in the same household as them. It may be that Helena herself is a ward, but this is uncertain. In any case the Countess insists that she is 'a mother' to Helena (1.3.133–50), and, despite Helena's lower social rank, approves of and even promotes a marriage between Helena and her son.

The King insists on this same marriage to reward Helena for her abilities in curing him. In so doing he gives up the considerable financial advantages he might receive on Bertram's marriage. He does not, however, give up the power he has to determine that marriage; does this make the King a good father to Bertram?

It is open to question whether the King 'disparages' his ward Bertram by demanding that he marry Helena.[50] This may be complicated because a king could ennoble a commoner.[51] Yet, after the King shows his fury at Bertram's refusal to marry as he commands (the vindictive anger of thwarted authority?), Bertram submits with:

> Pardon, my gracious lord, for I submit
> My fancy to your eyes. When I consider
> What great creation and what dole of honour
> Flies where you bid it, I find that she, which late
> Was in my nobler thoughts most base, is now
> The praised of the King; who, so ennobled,
> Is as 'twere born so.   (AWW 2.3.168–74)

The phrase 'as 'twere' suggests Helena is not actually ennobled for services or merit (such elevation is treated with rich irony in *The Winter's Tale* 5.2.125–43). Rather, in the succeeding lines the King promises to Bertram only that he will supply a marriage portion for Helena constituting 'A counterpoise, if not to thy estate / A balance more replete' (AWW 2.3.176–7). Thus it does not seem that the King raises Helena to Bertram's full social or economic level. In any case, he utterly disregards Bertram's clearly expressed wishes.

Lest we think that asserting a principle of 'voluntary' choosing of marriage partners is for Shakespeare a progressive step towards 'democracy', as one critic claims,[52] we must recall that the consensual model for marriage dates to the twelfth century and is theological in basis. And the outcome of *All's Well*, in which it appears that Bertram may finally be happy to have been forced to marry Helena, certainly contradicts earlier aspects of the play showing sympathy with objections to arranged marriage. Such pluralism of outlook is a hallmark of *All's Well*, the play in which Shakespeare most directly treats wardship. In it a mixed picture emerges in which loving care, sound education, heedless coercion, or tyrannous bullying are all seen as possible aspects of guardianship.

Wardship also collides with free marriage choices in the thematically overcrowded play *Cymbeline*. We have already discussed the pressure to marry her gruesome step-brother Cloten that is imposed on Imogen, and mentioned the images of good guardianship shown in the care of Imogen's two brothers by Belarius. In addition to these matters, the play presents the linked issues of Posthumus' unauthorised marriage despite his apparent royal wardship, and the violation of restrictions on royal marriages by Imogen. The first of these issues will be discussed here, and the second will be addressed in chapter 8, on divorce.

At the play's start we hear from gossiping courtiers that the orphaned Posthumus Leonatus was raised from birth at court as a favourite of King Cymbeline, and since Posthumus' deceased father had been an aristocratic warrior it seems likely that Posthumus is a royal ward. We learn also that he is about to be exiled by the outraged King because he has privately been married with Cymbeline's daughter Imogen, despite Imogen having been intended for the despicable Cloten.

Cymbeline expresses his anger to Imogen, claiming derogation through her marriage choice: 'Thou took'st a beggar, wouldst have made my throne / A seat for baseness' (*CYM* 1.1.142–3).[53] Imogen replies forthrightly: 'No, I rather added / A lustre to it' (1.1.143–4). Behind this exchange lies Imogen's counter-claim of a derogation had she been forced to marry Cloten. So she has replied to her father's 'That mightst have had the sole son of my queen!': 'O blessed that I might not! I chose an eagle / And did avoid a puttock' (1.1.139–41). Here Imogen asserts the naturally noble Posthumus is an eagle, and Cloten a puttock due to his mental poverty.[54]

Imogen's further assertions of Posthumus' natural superiority (1.1.145–51), despite Cloten's higher rank, might seem to express a principle of natural virtue outweighing birth and position. But such an interpretation is quite problematic for this play, as we shall see. Certainly Shakespeare sets up an unusual circumstance in showing a king deprived of his powers to direct the marriage of a ward, and to dispose of his royal heir in marriage.

But, as we have said, the planned match of Cloten with Imogen is, in terms of Christian marriage, sinful. It is also, in the opinion of Cymbeline's royal court, unworthy and odious (1.1.16–17). These and other complications of the dramatic postulates of *Cymbeline* let Shakespeare 'off the hook' in the sense that his play does not simply favour a child's full freedom to choose a mate, regardless of the social standing of the person chosen and even regardless of royal descent. But an intriguing question remains, which is why an artist of great wit and subtlety chose to get himself on such a 'hook' in the first place.

In a similar way, *Cymbeline* veers towards, but then swerves away from, a notion that a 'natural virtue' may override 'good birth' in other than matrimonial spheres. The play shows the Princes, raised without knowledge of their ancestry, demonstrating noble characteristics because 'How hard it is to hide the sparks of nature! / These boys know little they are sons to th' King' (3.3.79–80). Thus they insist on attempting martial prowess, showing an inherent impetus to chivalry. They do this despite their apparent father Belarius' objections; although wishing his blessing, they will still go to war with or without it (4.4.43–7). In an interesting parallel, their sister Imogen marries without her father's blessing, but does eventually crave and receive it (5.6.266, 5.6.269). Far from being egalitarian in thrust, the play *Cymbeline* demonstrates that 'sparks of nature' in the sense of high birth predetermine individual nature in the sense of audacity, courage, talent, and inclination.

But this conservative position is refracted further through the peculiar convolutions of the fabulating plot of *Cymbeline*, yielding some strange and challenging images. The first of these images begins with the encounter between Cloten and the royal brothers; the boys, who think themselves rough mountaineers, nonetheless demand civility of the courtier they meet. Uncivil Cloten is consequently killed by Guiderius/Polydore in a fair fight; when this becomes known the unknown Prince is convicted of *lese-majesty*, stripped of his hero status, and condemned to die. But then Belarius reveals the two Princes' true identities, and merely because 'This boy [Guiderius] is better than the man he slew' (5.6.303) his crime dissolves into a wholly forgivable act of self-defence. This odd twist resembles more than a little the subversive conclusion of *The Pirates of Penzance*, in which the pirates are pardoned following the revelation of their high birth. That is to say, it wryly moots circumstances where a judgment of capital guilt or innocence is made based on social standing.

In a second thought-provoking image of *Cymbeline*, simultaneous with the subversive twist of Guiderius' pardon Cymbeline's true (male) heir is revealed. This changes Imogen's status from royal heir-apparent to a mere daughter only third in line to the throne (5.6.374). That change of status makes pardonable her initial serious offence of marrying the well-parented (and well-educated) royal ward Posthumus.

Multiple interlinking enigmas in *Cymbeline* about nature, nurture, birth, wardship, autonomy, marriage, and succession are near the play's end all suddenly resolved in a manner that may make the head spin. Yet, despite even Cymbeline indicating that the play's complex sleight-of-hand denouements are somewhat incomprehensible (5.6.383–93), the whole play concludes on a note of simplicity and grace. This is due in large part to the transformation seen in King Cymbeline himself, who has been woodenly wrong-headed in judgment and in attitude until very near the play's end. But at the conclusion, when his prosaic speech finally acquires poetic

sinews and lustre, he gratefully accepts Imogen's runaway marriage,[55] proclaims 'Pardon's the word to all', makes peace with Rome, and leads all to
the temple in tones never heard before in this play:

> Laud we the gods,
> And let our crooked smokes climb to their nostrils
> From our blest altars. Publish we this peace
> To all our subjects. Set we forward, let
> A Roman and a British ensign wave
> Friendly together. So through Lud's town march,
> And in the temple of great Jupiter
> Our peace we'll ratify, seal it with feasts.
>   (*CYM* 5.6.477–84)

CHAPTER 4

Financing a marriage: provision of dowries or marriage portions

New plays and maidenheads are near akin:
Much followed both, for both much money giv'n
(*TNK*, Prologue, 1–2)

OVERVIEW

The family could become involved in a child's marriage in two ways, either by promoting the choice of a particular marriage partner, or by supplying material support. Unfortunately for the coherence of the subject, these two aspects of family involvement cannot be kept entirely distinct. In chapter 2 we have seen that the degree of involvement of families in the selection of a marriage partner ranged between the extremes of benign acceptance and a blessing of a child's own choice, and forcible coercion to accept a parent's choice of spouse. But when families gave property to newly marrying couples, their interest may not have been limited to the pecuniary. Since family material support could be withheld as well as offered, it could be used in coercive ways. Alternatively, support could be withheld, protectively, where a prospective marriage caused the family genuine concern for the interests of their offspring. For such reasons, financial arrangements for marriages will not divide on such simple lines as the laudable versus the detestable aspects of family involvement.

The present chapter will focus mainly on the provision of the dowries or marriage portions which brides typically brought into their marriages. The details of these portions were usually negotiated before marriage between the bride's and the groom's families, and once agreed marriage settlements specifying the conditions and the amounts of dowries were often fixed by common law contracts. Several scholars have given exemplary accounts of contracts for dowries;[1] these show clearly that such contracts were entirely distinct from the spousal contracts which alone made a valid marriage (see chapter 1). Nevertheless, sometimes literary scholars have in various ways confused the wholly optional contracts agreeing dowries, and the obligatory spousal contracts that formed marriages.[2]

So, to underscore the difference, the private early modern legal arrangements for property settlements often made in advance of marriage were voluntary and optional. They therefore had no fixed or required legal form, although they often followed local customary law or social traditions, and model versions were published in precedent books.

Families concerned for the future financial security and well-being of their children, and conscious of the dangers of litigation, produced written dowry agreements including carefully drafted clauses, as may be seen in some collections of private family papers. Since there was no straightforward means to register or record such agreements in courts, there must have been many more such agreements than have been preserved in historical records. Even when disputes over marriage settlements arose, these were not always litigated in courts, but were often settled by private arbitration and compromise. However, that was not the only available mode of seeking redress; even after her marriage an early modern Englishwoman mistreated in terms of her dowry settlement could apply for relief to the equity courts of Chancery or Requests (a married woman's legal standing, particularly in relation to the equity jurisdictions, will be considered in chapters 7 and 9). But when there were court records concerning marriage settlements, these reflected atypical circumstances; suits for action on the case, or in the equity courts, or in church courts, or local courts, concerned marital issues only when something went seriously wrong. Records of normal private arrangements for marriage settlements, where nothing went wrong, tend to be elusive.

It is a pity that this is so, for family legal arrangements were tied to everyday practices and common assumptions that must have been at least as significant to the texture of early modern life as the concerns of large political interests and the designs of the great and powerful. Any understanding we can gain of 'privately' made legal arrangements of the age by noting reflections in drama (taking heed of the 'distorting' lenses of genre,[3] artistic compression, possible exaggeration, etc.) may offer important opportunities for illuminating both Shakespeare's work and his world.

TERMINOLOGY AND HISTORY

We must first mention a terminological problem. Arrangements made by families and friends for the provision of dowries were often alluded to by Shakespeare, who used the terms 'dowry' or 'portion' to refer to the property given to new husbands. But, very confusingly, the term 'dower' also often appears in Shakespearian and other contexts with the meaning 'dowry' (as in *OED* 'dower' 2a). For, legally, the term 'dower' meant something quite different from 'dowry', and is sometimes used in this specific legal sense by Shakespeare as well.[4]

The full distinction between giving a dowry, a pan-European practice that was customary but not legally required for marriage, and a widow's rights to dower, a uniquely English institution embodied in the common law, will be discussed at length in chapter 9. To clarify briefly, the Roman practice of making a gift on marriage, or '*dos*', was accepted by the Christian Church and was once common throughout Europe. During the middle ages the English common law understanding of *dos* came to differ from that in the rest of Europe. In England the legal term 'dower' was reserved for the gift made on marriage by the husband to the wife (to take effect only on widowhood). In contrast, the term 'dowry', the bride-gift made by the woman's family to the man, was at first called a marriage-gift or *maritagium*,[5] and later a 'marriage portion'. Both 'dowry' and 'dower' mean endowment of a woman on marriage, but in the first case by her father (or family), and in the latter by her husband. 'Dowry', 'dower' and 'jointure' were terms used mainly by the landed aristocracy, while others, gentry and citizens, often used marriage 'settlement', 'agreement', 'covenant' or 'portion' to describe their arrangements.

Although, as seen above, the provision of portions or dowries was not a legal requirement for the formation of marriages, it was a common practice. By this custom of giving dowries, friends and families became crucial participants in marriages, although in law only the agreement of the prospective bride and groom was relevant to making marriages valid.

Chancery records of marriage settlement litigation among the aristocracy during the seventeenth century show a traditional reciprocity between the portion brought to the marriage by the wife and the jointure for her widowhood provided by the husband (jointures and other means to widows' maintenance will be discussed at length in chapter 9). In aristocratic families the pre-marriage agreement was likely to limit the wife's jointure to her widowhood alone; if she remarried then the husband's family were anxious to ensure her jointure ended, while in the pre-marriage negotiations the wife's family would attempt to secure for her a jointure for life. In a marriage agreement a wealthy wife's family would look to secure some of the property she brought into the marriage by means of a trust protected by the equity courts. Such arrangements for a married woman's separate estate are discussed in chapter 7.

Among particular groups, certain patterns of dowry provision are distinguishable. Most available written agreements for dowries concern the wealthy, who were most likely to leave documentary records of their lives. But other legal records such as wills, and some literary representations, indicate that negotiations over marriage portions were of great importance in early modern England at every social level. Families sought to help set up the new household, to secure the wife's future in widowhood, and often to enhance their own social position by seeking advantageous alliances. For the landed aristocracy a large dowry brought an increase in wealth and social standing to the man, and it was used to provide for the woman's support in widowhood. For gentry and merchant families, whose dowries did not increase at the same rate as the aristocracy's during Shakespeare's period, dowry still remained a significant part of marriage negotiations. Women from families of yeoman status and even daughters of poorer craftsmen attempted to bring some property into their marriage. Their marriage agreements were often made orally, but when found reported in wills or litigation show that the understanding between husband and wife was that the portion would be returned to the wife on widowhood in the form of some kind of provision for her.

'REALISTIC' PORTRAYALS OF DOWRIES IN SHAKESPEARE

Marriage portions or dowries are referred to in many Shakespeare plays. When detailed negotiations over these are portrayed, for instance, in the Renaissance Padua of *The Taming of the Shrew*, or the ancient Athens of *Timon of Athens*, the bargaining seems to mirror current English practices.[6] The negotiations in *The Shrew*, which will be analysed in detail in chapter 9, indeed may cast an unexpected light on questions about the marriage between Petruchio and Katherina Minola. Petruchio's intent 'Happily to wive and thrive as best I may' (*SHR* 1.2.55) will there be argued to be based on complex, and specifically Elizabethan, models of reciprocity.

A much simpler conception of a dowry as a windfall is evident behind the facetious remark made by the marriage-scorning Benedick of *Much Ado About Nothing*, who says of Beatrice: 'I would not marry her though she were endowed with all that Adam had left him before he transgressed' (2.1.234–6). The suggestion is that if Beatrice's ancestor Adam were able to give her the Garden of Eden, that dowry would not tempt Benedick; here the dowry is seen as a prize, an inducement to marry. The lure of immense property or wealth also motivates Portia's suitors in *The Merchant of Venice*, where capitalist investment in dowry-hunting in fantastic Belmont mirrors actual Elizabethan practices.[7]

The sub-plot of the Jailer's daughter in *The Two Noble Kinsmen* is also down-to-earth in several ways, although it meshes with the chivalrous tale of Palamon and Arcite. This young woman has a father unhappy about the scant dowry he can offer. Yet her unnamed Wooer is content to marry with no more than a promise of future consideration in her father's will, saying: 'Sir, I demand no more than your own offer' (*TNK* 2.1.10).[8] Because (by Shakespeare's time) property could be willed away from an heir at any time, the Jailer's 'offer' gives no basis for a pre-marital agreement, and so the Jailer replies without guile: 'Well, we will talk more of this when the solemnity is past. But have you a full promise of her? When that shall be seen, I tender my consent' (2.1.12–14). But then the daughter falls desperately in love with Palamon, and risks releasing him from prison. Even this desperate act does not win her his love, and so she goes mad. Subsequently Palamon obtains the Jailer's and his daughter's pardons, and

> Not to be held ungrateful to her goodness,
> Has given a sum of money to her marriage –
> A large one, I'll assure you.   (*TNK* 4.1.22–4)

So then the daughter has a dowry and a steadfast Wooer, but not the sanity that would make marriage possible. Sexual healing is prescribed by the wise Doctor, and then marriage with the loyal Wooer arranged. Finally Palamon and his three kinsmen knights bequeath their purses 'to piece her portion'.

The fable of chivalry in this play does not preclude a quite realistic mirroring of help given to a poor but worthy girl to 'piece' her dowry. For dowries were on occasion charitably 'pieced out' by well-wishing masters or local notables.[9] (As we shall see, Shakespeare's *All's Well That Ends Well* concludes with just such a gesture.)

Particularly mirror-like, in spite of another fabulous and ancient Athenian setting, is a depiction of the financial aid given by Timon of Athens to his loyal servant Lucilius in order to help bridge a social and financial gap that threatens Lucilius' love-match. Following negotiations with the prospective bride's father, Timon makes a generous gift to Lucilius enabling him to marry a young woman despite her family's higher status. These negotiations include careful questioning by Timon about the extent of the girl's dowry. This gives him an accurate measure of her family's social standing, and so what they would expect of a suitable, or 'equal', bridegroom:

TIMON   How shall she be endowed
    If she be mated with an equal husband?
OLD ATHENIAN Three talents on the present; in future, all.
TIMON This gentleman of mine hath served me long.
    To build his fortune I will strain a little,
    For 'tis a bond in men. Give him thy daughter.
    What you bestow in him I'll counterpoise,
    And make him weigh with her.   (*TIM* 1.1.143–50)

These dealings show a financial weighing or measuring of social standing, reflecting tendencies of the early modern world in which wealth was flowing away from the aristocracy, and yet inherited status was still of great importance. They also reflect how the financial arrangements made by family or friends in advance of marriages could be very costly. For we see, just before the Old Athenian arrives, that Timon pays five talents to relieve a friend of a heavy burden of debt (1.1.97–105). Hence, to offer to give his servant a sum that will 'counterpoise' a dowry of three talents does indeed require of Timon a significant sacrifice or 'strain'. The episode produces an image of social standing frankly measured by money, here in a dowry, but also of a contrary 'noble' indifference to monetary advantage typical of Timon.

It is worth noting that in terms of English common law the Old Athenian's conditional promise to give his daughter his whole estate in inheritance, 'in future, all', would not have been binding on him (any more than would the Jailer's intent in *The Two Noble Kinsmen*). In England after the 1540 Statute of Wills most parents could, by making a will, disinherit an heir (see chapter 9). Shakespeare's Old Athenian at first threatens to do just that, should his only child continue disobedient: 'If in her marriage my consent be missing, / I call the gods to witness, I will choose / Mine heir from forth the beggars of the world, / And dispossess her all' (1.1.140–3).[10] Yet the Athenian has stated his daughter might be 'endowed' with three talents and by being his sole heir. A promised inheritance of land is also part of the dowry negotiations depicted in *The Shrew* (2.1.121). No doubt expectations of inheritance did feature in pre-marital negotiations; we are very much in mirrorland here, for the legal doctrine of coverture (to be discussed in chapter 7) assured early modern husbands control over most of the property their wives might bring into marriage or acquire later, for example through inheritance.

It is also notable that the empirical studies of some social historians have modified a former view that early modern English, as opposed to continental, parents were more likely to confer property rights to the households of the subsequent generation through wills, rather than through *inter vivos* transfers of support or property. That is to say, the Old Athenian's threat to disinherit his daughter is less typical of an English pattern than was formerly thought; however, his intervention in her marriage choices made through economic pressures was still typical, and it mirrored realities.[11]

ECONOMIC COERCION AND MARRIAGES IN SHAKESPEARE

We have seen that the Old Athenian tries to direct the choice of his daughter's marriage partner by means of his control of her dowry. The issue of parents' economic power used to control free choice in marriage is logically analysed by the structure of *The Merchant of Venice*.

Although this play stretches away from legal mirrorland and towards fantastical mooting, it analyses by exaggeration real pressures placed on daughters. The play juxtaposes two highly contrived and contrasting versions of obtaining bridal portions: despite his wealth, Jessica's living father has no power at all over his absconding and apostate daughter, while Portia's father keeps his daughter under his control even from beyond the grave. Thus the financial aspects of the marriages of Jessica and Portia each present different 'as-if' or testing premises of fantastical mootings. The complications of the two marriages are partly symmetrical, for in each a 'foreign' bride conveys to a penniless but romantic Venetian bridegroom the great wealth that she has from her love-restricting father. But also an antisymmetry is posited in the power of the fathers. We may presume in Jessica's case that no dowry (or parental blessing) would be forthcoming from her father in the event of her marriage with Lorenzo, and so she must elope to marry him (yet finally, Shylock *is* forced to fund the marriage). To marry, Jessica must defy her father's will. Conversely, to get a husband Portia must exactly do her father's will.

In advance of her marriage Jessica provides herself with a dowry of sorts (to be squandered by Lorenzo) by stealing from her father's house. Eloping with an heiress, as well as the theft of ducats, would be understood by Elizabethans to be a crime (see chapter 6). These are also seemingly felt as wrongs by Jessica herself, as heard in her 'guilt/gild' punning during the elopement. So, pathetically obeying her father's last behest, Jessica locks the house she has just pillaged saying, 'I will make fast the doors, and gild myself / With some more ducats, and be with you straight' (*MV* 2.6.49–50).[12]

The contrived premise complicating Portia's marriage is her dead father's unusual will. This will was probably just within the bounds of Elizabethan law, as it does not prevent marriage absolutely (which would be unlawful), but does make compliance with the father's wishes a condition for inheritance. As such it resembles typical financial pressures on marriages, but in imposing a kind of marital lottery it takes these to a wild extreme. Thus Portia's choice in marrying is wholly governed by the fantastic casket test; even more in line with a fabling mode the conditions of the will punish suitors who fail the test with the loss of their legitimate procreative potential (they must promise never to marry another).[13]

Yet Portia's great wealth, which by the doctrine of coverture will become her husband's (as noted in *The Merchant* 3.2.16–18 and 3.2.164–71), draws several daring suitors. Bassanio himself is at first a self-confessed fortune-hunter; he sees as one and the same Portia's blonde 'sunny locks' and her wealth, figuring both as a second 'golden fleece' drawing many Jasons (1.1.167–72). This allusion to Medea might be seen as ominous in a play in which mothers are generally ignored, condemned, or scorned (Medea is recalled again with illusive innocence in 5.1.12–14). Yet Bassanio may be seen to reform his earlier attitude when he speaks out against gold at the moment of 'winning' the casket contest. He rejects the golden casket, which like all outward beauty may be 'purchased by the weight' (3.2.89), and chillingly likens all outward show to a blond wig taken from a corpse. Here he reiterates but inverts his former reference to beautiful golden female 'locks':

> So are those crisped, snaky, golden locks
> Which makes such wanton gambols with the wind
> Upon supposed fairness, often known
> To be the dowry of a second head,
> The skull that bred them in the sepulchre.
>
> (*MV* 3.2.92–6)

This macabre association of a golden 'dowry' with images of death and dismemberment may suggest a conversion to radical indifference with regard to Portia's rich dowry; this transformation may or may not be believably sincere in a Bassanio, or in Shakespeare's Belmont.

If Portia were to marry outside the terms of her father's will she would lose not only ease and wealth, but also her standing as the great lady of Belmont. Yet the patriarchal restrictions placed on her freedom to marry whom she chooses are not as murderous as those in the imaginary Athenian law we have seen invoked by Egeus in *A Midsummer Night's Dream* 1.1.42–5, or in the suitor-destroying ploys of fabulously monstrous King Antiochus in *Pericles*. Accordingly, Portia's plight does not terrify her, but it does depress her: 'O me, the word "choose"! I may neither choose who I would nor refuse who I dislike; so is the will of a living daughter curbed by the will of a dead father' (*MV* 1.2.21–4).

The carefully calibrated dimensions in Portia's mooted case and in the above-cited more 'realistic' Shakespearian portrayals of dowries illustrate how in Shakespeare's society the law countenanced a great deal of patriarchal control over wives, sons, and daughters. Extreme coercion by the family over marriage choices was not lawful because a valid marriage depended on the free consent of the parties. But family persuasion that fell short of duress was lawful.

In several places in Shakespeare's plays angrily expressed economic threats are used in attempts to influence recalcitrant daughters. Old Capulet threatens in *Romeo and Juliet* 3.5.191–4: 'An you be mine, I'll give you to my friend. / An you be not, hang, beg, starve, die in the streets, / For, by my soul, I'll ne'er acknowledge thee, / Nor what is mine shall never do thee good.' As we have seen, the Old Athenian of *Timon* only slightly less vehemently threatens to disinherit his daughter for similar reasons, and the Duke of Milan does the same in *The Two Gentlemen of Verona* 3.1.76–9.

But in the bourgeois or city comedy *The Merry Wives of Windsor* both parents fail to control the determination of Anne Page to marry her own chosen Fenton. Anne's father threatens (without excessive rancour) to withhold her dowry if she does so: 'If he take her, let him take her simply: the wealth I have waits on my consent, and my consent goes not that way' (*WIV* 3.2.69–71). In the event Anne does marry Fenton, relying on her independent inheritance to fund her marriage. No further dowry appears to be paid; nevertheless, all except Falstaff seem reconciled at the play's end.

HETEROGAMY, NON-ACQUISITIVE SUITORS, AND MISSING DOWRIES IN SHAKESPEARE'S PLAYS

Parents stubbornly interfering with courtship are common in Shakespeare's plays, and are usually defeated in accord with New Comedy conventions. Yet social historians tell us that among the middling classes of early modern England couples typically made their own marriage choices autonomously, and then only later submitted them to their parents for approval and for the making of dowry arrangements.[14] The contemporary drama may seem leery of even this pattern, as in Dekker's *The Witch of Edmonton* where Carter's generous readiness to provide a good dowry on the sole basis of his Susan's liking for Frank Thorney leads to her death and disaster.

In Shakespeare's plays the concerns of parents leading to a denial of dowries may have more or less good motives. The choleric dowry-denying

Old Athenian of *Timon* mentioned above may be snobbish and greedy (and yet biddable to bribery), but he may also be protective of his daughter. For a mistrust of heterogamy or social misalliances was in accord with the general social attitudes and fears of Elizabethans.[15]

Some of these attitudes involved suspicions that a man (or a woman) wooing a poor but attractive partner might seek only a sexual conquest.[16] Indeed, as seen in cases heard by the bawdy courts, irregularly contracted marriages were often pretexts for seduction. Thus is Touchstone's, who says to a woman of lower social standing: 'Come, sweet Audrey. / We must be married, or we must live in bawdry' (*AYL* 3.3.86–7).

Similar ribaldry is depicted by Shakespeare at a slightly higher social level when he renders ridiculous the heterogamic marriage of the absurd Spaniard Don Armado in *Love's Labour's Lost*. In his self-conscious preening over the innate nobility of his love for the clearly 'dowerless'[17] country wench Jaquenetta, Armado intends to have an old ballad on King Cophetua updated to celebrate himself (*LLL* 1.2.104–11). Armado's preposterously high-flown marriage proposal, written to the illiterate (and pregnant) Jaquenetta, also cites Cophetua as a precedent (4.1.64–79). In parallel with his literary pretensions, Armado's fate is ridiculed; this is 'To hold the plough for her sweet love three year' (5.2.870). In Armado's case lustful misalliance is shown to be a social disaster, and romantic illusions absurd.

Armado's extreme folly foregrounds real concerns. Dowerless marriages were regarded with suspicion by parents not only for reasons of their own lost opportunities for power, status, or wealth; many parents may have also been concerned about their children's potential unhappiness in unequal alliances. There was also, in accord with some ideologies of the age, a conventional vein of disapproval of the motivation of immoderate marital sexuality. So, in 'Of Moderation', Montaigne reproves 'the verie pleasures [husbands] have by the familiarity of their wives, except moderately used', and approves the thought that 'marriage was a name of honour, and dignity, and not of foolish . . . lust'.[18] Accordingly, the new husband Othello, for instance, denies that his wish to have Desdemona with him is 'To please the palate of my appetite, / Nor to comply with heat' (*OTH* 1.3.262–3). This kind of thinking seems to affect the Shakespearian parents Lear, Polixenes, and Prospero, all of whom seem to suspect that sexual desires will lead their children into inappropriate and unhappy dowerless marriages.

The withdrawal of Cordelia's dowry in *King Lear* is due to Lear's wrath in the division of the kingdom scene. This is a scene set in a kind of fableland, outside of all familiar economic, temporal, and religious territories, and so the King of France in it may seem only noble in saying of

Cordelia 'she is herself a dowry' (*LRF* 1.1.241). He then takes her as his wife with:

> Fairest Cordelia, that art most rich, being poor;
> Most choice, forsaken; and most loved, despised:
> Thee and thy virtues here I seize upon.
> Be it lawful, I take up what's cast away.
> Gods, gods! 'Tis strange that from their cold'st neglect
> My love should kindle to inflamed respect. –
> Thy dowerless daughter, King, thrown to my chance,
> Is queen of us, of ours, and our fair France.
> Not all the dukes of wat'rish Burgundy
> Can buy this unprized precious maid of me. –
> Bid them farewell, Cordelia, though unkind.
> Thou losest here, a better where to find.
>
> (*LRF* 1.1.250–61)

Yet this fine gesture is understood less than romantically by the conventionally minded courtier Gloucester. Just before reading Edmund's forged letter Gloucester remarks on disturbances of the times not in astrological, but in political terms:

> Kent banished thus, and France in choler parted,
> And the King gone tonight, prescribed his power,
> Confined to exhibition – all this done
> Upon the gad? –   (*LRF* 1.2.23–6)

It is only after the shock of accepting Edmund's falsified evidence of Edgar's conspiracy that Gloucester attributes all to 'These late eclipses in the sun and moon' (1.2.101), to Edmund's derision. So we may take Gloucester's remark on France's departure as an expression of a political creature's genuine worry over international and national disruptions, partly occasioned by a marriage without dowry.

We may further wonder about Gloucester's mention of the French King's 'choler'. Is the absence of a dowry a cause of his anger? Or have further harsh words passed between France and Lear off stage as indicated by Goneril's sarcastic 'There is further compliment of leave-taking between France and him' (1.1.301–2)? In any case, there is another sense in which France, who has spoken of his 'inflamed respect' for the truth-telling Cordelia, may be read by some as being hot. There is on Lear's part at least an innuendo that France's acceptance of a dowerless maid was driven by 'heat' in a sexual sense, when with anger and disgust Lear describes his loathing of the idea of returning to live with Regan:

Why, the hot-blooded France, that dowerless took
Our youngest born – I could as well be brought
To knee his throne and, squire-like, pension beg
To keep base life afoot.   (*LRF* 2.2.385–8)

A parallel to such an attitude to France may appear in *The Tempest* where, for often-debated reasons, Prospero repeatedly admonishes Prince Ferdinand's potential unchastity. Although on an island where titles are ineffectual, Ferdinand offers to just-met Miranda: 'O, if a virgin, / And your affection not gone forth, I'll make you / The Queen of Naples' (*TMP* 1.2.450–2). Hearing this King Cophetua-like offer, Prospero punishes Ferdinand as a 'traitor' with Caliban's task of log-carrying; then Prospero overhears Miranda's artless 'by my modesty, / The jewel in my dower, I would not wish / Any companion in the world but you' (3.1.53–5). With no further mention of a dowry or parental blessing than that, Miranda offers herself to Ferdinand with: 'I am your wife, if you will marry me' (3.1.83). Following this Prospero overhears Ferdinand's impassioned acceptance and the couple's interchange of mutual present-tense vows asserting that they have taken the status of 'husband' and 'wife'. He also sees the confirmation of this by a traditional handfasting, forming a fully binding marriage by spousals, as we have said. After some delay Ferdinand is released from his servitude, but even then he is subjected to Prospero's dinning insistence that he delay sexual consummation of his marriage until 'All sanctimonious ceremonies' are 'ministered' (4.1.16–17). Here a possible verbal parallel appears with King Lear's remark on 'the hot-blooded France' in Prospero's suspicion that 'th' fire i' th' blood' (4.1.53) may have led Ferdinand into marriage. This would not be the only parallel between the patriarchs Prospero and Lear. A great difference, however, is implied in the fact that, in his spite and fury and probably guilt as well, Lear cannot even bring himself to name Cordelia, but is forced into the circumlocution, 'our youngest born'.[19] Prospero, in the end at least, conversely proves to Miranda he has acted as promised 'in care of thee'.

In *The Winter's Tale* the choleric King Polixenes spies on the festive – but also anxious – sheep-shearing revels, fearing that his son will be misled into an unequal match. Even before Polixenes' arrival, the wooing of the seemingly lowly Perdita by Prince Florizel is beset with fears of a lascivious misalliance. Perdita's fears are not well assuaged by Florizel's learned comparisons of his disguised self to classical gods who have inhabited lustful animals to further sexual pursuit of beautiful mortal women. But of course Florizel disowns his own comparisons: 'Their transformations / Were never

for a piece of beauty rarer, / Nor in a way so chaste, since my desires / Run
not before mine honour, nor my lusts / Burn hotter than my faith' (*WT*
4.4.31–5). Florizel also highlights the inequality in his marriage by belittling
a generous dowry offered by the Old Shepherd:

> OLD SHEPHERD   I give my daughter to him, and will make
>   Her portion equal his.
> FLORIZEL   O, that must be
>   I' th' virtue of your daughter. One being dead,
>   I shall have more than you can dream of yet,
>   Enough then for your wonder.   (*WT* 4.4.383–7)

Although chastity is averred, and 'virtue' is a dowry, there is still a strong
link between this fabulating pastoral scene and mirror-like allusions in the
play (and its source) to the actually rapidly declining medieval institution
of heterogamic concubinage.[20] Certainly Polixenes thinks Perdita unchaste
(4.4.438–9); the tendencies of royal sons to pseudo-marry or cohabit at will
did not terminate in Shakespeare's England.

Despite the great interest, reflecting their social importance, shown in
dowry arrangements in many of Shakespeare's plays, in a number of these
a bride's marriage portion is said either to be not paid (*TGV* 3.1.78–9; *MM*
1.2.137–9 and 3.1.219–32; *LRF* 1.1.128–9), or to exist only in the form of her
great virtue (*TGV* 3.1.68–79; *LRF* 1.1.108–20; *WT* 4.4.384–5; *TMP* 3.1.53–4;
implicitly *AYL*, *TN*, *MM*, *PER*). Depending on the mode of the play,
such a lack is not always an occasion for trouble. In general, Shakespearian
bridegrooms who happily marry dowerless brides inhabit fableland (being
neighbours with Cophetua, the Prince and the Beggar Maid, and Prince
Charming and Cinderella), not mirrorland. Often there is no actual misalliance in apparently heterogamic Shakespearian marriages; pastoral conventions allow the apparent low status of heroes or heroines to be illusory, with
their disguises as countrymen or countrywomen only temporary accidents
befalling the wealthily well-born.[21]

There are also, however, painful Shakespearian instances of missing or
withdrawn dowries. For instance, in *The Two Gentlemen* an expected dowry
is (at least in pretence) withdrawn by Silvia's father, the Duke of Milan. He
claims that he will remarry and so disinherit her, his purpose being to trick
Valentine into revealing their plans for elopement. Despite the fantastic
nature of the ruse, the Duke's description of how he has decided to remarry
rather than be dependent on his daughter has interestingly mirror-like
aspects. His threats seem to express an assumption that his future care in
old age merits present material support:

> Proud, disobedient, stubborn, lacking duty,
> Neither regarding that she is my child
> Nor fearing me as if I were her father.
> And may I say to thee, this pride of hers
> Upon advice hath drawn my love from her,
> And where I thought the remnant of mine age
> Should have been cherished by her child-like duty,
> I now am full resolved to take a wife,
> And turn her out to who will take her in.
> Then let her beauty be her wedding dower,
> For me and my possessions she esteems not.
>
> (*TGV* 3.1.69–79)

This may seem to mirror a social reality, although social historians have pointed out that for demographic reasons (normal late marriage, early death) in practice 'extended family' households were not at all common in early modern England.[22] A similar motive is implied in the premising fable of *King Lear* when Lear connects his withdrawal of Cordelia's marriage portion with his lost hopes of his original plans for old age, 'to set my rest / On her kind nursery' (*LRF* 1.1.123–4).

Another case of missing dowries arises, or rather two cases arise, when *All's Well* emphasises the dowryless conditions of otherwise marriageable Helena and Diana. Romantic fabulation gives way to practical mirroring when the King says of Helena 'Virtue and she / Is her own dower', but then adds that preceding her marriage there will also be a supply of 'honour and wealth from me' (*AWW* 2.3.144–5). However, the play thoroughly confounds the romantic thrust of Helena's good fortune, for her virtues (and new dowry) prove unattractive to the young Count Bertram who is ordered to marry her (in our discussion of wardship in chapter 3 we have considered the possibility of his 'disparagement').

The forced marriage of Bertram to Helena collides with a model of a love-led 'companionate' marriage choice. Indeed a tension between this ideal as it was expressed in the relatively free choice of marriage partners for many of Shakespeare's middling-class contemporaries, and the expression of different priorities underlying the operation of a distinctly economic 'marriage market' in Shakespeare's London,[23] may have inspired some of the peculiar ironies of *All's Well*. For instance, the unhallowed 'bed trick' is offered by Helena as a holy means to provide virtuous but poor Diana's dowry: 'Doubt not but heaven / Hath brought me up to be your daughter's dower' (4.4.18–19). And then the French King seemingly repeats the ill-considered offer he made to Helena, by offering to Diana: 'If thou be'st yet a fresh uncropped flower, / Choose thou thy husband and I'll pay thy dower' (5.3.328–9).

A similar economic means 'To buy you a better husband' is offered to Mariana late in *Measure for Measure* (5.1.422). This play is built around missing dowries; both Mariana's and Juliet's lost dowries bring confusion into their marriage contracts, as we have seen in our discussions of 'pre-contracts' in chapter 1. Moreover, Isabella may be implied to be dowryless by certain details of the play. For in general the families of well-born women entering convents paid dowries on their behalf, but this was not the case for women joining the Poor Clares.[24] It has therefore been argued that this explains Isabella's choice of 'the sisterhood, the votarists of Saint Clare' (1.4.5) when she decides to enter a convent.[25] The implied straitened circumstances of Isabella's family might motivate her brother's near-fatal postponement of the 'outward' forms of marrying, which was occasioned, he says, 'Only for propagation of a dower' (1.2.137–8). And so Isabella, nearly the only young woman in Shakespeare's plays choosing not to marry,[26] might be understood as constrained in part by a lack of dowry, as well as guided by her inclination. This understanding of an additional motivation may have a significant bearing on the notorious question of her willingness, or not, to marry at the end of *Measure for Measure*.[27]

ROYAL MARRIAGES AND DOWRIES IN SHAKESPEARE

In Shakespeare's history plays, where actual dynastic issues are at stake, a royal misalliance or royal marriage without a suitable dowry is seen as either impossible or highly ill advised. So Shakespeare's King Henry VI at first accedes to a marriage bringing 'a large and sumptuous dowry' (*1H6* 5.1.20), and also probable peace with France. But soon after he is influenced by Suffolk to marry Margaret, who brings neither dowry nor political advantage. When the English nobles complain, Suffolk expresses an unrealistic (for royals) notion of marital free will and chides:

> A dower, my lords? Disgrace not so your King
> That he should be so abject, base, and poor
> To choose for wealth and not for perfect love.
> Henry is able to enrich his queen,
> And not to seek a queen to make him rich.
> So worthless peasants bargain for their wives,
> As market men for oxen, sheep, or horse.
> Marriage is a matter of more worth
> Than to be dealt in by attorneyship.

Not whom we will but whom his grace affects
Must be companion of his nuptial bed.
And therefore, lords, since he affects her most,
That most of all these reasons bindeth us:
In our opinions she should be preferred.
For what is wedlock forced but a hell,
An age of discord and continual strife,
Whereas the contrary bringeth bliss,
And is a pattern of celestial peace.

(*1H6* 5.7.48–65)

But Henry's adventure in companionate marriage, or the individualistic 'heroics of marriage',[28] soon begins to have disastrous consequences. This is underscored, for instance, when Margaret's family's poverty is recalled in the Yorkist Edward Plantagenet's insulting description of Henry's marriage, again debasing the legend of King Cophetua: 'he took a beggar to his bed' (*RDY* 2.2.154).[29]

Shakespeare's much more astute King Henry V demands great territories in France for Princess Katherine's marriage portion. Hal uses considerable diplomacy and wit in this marriage negotiation, which is also a peace negotiation with France. So, following the model that dowry negotiations were privately arranged, he deliberately dismisses the court audience to avoid the sort of disastrous excessive publicity of royal affairs seen during the kingdom's division in *King Lear*. Henry then punningly woos Katherine with:

No, it is not possible you should love the enemy of France, Kate. But in loving me, you should love the friend of France, for I love France so well that I will not part with a village of it, I will have it all mine; and Kate, when France is mine, and I am yours, then yours is France, and you are mine. (*H5* 5.2.171–6)

This demand is potentially offensive, but so framed that it humorously side-steps the fact that the victor at Agincourt can demand what territory he wants for a dowry as well as the charming princess, whom he will not have as wife without it.[30] And again showing that royal dowries portrayed by Shakespeare involved great political matters, we see an offer of whole French provinces in *King John*. Having ascertained a willingness to consent to marriage on the part of his niece Blanche and Louis the Dauphin of France, King John offers as her dowry:

Volquessen, Touraine, Maine,
Poitou, and Anjou, these five provinces,
With her to thee, and this addition more:
Full thirty thousand marks of English coin.

(*JN* 2.1.528–31)

Having observed these patterns, we may return to reconsider the dowry-seeking motives of Burgundy in *King Lear*. Before learning of Cordelia's disgrace, Burgundy had demanded no more in dowry than the offer Lear originally made (1.1.192–4). This is generous, as a bridegroom's representatives would normally try to increase an opening offer. After learning that Cordelia will bring little political advantage, Burgundy merely reiterates his first modest demands of Lear:

> Give but that portion which yourself proposed,
> And here I take Cordelia by the hand,
> Duchess of Burgundy.   (*LRF* 1.1.242–4)

This is hardly despicable. Despite its fabulating premises, *King Lear* is not sealed against political truths; for Burgundy to take a wife with neither dowry nor influence would be abnormal and unwise. Yet having to admit this is difficult and embarrassing for Burgundy. He is placed in a most uncomfortable position due to the glare of publicity used by Lear to punish and humiliate Cordelia. Unlike Hal, Burgundy has no opportunity to stipulate in private, with a humorous phrase, that his demands must be met; he is forced rather to fall back stammeringly on phraseology which may echo the equitable doctrine of legal 'election' (1.1.204–5).[31] The discomfort and political unwisdom of the whole affair is underscored when, with waspish wit, Cordelia exactly inverts Prince Hal's jest, saying: 'Peace be with Burgundy; / Since that respect and fortunes are his love, / I shall not be his wife' (1.1.247–9).

There is no sign that Cordelia is dismayed when Goneril says she has been received as a wife 'At fortune's alms' (1.1.278); Cordelia at least maintains the myth of the superiority of a marriage without regard for pelf. This relates to a difference of mode between the fabulating first act of *King Lear* and the mirror-like last act of *Henry V*. But, for Shakespeare, that difference is not that between an ideal and a fallen world: *Henry V* ends with international peace and family happiness, while *King Lear* ends with both family and trans-national disaster.

In general, Shakespeare implies the view that dowries were of enormous importance. His many and varied dramatisations of dowry arrangements made preceding marriages make clear that the foundation of new households was perceived in his time as a matter of fundamental economic, social, and family significance. Thus Shakespeare's portrayals of marriage did not end with an automatic 'happily ever after'. Rather, marrying is seen to have great import for the future, as well as being the outcome of the romantic trials and adventures leading up to it.

CHAPTER 5

The solemnisation of marriage

INTRODUCTION

As we have seen in chapter 1, John Webster's Duchess of Malfi and her steward Antonio marry privately by mutual consent. Each uses unconventional and metaphorical language to express their intent to marry one another, and yet by this they are married. For, as discussed above, any expression of genuine present intent, with no need for a particular formula or type of words, created a valid and binding marriage contract by spousals. The Duchess then says, using the word 'force' with a meaning perhaps hovering between legal 'enforcement' (*OED* 'enforce' III, 14) and moral compulsion: 'What can the church force more?' Antonio hints at misgivings, but she reiterates:[1]

> How can the church bind faster?
> We are now man and wife, and 'tis the church
> That must but echo this:–

No clearer statement could be made of the rules, which we have previously examined, governing consensual marriage. These rules, current in Shakespeare's England, did indeed ensure the inability of the Church or its ceremonies to 'bind faster' in marriage than spousals did. Church solemnities, the Duchess says, are merely an echo of what went before.

Webster's play makes equally clear, however, that such a marriage by spousals alone could be disastrous for all concerned. The not uncommon practice of unsolemnised or 'clandestine' marriage was much debated, as we shall see in chapter 6. Here we will consider the other side of the same coin, the question of solemnisation itself. Clearly solemnisation and clandestinity were paired as inverses; they will be discussed in two separate chapters simply because there is so much to explore in relation to each.

Before going on to examine the history of solemnisation, we must point out that contemporary English marriage laws provide the inevitable background for Shakespeare's plays. Indeed we have found, as a general rule, that law in Shakespeare's plays usually accorded with the laws currently in force in England, regardless of the setting in time or place of the dramatised action. This principle applies in most places concerned with solemnisation of marriages; we will note some exceptions where either fabulating or fantastically mooted modes of dramatic construction are more consequential than mirror-like modes. Understanding that will lead to the uncovering of some peculiar complications. For instance, the next chapter will explore the strange-seeming paradox that a person clandestinely married, like the Duchess of Malfi, was by Elizabethan law both legally married and guilty of a punishable offence. And in the present chapter we will demonstrate that – in subtle ways not noted before – Shakespeare responded to contemporary disputes over the prescribed methods for solemnising marriages.

SOLEMNISATION OF MARRIAGE AND ENGLISH LAW

Various suggestions have been advanced to explain a widespread lack of confidence in early modern England about what actions were needed to make a marriage. Some historians point to the break with the Church of Rome. While Catholic Europe carried out marriage law reforms, Tudor and early Stuart England were unable to do so because of royal conservatism and aversion to radical change (Henry), or early death (Edward), or royal hostility to marriage in general (Elizabeth), or lack of agreement among the various groups of moderate Protestants, reforming Puritans, and Catholics or quasi-Catholics who vied for power.

In fact difficulties caused by lack of an agreed form for contracting marriage were not unique to England, nor new in the sixteenth century, and were rather the result of very longstanding disagreements over the role, if any, that should be played by the Church in marriage. In the first century after Christ the early Church fathers had no historical model for Christian marriage. Being either unable or unwilling to accept that marriage was the concern of the Church, they did not set out any code or official policy on marriage. Rather than seeking to regulate secular life, the early Church promoted an ideal of a life of contemplative prayer and celibacy.[2] As a result, uncertainties over whether the Church needed to bless or solemnise a marriage continued throughout medieval and early modern England.

The Church did eventually accept a responsibility for legislating on marriage. In the late twelfth century Pope Alexander III made an attempt to compel the use of a validating church marriage ceremony, but this attempt was unsuccessful. Instead, as we have seen, the Roman Church accepted the doctrine of consent, which held that a valid marriage was contracted solely by the consent of both parties and that the Church played no part in legal formalities necessary for marriage formation.

The Alexandrine doctrine of consensual marriage remained controversial, and was long criticised by both reformers and scholars. However, as E. J. Carlson has pointed out, the early theologians were limited because 'there was no scriptural warrant for a requirement of ceremony, banns, endowment or parental consent for a valid marriage'.[3] Neither did Roman law provide helpful precedents, as it allowed informal secular marriage by consent alone.[4]

Although the Church failed to regulate marriage formation, it did claim a special interest in marriage. At the Council of Florence (1431–46) theologians confirmed that marriage was a sacrament, that is, an outward sign of inward grace. In consequence, when husband and wife contracted before God, an indissoluble bond was created between them. The two theories of marriage, that it was a sacrament, and also that it was created solely by consent of the parties, coexisted uneasily until the implementation (for most of Catholic Europe by 1564) of the decree *Tametsi* of the Council of Trent.[5]

In England, by contrast, marriage was dropped from the list of sacraments during the Reformation, but consensual marriage continued valid until 26 Geo. II c.33 (1753), known as Lord Hardwicke's Marriage Act. There were earlier short-lived attempts at reform, but none of these applied in Shakespeare's time.[6]

There is, however, no doubt that even before the 1564 counter-Reformation Tridentine reforms, or the 1753 English Marriage Act, Churches strongly discouraged marriages that were made with lack of formality. In 1215 at the Fourth Lateran Council Pope Innocent III insisted on the public announcement in church of a proposed marriage on three separate occasions. In England this requirement for the publication of banns had already been made in 1200 by the Archbishop of Canterbury, Hubert Walter, for the province of Canterbury. Between 1200 and 1342 more than thirty canons and diocesan statutes attempted to regulate marriage in England. In particular a marriage was to be a public ceremony conducted by a priest before witnesses. This ceremony could take place inside the church during mass, or outside at the door of the church, with an exchange of rings and the endowment of the woman.[7] Other regulations required the public declaration of impediments, and set out times and seasons allowed for the marriage to take place. For example, the ceremony was to be held in the morning, and certain days and seasons (Sundays, Lent) were to be avoided.

Henry VIII declared himself the temporal head of the Church in England in 1534 by the Act of Supremacy. The English Reformation was then put in place by piecemeal legislation during Henry's reign and later during the reigns of his son Edward and daughter Elizabeth. The law of marriage was a central concern to Henry because of his struggles with the Pope about his desire to divorce and marry again, and his 'marital problems would affect the theory and law of marriage in the Western European tradition for centuries to come'.[8] But despite Henry's concerns with divorce, any general reform of marriage laws met with little royal sympathy. Before the break with Rome, Henry had been scathing of the opinions of continental reformers. In response to Martin Luther's 1520 book, *The Babylonian Captivity of the Church*, which attacked the Church of Rome and the Holy Sacraments, Henry in 1521 had written *Assertio Septum Sacramentorum*.[9] In this work Henry poured scorn on Luther's objection that there was no scriptural authority for considering marriage to be a Holy Sacrament, holding Luther's comments to be a preposterous questioning of centuries of Church teaching. It seems that twenty or so years later he remained just as unwilling to contemplate alterations to long-established tenets of the Church, unless, of course, these conflicted with his claim to temporal supremacy in England.

In a series of legislation just before and after his 1534 marriage to Anne Boleyn, Henry and his ministers acted quickly to end religious submission to Rome.[10] Following the agreement with the clergy embodied in The Submission of the Clergy 1532, the statute 25 Hen. VIII c.19 (1534) proposed the replacement of canon law with revised Church canons. This Act contains a clause, numbered 3, which is still in effect, that limits the powers of Convocation: 'no canons, constitutions or ordinances shall be made . . . which shall be contrary or repugnant to the King's prerogative royal, or the customs, laws, or statutes of this realm'.[11] Convocation's subordination thereafter became a running theme especially in relation to regulation of marriage. A complete draft of revised canons was produced within eighteen months, but then was never implemented.[12] In 1536 Convocation again tried to press Henry to move ahead with the revised canons, and again Henry did nothing. In 1544 another Parliamentary Bill provided that a new code of canon law should be drafted for England. This did receive the King's signature, but once again Henry took no further action.[13]

Although Henry argued with his Archbishop Cranmer for its retention,[14] marriage ceased to be a Holy Sacrament in England in 1536 when the Ten Articles, written to provide a doctrinal statement for clerical marriage, omitted marriage from the list of sacraments.[15] 'Holy matrimonie' is named rather as an 'honorable estate instituted of God in paradise' in the first Book of Common Prayer of 1549, and in the Tudor revised reissues.[16]

Following the 1549 Act of Uniformity (2 & 3 Edw. VI c.1), the Prayer Book became the only legal form of worship, and it finally provided the new English Protestant Church with a form of marriage ceremony, 'The Forme of Solemnization of Matrimonie'.[17] Significant innovations made there by Cranmer included the use of the vernacular, and a requirement that the whole ceremony take place inside the church and not outside it at the church door. Also, importantly, at the very start of the ceremony, marriage is said to be made firstly for the purpose of procreation, next for avoiding fornication and sin, and lastly (innovatively) for 'mutuall society, helpe and coumfort'.[18] The old and new were both represented in the new Prayer Book marriage ceremony. For instance, the old popular rituals of handfasting and ring-giving were retained and formally incorporated; in the 1549 version the priest joins the hands of bride and groom and the groom gives a ring and 'other tokens of spousage, as golde or silver' to the bride. The groom then tells the bride 'with thys ring I thee wed: Thys golde and silver I thee geve.'[19]

Cranmer's new Prayer Book aimed to conciliate both conservative and reformed opinion by making concessions to each. For example, it retained ceremonies and symbols such as confirmation, and the use of vestments and candles, as Martin Bucer said, 'lest the people, not yet thoroughly instructed in Christ, should by too extensive innovations be frightened away from Christ's religion, and that rather they may be won over'.[20] The mass was retained even though the service was now more lengthily described as 'The Supper of the Lorde and the holy Communion commonly called the Masse'. This retention was intended to avoid open and bitter dispute about transubstantiation and the real presence in the mass while reassuring conservative opinion. The introduction of the vernacular and the form taken by the prayer of consecration at the heart of the mass, on the other hand, emphasised the spiritual nature of the communion, which satisfied reformers, or some of them.

In 1551 the Commons again approved the appointment of a Commission to draft new Church canons. Although the resulting *Reformatio Legum Ecclesiasticarum* was completed by 1553, it met with opposition in the Lords and Commons and 'died with the King [Edward VI] on 6 July 1553'.[21] The Code included the innovations that a valid marriage could only be contracted 'openly in front of the church' following banns and that it required parents' or guardians' consent. The *Reformatio* also would have abolished divorce *a mensa et thoro*, and would have allowed divorce and remarriage for both men and women if they were the 'innocent party' following adultery, or in cases of desertion, 'deadly hostility', or criminal ill-treatment. It also would have required mothers to breast-feed their own children![22]

Although the *Reformatio* was halted, further reform of the 1549 Prayer Book was brought forward. Perhaps because the 1549 version was a compromise and conciliatory, always intended to be temporary, it was soon followed by a more radically Protestant version which satisfied among other demands some Puritan desires for reform of the marriage ceremony. This 1552 Prayer Book, completed by Cranmer before Edward's death, was authorised for use by Parliament by a new Act of Uniformity in 5 & 6 Ed. VI c.1 (1552).[23] This second Prayer Book made few, but very significant, changes to the initial version of 1549. These alterations included the reading of the Ten Commandments, a new form of words to be said by the priest to communicants, and new directions on the kind of bread and wine to be used in the communion service which gave unequivocal expression to reformers' denial of the real presence in the elements of bread and wine. This was to be everyday bread, not specially made wafers, and if any remained left over the priest could take it home for his own use; there was to be no consecration of the elements of bread and wine.[24]

Another, very visible, change made in 1552 was an instruction that altars be replaced by plain wooden tables set in the body of the church or in the chancel. There was also a revision of the 1549 Prayer Book's instruction that before a communion service priests were to call on known 'open and notorious evill livers' to confess their sins before the congregation, and call on those known to bear malice towards each other to reconcile their differences before they took communion. There was a concern that these instructions, added to the Prayer Book exhortations to communicants to practise exercises of critical self-examination and confession, had the unintended but unsurprising result of discouraging church attendance.[25] Parishioners were very afraid of the consequences of inadequate preparation, and were anyway unused to frequent taking of communion, which the old Catholic pattern of worship had not required. To overcome this problem the 1552 Prayer Book elevated the offices of matins, and then evensong (which are not mass), into the main church services for most parishioners, with tolling of church bells to remind them the office was about to begin.[26] In the marriage service in particular, the 1552 Prayer Book removed the groom's spousal gifts to his bride of gold and silver, and only the ring remained.[27]

The 1552 Prayer Book was outlawed when the Catholic Queen Mary came to the throne in 1553. In its place Mary restored the Latin Breviary and Missal to general use. Arguably, this was not an unpopular move; there was widespread support for Mary's claim to the throne, perhaps showing how fragile the new religious order had been. In contrast to earlier historical readings, Christopher Haigh and others claim that in the middle sixteenth century English Protestantism had a limited popular appeal because its concentration on Bible reading, and its insistence on justification by faith and on predestination, did not readily motivate a largely illiterate population. While elsewhere in northern Europe mobs destroyed altars and images, in England these were taken down by state-hired masons and carpenters and sometimes quietly replaced by the parishioners later.[28] David Starkey claims that in its English beginnings Protestantism was not a broadly based ideological uprising (and neither was it the result of Henry VIII's megalomania) but rather the battleground of factional politics at the royal court.[29] Haigh contends that, except in London, it was not until the reign of Elizabeth that the widespread teaching of the reformed religion first took place, and 'the establishment of protestantism as a mass religion was thus a consequence, not a cause, of the political Reformation'.[30]

In 1559 Queen Elizabeth issued a new Act of Uniformity (1 Eliz. I c.2) slightly moderating the Reformation trend of the 1552 Act of Uniformity; this Elizabethan Act continued in force until 1640. The Act authorised and imposed the use of a slightly more conservative revision of the martyred Cranmer's 1552 Prayer Book.[31] This version omitted Cranmer's 'black rubric', which had been a last-minute amendment to assuage Protestant sensibilities and which explained that communicants could kneel when receiving communion without acknowledging the real presence in the elements of bread and wine. Despite her own 1559 Act, Elizabeth personally used Catholic ritual symbols in the royal chapel,[32] and it has recently been proved that she used the 1549 Prayer Book there as well.[33] But 'to reintroduce 1549 was not practical politics',[34] for Elizabeth was supported by the surviving Protestants from King Edward's Council, and had to contend with strongly Protestant returning Marian exiles.

Elizabeth's settlement, however, did not satisfy some of the exiles' and others' fervent wishes for further reform. It rather established a Church nearly 'frozen in time' as of 1552.[35] An uneasy compromise between those who wanted further radical religious changes and those who supported the Queen continued until the appearance in the 1580s of the anti-Calvinist Arminians, who laid renewed emphasis on the sacraments, in particular the real presence in the eucharist, and looked to the 1549 Prayer Book. On the other hand, in reaction to their disappointment about the 1559 Prayer Book some Puritans turned to other liturgies. For example, the 1576 Liturgy of

Compromise was sometimes used, or 'doctored' versions of the Prayer Book rites, and expurgated or edited editions of the Prayer Book were sometimes bound with the Geneva Bible for use.[36]

Gerald Bray explains that further attempts to enact the 1553 *Reformatio Legum* in the Parliaments of 1571 and 1572 came to nothing partly because the Queen suspended all religious bills on 22 May 1572 to avert 'trouble over prayer book reform'; the next day she had to reassure Parliament that there was no 'royal retreat from protestantism' and 'the reformed faith was safe in her hands'.[37] Clearly religious reform, and especially Prayer Book reform, were long-running and highly contentious issues.

When Scottish James came to the English throne, Puritan hopes for further religious reform were again raised. A petition, called the Millenary Petition because of the supposed one thousand clergy who signed it, was presented to James in April 1603. This asked for relief from grievances, and in particular the removal of church ceremonies offensive to Puritan sensibilities. These included confirmation, private baptism, and baptism administered by women (midwives). The petitioners also requested that the use of clerical surplices and caps should be abolished, that the term 'priests' should go, that a sermon and examination should take place before communion, that long services should be abridged, that church music should edify and not entertain, and that a stricter uniformity of doctrine (along their own lines) should be prescribed. They also asked that the obligatory use of the wedding ring be abandoned. Other grievances in the Petition concerned the church courts, compulsory subscription to articles of religion, and the use of *ex officio* oaths by the Court of High Commission.[38] The Hampton Court Conference, called by James to listen to these complaints, took place on 15, 16, and 18 January 1604 in the royal presence chamber. The outcome was disappointing for Puritan hopes, for James agreed to only very moderate reforms.[39] The resulting changes included small textual variations in the Prayer Book but without eradication of use of the sign of the cross, surplices, or wedding rings. New Church canons which slightly limited episcopal government were issued in 1604, but these were used by the newly appointed Archbishop Bancroft in an attempt to 'crush nonconformity' among the clergy.[40] All in all, James showed himself unimpressed with the Puritan arguments, while the representatives at the conference who had demanded only moderate changes and obtained almost nothing became 'victims of their own strategy'.[41]

The great lasting outcome of Hampton Court was an order for the preparation of the King James Bible. With regard to marriage law, the new canons of 1603–4 had no great effect. These included Canon 99, which made void marriage within prohibited degrees, re-enacting the table of 1563. The next, Canon 100, prohibited marriage and contracts of marriage for those under twenty-one without parental consent.[42] It did not declare such marriages void. Parliament did not enact the 1603–4 canons, and indeed passed a bill declaring that no recent (within ten years) or future Church canon could result in loss of life, liberty, or goods unless it was confirmed by a statute.[43] So, despite contrary assumptions of some Shakespeare critics,[44] the proposed 1603–4 Canons 99–108 concerning marriage and divorce had at best equivocal force on the laity unless they reiterated older Church laws.

Therefore, despite the great change made by the separation from Rome, and despite Protestant doctrinal reforms, unsolemnised marriages contin-ued to be accepted as valid in Shakespeare's England. Why this was the position in England when some other Protestant countries had managed to mandate the solemnisation of marriage in their laws, and counter-Reformation Catholic Europe did the same, is an unanswered question. It has been argued that while Englishmen were eventually able to accept the legislation of religious doctrine and their forms of worship, they were not happy to have legislation decide personal behaviour or 'discipline' be-cause of the power over them that would be given to the Church or state.[45] The Queen's personal dislike of marriage has also been suggested as a rea-son for refusal to countenance reform.[46] Also Elizabeth's father Henry 'had not made himself Pope of England to give away his power',[47] and proba-bly Elizabeth and certainly James echoed his sentiments. And finally, the Protestant reformers were not united and their bitter differences prevented effective agreement. Some, sympathising with Luther, preferred to believe marriage was mostly a secular concern,[48] while others either sought or feared an increase in power for the Church.[49] That the regulation of marriage was one of the central concerns of the English Reformation paradoxically de-layed the implementing of its reform.

SOLEMNISATION OF MARRIAGE AND THE SHAKESPEARIAN STAGE

As the law stood in Shakespeare's time, solemnisation of a marriage, using the 1559 Prayer Book, was prescribed by the 1559 Act of Uniformity. This Act 'invoked sanctions as severe as life imprisonment for . . . refusal to use the prayer book or for denouncing it', but as Collinson further comments, like many statutes this one was not effectively applied and so shows 'evi-dence for the aspirations of government, not a record of social reality'.[50] Although it has not been noted before, Shakespeare made indirect adverse comments on the Prayer Book marriage ceremony, as we shall see. Others made very explicit objections to this ceremony, so the sanctions were clearly no deterrent to public interest or debate.

The mandatory form for the marriage ceremony met with opposition from both ends of the religious spectrum. Catholics would have found objectionable the Reformation bias especially of the 1552 and 1559 Prayer Books. They also might not have liked the inclusion in all three Tudor Prayer Books of the companionate thesis that marriage is for 'mutuall societie, helpe and coumfort', which was included by Cranmer supported by the strongly Protestant Martin Bucer.[51] Puritans repeatedly and vociferously objected to the obligatory giving of a ring during the Prayer Book marriage ceremony, which they saw as idolatrous,[52] and to the inclusion of taking communion in the ceremony, which they saw as a popish custom.[53] Indeed the entire compulsory ceremony, as not one enjoined by the Bible and as one empowering the Church hierarchy, could have offended Elizabethan Puritans according to some interpretations.[54]

Opposition to the marriage ceremony was of course only a part of a wider range of objections to the religious compromises in the Tudor Prayer Books. The unacceptability of parts of the Prayer Book made the second of the 1583 Three Articles of the new Archbishop Whitgift intolerable to even moderate Puritans. This article required each clergyman to accept that 'the Book of Common Prayer . . . containeth nothing in it contrary to the word of God . . . and that he himself will use the form of the said book'. That stipulation, rather than the constitutional and doctrinal tenets of the two other of the three articles, 'touched the conscience of all precisions in the most tender place'.[55]

We will next argue that Shakespeare definitely addressed such controversies; by the varied means of significant silences, precise parodic parallels, and somewhat wild travesties, Shakespeare's plays responded to these matters in subtle ways.

In Shakespeare's plays the solemnisation of a marriage is frequently referred to as a future event, or is reported to have taken place offstage. Yet solemnisation is not seen as an act completed, and hardly ever seen as an act undertaken, on the stages of Shakespeare or his contemporaries. Was this omission due only to reasons of artistic expediency, or was it the result of external laws or other limitations on the playwrights' options?[56] It has been suggested, for instance, that 'Shakespeare's reluctance to represent any marriage but spousals on stage probably proceeds from religious scruple, from avoiding profanation, if not outright censorship'.[57] But solemn ceremonies at least as important as marriage, such as coronations, are portrayed on the Elizabethan stage. There is certainly no basis for an external reason sometimes alleged for an avoidance of theatrical portrayals of the Prayer Book marriage ceremony: a notion that even in representation this ceremony might have some sort of legal force. Spousals by handfasting or other gestures and by *verba de praesenti*, which did have binding legal effect (and were for that reason made parts of the Prayer Book ceremony), were frequently enacted on Shakespeare's and his contemporaries' stages; the fact of play-acting made theatrically imitated spousal contracts void.

There might have been artistic reasons for the same avoidance, due, for example, to theatrical condensations of time or detail, or perhaps to a wish to avoid representing the too familiarly commonplace. But marriage ceremonies are frequently seen, in our time, in cinematic representations, adding suspense, emotion, and dramatic colour. Therefore we find it strange that solemnised marriages did not have Shakespearian stage representations, while marriages by spousals were often portrayed in minute detail. We believe this absence may connect with historical tensions in Shakespeare's time concerning church rituals, and especially rituals prescribed in the Prayer Book.

It is useful to begin by considering some senses of 'solemn', 'solemnity', or 'solemnities', words often heard in Shakespeare's plays. A 'solemnity' could simply refer to a festive occasion, as in *Romeo and Juliet* 1.5.56 and 62, but in the same play these words refer figuratively to a marriage, as in 'murder our solemnity' (4.4.88), or 'solemn hymns' (4.4.115). In other places Shakespeare simply used 'solemnity' or 'solemnities' as a synonym for 'marriage', as in 'we will talk more of this when the solemnity is past' (*TNK* 2.1.12–13) or 'the moon, like to a silver bow / New bent in heaven, shall behold the night / Of our solemnities' (*MND* 1.1.9–11). Yet in other places the same terms refer either to social events unrelated to marriage, such as the Capulets' masked ball,[58] or to celebrations of marriage not part of a religious ceremony, as in 'A fortnight hold we this solemnity / In nightly revels and new jollity' (*MND* 5.1.362–3).

However, solemnisation is also referred to by Shakespeare in contexts where he indicates a practice that follows a spousal contract, and which enhances the lawfulness or the social acceptability of that marriage. Sometimes a gap of time between the making of a marriage contract and the solemnisation of the marriage is represented as having a particular purpose. In reality such postponements were not unusual where dynastic issues were at stake, and Church law required delays in marriages *de futuro* of underage children, or marriages made by proxy needing confirmation. Also marriage contracts could be conditional upon, for instance, the arrangement of dowries or granting of parental consent; then an interval between *de futuro* spousals and solemnisation simply indicated that further conditions had still to be met.

There are many examples of delayed solemnisation mentioned in Shakespeare's plays. For instance, Suffolk, the proxy wooer for King Henry VI, says 'I'll over then to England with this news, / And make this marriage to be solemnized' (*1H6* 5.5.123–4). Duke Vincentio probably implies there were conditional spousals when he recalls a delay between 'the contract and limit of the solemnity' during which time Mariana's 'brother Frederick was wrecked at sea, having in that perished vessel the dowry of his sister' (*MM* 3.1.217–19).[59] Conversely, when a marriage made by spousals bears the burden of urgent political purposes, as does an expedient marriage made in *King John* 2.1.534–6, the interval between handfasting and solemnisation can become negligibly short; this is seen in the lines: 'at Saint Mary's chapel presently / The rites of marriage shall be solemnized' (2.1.539–40).

Normally both canon law and the Prayer Book demanded the thrice reading of banns between spousal contracts and a church marriage ceremony. Such are the banns referred to when, seeking to make commodity out of others' frustration, Falstaff seeks out, for purposes of pecuniary exploitation, 'contracted bachelors, such as had been asked twice on the banns' (*1H4* 4.2.17–18).

Smacking of motives perhaps still dubious, yet more respectable than Falstaff's, Duke Prospero harshly insists that 'All sanctimonious ceremonies may / With full and holy rite be ministered' (*TMP* 4.1.16–17) before the marriage by *de praesenti* spousals of Ferdinand and Miranda is sexually consummated. Then Prospero echoes (with some obliquity in the changed referents) the opening words of all the Tudor Prayer Books' marriage ceremonies, 'Deerely beloved frendes, we are gathered here'.[60] Thus Prospero sets his course 'to Naples, / Where I have hope to see the nuptial / Of these our dear-beloved solemnized' (5.1.311–13).

As we shall see, Prospero's allusion to the language of the Prayer Book marriage ceremony stands out as uniquely positive in contrast to other Shakespearian allusions to this ceremony, which are generally satiric or parodic. But before exploring that, we will consider the contexts of Prospero's insistence on sexual abstinence before that ceremony. Officially, to avoid sinfulness, consummation required solemnisation, and normally solemnisation meant delay. In fact, the interval between the making of a marriage contract and the time for the sexual consummation of the marriage is perceived in widely diverse ways in varied Shakespearian instances. Some contracted couples in the plays awaiting solemnisation find this delay irksome,

some consciously 'rise above it', some attempt to or do 'jump the gun', and some are even pleased to wait. Strong contrasts are seen in Shakespeare's last plays concerning the frustrations of awaiting a marriage solemnisation. Prince Ferdinand not only accepts Prospero's insistence on deferring the sexual consummation of his marriage (which Prospero himself calls a 'contract' in *The Tempest* 4.1.19), but actually shows zeal for this temporary frustration until solemnisation:

> As I hope
> For quiet days, fair issue, and long life
> With such love as 'tis now, the murkiest den,
> The most opportune place, the strong'st suggestion
> Our worser genius can, shall never melt
> Mine honour into lust to take away
> The edge of that day's celebration;
> When I shall think or Phoebus' steeds are foundered
> Or night kept chained below.   (*TMP* 4.1.23–31)

Ferdinand thus expresses relish at how his very impatience will give 'the edge' to his marriage's 'celebration'. Quite on the contrary, Leontes recalls with lasting bitterness his prolonged wooing of his wife in which 'Three crabbed months had soured themselves to death', although this may suggest the interval either before handfasting or before the church marriage ceremony, for he describes it as 'Ere I could make thee open thy white hand / And clap thyself my love. Then didst thou utter, / "I am yours for ever"' (*WT* 1.2.104–7).[61]

Contrastingly again, when the Theseus of *The Two Noble Kinsmen* is persuaded to undertake a charitably motivated military campaign that will delay his wedding to Hippolyta, he is therefore praised for making 'affections bend / To godlike honours', and he replies 'As we are men, / Thus should we do; being sensually subdued / We lose our human title' (1.1.228–32). Not called away to such a noble enterprise, the Theseus of *A Midsummer Night's Dream* awaiting the same wedding repeatedly expresses great impatience, beginning the play with a complaint that the remaining four days of waiting 'lingers my desires', and nearly ending it with his comment on 'this long age of three hours' (5.1.33). Although she has only one day to wait for her secret wedding (*ROM* 2.2.63–4, 2.3.169–72), Juliet expresses a similar impatience in her soliloquy beginning: 'Gallop apace, you fiery-footed steeds, / Towards Phoebus' lodging' (3.2.1–31). Again acknowledging female desire, Rosalind jests that time: 'trots hard with a young maid between the contract of her marriage and the day it is solemnized. If the interim be but

a se'nnight, time's pace is so hard that it seems the length of seven year'
(*AYL* 3.2.306–9).

In fact the minimum delay for reading banns was usually two or three
weeks, for it required 'three several Sundays or holy days',[62] one of which
might be a weekday. So, if understood in terms of Elizabethan legitimacy,
the sort of hurried marriages referred to by Rosalind would have been by
a special licence allowing the omission or reduction of banns (such as was
Shakespeare's own marriage). Special licences, which were controversial,
were available from the bishop at a price; normally a substantial bond had
to be offered to guarantee against impediments.

However, it is quite possible that the hasty marriage in *Romeo and Juliet*
is intended only for dramatic effect. It would then employ the principle
of fabulation which relies on audiences overlooking detail and accepting
instead conventionalised dramatic time-compression.[63] Similar fabulation
may apply to the even greater haste seen in Portia's intent that, when the
right casket choice is made, 'straight shall our nuptial rites be solemnized'
(*MV* 2.9.6), and there is only an afternoon's delay between the spousals
by handfasting and the 'ceremony' confirming the marriage of Helena and
Bertram (*AWW* 2.3.179–81).

But no such fabulating compression for dramatic purposes applies to
Rosalind's jests about an 'interim' of only 'a se'nnight' between contract
and solemnisation. We suspect here rather a mirror-like dramatic mode,
although humorous, and that Rosalind's mention of a one-week delay for
solemnisation contains a deliberate allusion to the controversies surrounding banns. The possibility of this is increased because in the same series of
jests she gibes both at ignorant priests, and at idle lawyers and the seasons
of their inaction (*AYL* 3.2.311 and 3.2.322–3).

Another period of one week until solemnisation is imposed in *Much Ado*
on an impatient Shakespearian bridegroom, who just after contracting a
marriage seeks its overnight completion:

> DON PEDRO County Claudio, when mean you to go to church?
> CLAUDIO Tomorrow, my lord. Time goes on crutches till love have all his
>   rites.
> LEONATO Not till Monday, my dear son, which is hence a just sevennight,
>   and a time too brief, too, to have all things answer my mind.
>
> (*ADO* 2.1.332–8)

The ensuing wedding is made without any sign of banns (asking for objections) having been read. For the impediment of unchastity (to be discussed
in chapter 8) is not alleged by Don John until the ceremony itself. This
anomaly does allow for a great dramatic impact; there seems a deliberate

allusion to omission of the full requirements for solemnising marriage, and the consequences of such neglect.

Before further investigation of Claudio's and Hero's irregular and truncated marriage ceremony, which in fact traduces the controversial Prayer Book form, it is useful to take a slight detour through various Shakespearian allusions to the Prayer Book marriage ceremony.

When Shakespeare echoes the language of the Prayer Book marriage ceremony, the contexts are usually satiric or parodic (the exception being Prospero's allusion, noted above).[64] These echoes include 'Is not marriage honourable in a beggar?' (*ADO* 3.4.27–8) mocking the Prayer Book's distinctive phrase 'an honorable estate'.[65] Benedick's reference to 'the state of honourable marriage' in 5.4.30 is hardly less wry in effect, as it immediately precedes Claudio marrying a veiled woman whom he does not know. In another example Jaques remonstrates with Touchstone: 'This fellow will but join you together as they join wainscot; then one of you will prove a shrunk panel and, like green timber, warp, warp' (*AYL* 3.3.78–80), echoing the Prayer Book's distinctive 'joined together in matrimony', which differs from the phrase 'coupled together' translating Matthew 19.6 and Mark 10.9 in 'all Protestant Tudor Bibles'.[66]

Such echoes of the Prayer Book marriage ceremony that parody its language do not mock the meaning of the ceremony as subversively as does the (reported) physical travesty in Petruchio's marriage solemnisation. A wholly proper marriage ceremony (presumably using the Prayer Book) is arranged, but the groom Petruchio appears late, dressed as a tramp, an 'eyesore to our solemn festival' (*SHR* 3.2.101), and refuses to change into more fitting clothes to 'go to church'. And then, in recounted offstage action (3.3.30–56), Petruchio commits near sacrilege firstly in swearing 'Ay, by Gog's woun's' in place of the words of consent specified by the Prayer Book,[67] either 'I will' or the sacred words to be 'taught by the priest' accompanying the giving of a ring (no ring is ever mentioned in connection with this marriage). Secondly Petruchio strikes down the astonished priest, stamping and swearing. Thirdly he loudly kisses the bride on her lips in the church, which was also not part of the rubric of the Prayer Book ceremony. Indeed Petruchio is reported to assault the use of the Prayer Book itself:

> the priest let fall the book,
> And as he stooped again to take it up
> This mad-brained bridegroom took him such a cuff
> That down fell priest, and book, and book, and priest.
> 'Now take them up,' quoth he, 'if any list'.
>
> (*SHR* 3.3.34–8)

Whether this sort of behaviour, which causes its narrator to leave the church 'for very shame' (3.3.53), is simply mad-brained or has a further meaning, is our quest.

We may mention that the travesty of a marriage solemnisation in the description of Petruchio's wild behaviour has other relevance to controversies over the English Prayer Book's rubrics. The act of Petruchio throwing the 'sops' of his glass of wine into the face of the 'hungerly' appearing sexton (3.3.42–9) may well allude to the Prayer Book's rubric that the priest should take home for his own consumption the leftovers of the communion table including the wine.[68] The description of the 'hungerly' sexton's thin beard begging for sops may refer also to the notorious poverty of many English clerics. Petruchio's stamping and swearing 'As if the vicar meant to cozen him' (3.3.41) may be a less distinct allusion to the practice of the groom placing gold or silver on the Prayer Book,[69] an option allowed in the rubric of the 1549 first Prayer Book which was objectionable to reformers and removed in the 1552 and 1559 versions.

Having seen a range of Shakespearian parodies and a reported travesty of the Elizabethan Prayer Book marriage ceremony, we may return to the marriage ceremony of Hero and Claudio in *Much Ado* 4.1. This, although aborted, is the only such ceremony even partly enacted on Shakespeare's stage. Because of our illustrations of parodies, we might expect this staging to defy official Elizabethan standards. As far as it progresses, it appears to do so, for it diverges significantly from the prescribed form.[70] For instance, from the start Leonato, the bride's father (and Governor of Messina), is not obedient to the passive and silent role assigned the father by the rubric of the Prayer Book.[71] Instead he orders the officiating clergyman: 'Come, Friar Francis, be brief. Only to the plain form of marriage, and you shall recount their particular duties afterwards' (*ADO* 4.1.1–3). Thus the compliant Friar omits the beginning of the English marriage ceremony, including the controversial recitation of the three Protestant reasons for marriage, and asks only if the couple have come to be married. An unsatisfactory or equivocal answer from Claudio provokes a second intervention from impatient Leonato (4.1.7–8). The ceremony continues only as a sort of bitter sham, for Claudio's sole aim is the public shaming of Hero. The Friar asks 'If either of you know any inward impediment why you should not be conjoined, I charge you on your souls to utter it' (4.1.12–14). This recalls the Puritan emphasis on self-examination, and echoes the Prayer Book's 'I require you and charge you (as you will answer at the dreadful day of judgment, when the secrets of all hearts shall be disclosed) that if either of you do know of any impediment why ye may not be lawfully joined together in matrimony, ye may confess it.' But Shakespeare's Friar's exhortation of the bride and groom to reveal 'inward' impediments or else they will risk their souls varies slightly in emphasis, and indeed may resemble the much-decried ordeals that Puritan clergymen were subjected to when forced by the two Courts of High Commission to take *ex officio* oaths and then reveal any inward reservations they may have had about religious conformity. It may recall also the exhortations removed from the latest Prayer Book for public self-examination and confession before taking communion.

So the depiction of the failed marriage solemnisation in *Much Ado* is redolent of religious and legal controversy, although the cruel and bitter sarcasms Claudio heaps on falsely accused Hero undoubtedly bear the main emotional thrust of the scene. Here, alongside the bitterness of Shakespeare's representation of a marriage disrupted by error upon error, and in *The Shrew* alongside anti-establishment farce, an implicit questioning of what form marriage solemnisation should take features strongly.

Where that questioning leads is best illustrated in a scene of off-colour repartee in which a scurrilous clown abuses the official ideology of marriage specifically as it is set out in the Elizabethan Prayer Book marriage ceremony. This repartee includes a series of verbal allusions which have gone unnoted because they lampoon the structures and meanings of the Prayer Book, and do not simply echo its words.[72] Near the start of *All's Well That Ends Well* 1.3 the kindly Countess of Rousillon dismisses the clown Lavatch on account of rumours of his bawdry. Lavatch replies with a series of mock-godly jests using false logic in a manner not unlike Falstaff's,[73] wittily parrying well-founded accusations by presenting preposterous arguments to amuse and confound. Lavatch starts with a thinly disguised plea for money with which to marry: 'I am poor, though many of the rich are damned. But if I may have your ladyship's good will to go to the world, Isbel the woman and I will do as we may' (*AWW* 1.3.16–19). G. K. Hunter comments that the phrase 'go to the world' 'must derive from the Catholic view of the essential carnality of marriage'.[74] From that starting point, the Clown adds that 'I think I shall never have the blessing of God till I have issue o' my body, for they say bairns are blessings' (1.3.24–6). This catches the attention of the Countess who asks him to 'Tell me thy reason why thou wilt marry' (1.3.27). His reply parodies, with an increasing and cumulative satirical force, each of the three reasons given for marriage in the Prayer Book marriage ceremony. It should be noted that he parodies these reasons in exactly the same order as they are presented in all versions of the Prayer Book; this repetition of the distinctive ordering strengthens the force of the satiric allusion. For the sequencing in the Prayer Book was quite deliberately chosen by Cranmer as a compromise between suppressing and emphasising the innovative 'companionate' theories promoted by the more 'reformed' Protestant thinkers.[75] Martin Bucer, pleased that Cranmer included the companionate thesis, as MacCulloch says, 'for the first time in an official liturgical marriage text', suggested to the Archbishop that in the planned revision of the first Prayer Book the companionate reason should be placed first. That was in vain,[76] but the official Elizabethan *An Homilie of the State of Matrimonie* (commanded to be read out in church) does show Bucer's preferred ordering, with the companionate reason given not last but first.[77]

The first reason given by the Prayer Book for marriage is for 'the procreation of children to be brought up in the fear and nurture of the Lord', against which Lavatch has already mock-piously requisitioned 'bairns' in order to obtain for himself God's blessing. The second Prayer Book grounds for marriage, 'for a remedy against sin, and to avoid fornication', corresponds with Lavatch's next mock-pious point: 'I am driven on by the flesh, and he must needs go that the devil drives' (1.3.28–30). But it is in his parody of the third Prayer Book reason for marriage that Lavatch outdoes himself. Untangling his chop logic is not easy, but we see it as follows. He offers a sequence of 'other holy reasons' for marriage, starting with the proposition 'I have been, madam, a wicked creature, as you – and all flesh and blood – are, and indeed I do marry that I may repent' (1.3.35–7). The Countess points out the allusion here to the proverb 'marry in haste, repent at leisure', but Lavatch has yet to explain why he will repent of marriage. This is because of the cliché that a certainty of cuckoldry comes with a man's marriage, a stale enough piece of Elizabethan mock-wisdom which is here endowed with a new degree of high absurdity. Lavatch says 'I am out o' friends, madam, and I hope to have friends for my wife's sake' (1.3.39–40), which the Countess immediately understands to mean he will have 'friends' in his wife's lovers. This is indeed his meaning, which he paradoxically claims to be positive in a quibbling argument including 'he that cherishes my flesh and blood loves my flesh and blood; he that loves my flesh and blood is my friend; *ergo*, he that kisses my wife is my friend' (1.3.47–50). Now this wildly parodies the third Prayer Book reason for marriage, the specifically Protestant one that it is for friendly companionship.[78] From this vantage point Lavatch launches hoary jests about universal cuckoldry onto questions of religious dissension. He says 'young Chairbonne the puritan and old Poisson the papist, howsome'er their hearts are severed in religion, their heads are both one: they may jowl horns together like any deer i' th' herd' (1.3.51–5), suggesting the old fish-eating Catholic and the new flesh-eating

Protestant are cuckolds alike. This is Shakespeare's only direct reference to Reformation religious conflict, although Anne Boleyn is called 'A spleeny Lutheran' by Cardinal Wolsey in *All Is True* 3.2.100.

After some more scurrility and misogyny Lavatch exits on a note pertinent to Puritan objections to especially the 1559 Prayer Book's rubrics and rituals: 'Though honesty be no puritan, yet it will do no hurt; it will wear the surplice of humility over the black gown of a big heart' (1.3.91–3). The requirement for surplices in the first 1549 Prayer Book becomes tacit in the more reformed 1552 version, but then the 1559 Elizabethan Prayer Book added its notoriously vague Ornaments Rubric, which 'caused anxiety and dismay among protestant subjects'.[79] This demanded the use of 'such ornaments in the church as were in use by authority of Parliament in the second year of the reign of King Edward the Sixth'.[80] This was taken to require clerical use of ancient vestments, and these, according to Lavatch's upside-down logic, are surplices 'of humility'. He further alludes to secretive Genevan black ministerial gowns that some Puritan clergy wore under the requisite surplice as well as over a prideful 'big heart'.[81] In accusing Puritans of big-hearted pridefulness in their nonconformity, while making conformity in wearing a surplice a matter of due humility, Lavatch alludes to a long-running vestimental controversy, and seems to attack the sincerity of the Puritans. But this is half undone, because Lavatch is anyway given to using inverted logic,[82] and because the wearing of vestments is *prima facie* more ostentatious than that of plain gowns.

All this ridicule suggests that Shakespeare held in derision fundamentalism on any side of legal–religious controversies, especially over the rituals of marriage. The highly Protestant aspect of the Prayer Book ceremony, the naming of the three purposes of marriage, is elided or travestied in all Shakespearian contexts. On the other hand, the required giving of a ring or rings in the church ceremony, which was highly objectionable for Puritans, is also not seen in any Shakespearian setting in relation to solemnisation. This absence is all the more striking if we note that gifts of rings are frequently (but not inevitably) made either before, during, or after Shakespearian espousals (*TGV* 2.2.4–6, *R3* 1.2.189–212, *MV* 3.1.113, *ROM* 3.2.142, *WIV* 3.4.99, *TN* 2.2.5, *PER* s.22.61, *CYM* 1.1.113). Alternatively, Shakespearian rings sometimes feature symbolically within sexual intrigues involving cross-dressing or the bed trick (*AWW* 3.7.22, 4.2.39–52, 5.3.77–320, and in a crucial structural pattern throughout *The Merchant of Venice*).[83] Overall, no single referent or mysteriousness is allowed to attach to the 'signifier' in the material form of a ring;[84] a sentimental ring with a 'posey' inscribed is merely derided in *The Merchant of Venice* 5.1.147–50

and in *Hamlet* 3.2.145, and is imaged angrily broken in *A Lover's Complaint*
45. If a ring equals a marriage, as it does in the excellent song:

> Between the acres of the rye,
> With a hey, and a ho, and a hey-nonny-no,
> These pretty country folks would lie,
> In spring-time, the only pretty ring-time,ˆ
> When birds do sing, hey ding-a-ding ding,
> Sweet lovers love the spring.
>
> (*AYL* 5.3.21–6)

the equivalence is strictly in the form of a synecdoche or symbolisation of
the whole by a part (for example, 'pretty ring-time' equals marriage). For
Shakespeare a wedding ring does not in any mystical sense represent the
substantiation of an essence.

So in Shakespeare's satiric or subversive responses to the official English
marriage ceremony we see two opposed tendencies. These show an aversion
to the privatisation of spirituality implied in the Prayer Book marriage ceremony's exhortation to Protestant companionate marriage (a more extreme
privatisation, feared by Catholics, could be an alleged direct connection
to God obviating any need for an outward Church). They also show an
avoidance of any endorsement of the required use of a valuable physical
object, a ring, in a sacred context; this, for many Protestants, smacked of
idolatry.

More generally, Shakespeare's complex response to controversies over
marriage rites suggests that he was chary of tendencies to which Catholics
and Protestants each respectively objected: the elevating of private relationships and private convictions to a spiritual height, and the making of idols
where there are only symbols.[85] A sort of *via media* in religious sensibility
thus implied may have been more representative of the typical stances in
Shakespeare's world than those depicted in some views of history, which
seize on loud extremes.[86]

CHAPTER 6

Clandestine marriage, elopement, abduction, and rape: irregular marriage formation

THE PROBLEMS OF CLANDESTINE MARRIAGE

Any marriage that failed to meet all of the Church's demands for solemnisation was termed clandestine; this description therefore covered a large variety of ways in which unsolemnised consent could be given.[1] In Shakespeare's time there was also considerable dispute about the particular form of the Prayer Book solemnisation required by English law.

As we have said, even though the teaching of the Church of Rome was that marriage was a Holy Sacrament (or, in the Prayer Book of the Church of England, 'an honourable estate'), a failure to go through church solemnisation of a marriage was not fatal to its validity. Instead a clandestine marriage was treated as valid but a sin, and was punished as such in the church courts. Erring parties were usually ordered to comply with Prayer Book regulations for solemnisation and to do penance, and priests involved could be punished by suspension or loss of living. Such an outcome was unsatisfactory to many people. Wealthy families and patriarchs wanted more control over children's marriages. The more conservative Protestant reformers deplored the lack of regulation and wanted the validity of marriage controlled by the Church. Other Puritan reformers disagreed and objected to any clerical involvement at all in marriage. The clerical establishment complained about the activities of poor unbeneficed priests working outside Church hierarchies for profit. Common lawyers and Protestant reformers both complained that the church courts were insufficiently active in punishing those who flouted the law.

Dispensations were the focus for many other complaints. Clandestine marriages could be those that took place without banns being thrice read, or those not using all the ceremonies and following all the rubrics of the Prayer Book, or those that took place during disallowed times or seasons, or marriages that lacked more than one of these requirements for solemnisation.[2] Nevertheless a release from any of these requirements (or even from impediments, which will be discussed in chapter 8) could be obtained by a dispensation from the Church.

After the English Church separated from Rome, papal dispensations were replaced by the Act 25 Hen. VIII c.21 (1534) which allowed the Archbishop of Canterbury and bishops to grant licences and dispensations (in return for a fee). Licences were often purchased to give leave to marry without banns, and dispensations were also purchased by the nobility and the wealthy to allow marriages without public solemnities. Following many complaints made in books, in Convocation, and in Parliament, Archbishop Whitgift's 1583 'Articles for the Regulation of the Clergy' required a 'large and sufficient bond' to be given before a licence or dispensation was granted.[3] But this did little to prevent continuing complaints; the Millenary Petition of 1603 addressed by Puritan clergy to James I included the request that licences for marriage without banns should not be too readily granted, and the Canons of 1604 reiterated the need for banns and licences.

The Council of Trent in 1563 had solved some of the problems caused by clandestine marriages for the Catholic Church by requiring two witnesses to a valid marriage, one of whom was to be the parish priest. In early seventeenth-century England two witnesses were required by the church courts to give evidence in disputed cases, but the parish priest was not one of them. However, as an indication of the great disapproval the English Church extended towards unsolemnised marriages, witnesses to a clandestine marriage could be punished by the church courts, which not surprisingly made witnesses reluctant to testify. Other deterrents to witnesses were possible. In 1600 the Court of High Commission declared all the witnesses to John Donne's clandestine marriage excommunicate and imprisoned some; one witness was severely damaged professionally by being prevented from attending to his duties as a lawyer.[4] In the first decade of the seventeenth century the Bishop of London was so strict that he actually forbade admission of any evidence of clandestine marriages, on the principle that the witness was *ipso facto* excommunicate.[5] Therefore in contested cases clandestine marriages presented serious problems of proof.

Despite former views of high prevalence,[6] some recent investigations of records of consistory courts raise doubts that clandestine marriages continued to be very common in late sixteenth- and early seventeenth-century England. For example, records of Wiltshire courts show that between 1570 and 1640 the amount of contentious marriage litigation fell sharply, and this was matched by a similar fall in disciplinary prosecutions for marriage contracts and for failing to have banns read.[7] It has therefore been suggested that a change in popular understanding had occurred in this period, and that the Church's teaching and admonitions on the need for calling banns and going through a church ceremony had been generally successful. As a result, it has been claimed, ecclesiastical lawyers regarded unsolemnised marriage contracts as more or less unenforceable.[8]

But these findings do not agree with evidence presented from church courts in other parts of the country,[9] and so a widespread change in attitude of ecclesiastical courts and lawyers may be doubted.[10] Evidence for a decline in spousal litigation throughout the country remains inconclusive. Although the Church's exact requirements on solemnisation were not universally accepted, it still seems that popular opinion considered the Church's blessing a necessary part of the formation of a valid marriage. Old traditions in continental Europe and England, which typically demanded varied forms of ceremony or ritual, and which required sexual consummation for the validity of marriage, long continued to be regarded as significant although they had no legal basis. It has been suggested that the continuing numbers of clandestine marriages evidence the continuity of such traditions.[11]

Marriages made simply by handfasting or trothplight by the couple without a priest were most frequently found during the middle ages, but continued into the eighteenth century. The continuing use of secular methods of contracting marriage points to the persistence of ancient, often regional, popular customs and practices. But by Shakespeare's time a clandestine marriage in England was more likely to be a private marriage ceremony before a priest, but not in church, and without banns, licence, or publicity. Marriage in a 'lawless church' was also popular. These were churches, known as 'peculiars', which were outside the jurisdiction of bishops, and whose clergy claimed an autonomous right to issue marriage licences and conduct marriages.[12] Despite a 1597 complaint in Parliament directed towards marriages 'made in Places peculiar . . . By vagrant, unlearned, dissolute, drunken and idle Stipendaries, Vicars and Curates',[13] the abuse continued unabated. In London the most important peculiars were St James's Dukes Place, and Holy Trinity in the Minories, both of which conducted a very large and very profitable business in irregular marriages. Some prison chapels, like that at the Fleet, claimed the status of lawless churches and conducted irregular marriages. Although this trade became notorious in the late seventeenth and eighteenth centuries, and continued until prohibited by Lord Hardwicke's Marriage Act of 1753, it was already in existence in Shakespeare's age.[14]

Marriages failed to conform to the Prayer Book marriage service for a variety of reasons. The practice of making clandestine marriages in private houses or chapels may point to a desire to avoid publicity, perhaps to forestall possible objections to the marriage on the basis of impediments. Remote degrees of affinity or consanguinity were difficult to trace; it was relatively simple for couples at risk to purchase a dispensation from banns or licence, or to visit a lawless church for the ceremony.

Another reason for wanting privacy for a celebration of marriage was not to avoid publicity, but to circumvent the requirement to use the reformed English Prayer Book marriage service. Catholics, in particular, were suspected of undertaking clandestine marriages in order to celebrate their marriage using Catholic rituals and before a Catholic priest, and so avoiding a marriage solemnised according to the Prayer Book altogether. Or they may have had two marriage ceremonies; the second ceremony complied with the Act of Uniformity by using the Prayer Book, and allowed the marriage to be recorded in the parish register, as required by statute. Commissions to search out recusants, especially in the north of England, would investigate any report of a clandestine marriage on the presumption that there was a link between unsolemnised marriages and recusancy.

Puritans too had their own reasons for wanting to avoid a marriage solemnised according to the Prayer Book marriage service. Emmison's summary of records from Essex church courts describes several charges against priests and couples for omitting the obligatory wedding ring from the service. He describes a case in 1558 when a priest was reported to the court for halting the marriage service because the groom refused to be married with a ring.[15] The need for such a ring was regarded as idolatrous by Puritans, and was complained about in the Millenary Petition.

Religious scruples may have contributed to the odd behaviour of some highly placed people who undertook a clandestine marriage when they must have understood the consequences. In 1547, at the singular hour of 2 a.m., the remarkable Bess of Hardwick, who would marry four times amassing great wealth, married Sir William Cavendish, Treasurer of the King's Chamber, in the house of the Marquis of Dorset and his wife Frances, a grand-daughter of Henry VII and the mother of Lady Jane Grey.[16] It seems likely that their motives for avoiding church solemnisation were related to their strong Protestantism.

In another notable example, in 1598 the Attorney General Sir Edward Coke privately married his second wife, the young widow Lady Elizabeth Hatton, without either a church blessing or a public ceremony. They were married in the evening at Hatton House in the presence of her father Lord Burghley. Coke, Lady Hatton, Lord Burghley, and the priest who conducted the marriage were all cited to appear before the church court.

Coke gave as his defence his lack of knowledge of canon law. A fine and a dispensation from the bishop ended the matter.[17] It may be that Coke and Lady Hatton, who agreed on nothing thereafter, were united in the wish to avoid the Prayer Book marriage service.

Before returning to Coke's and other well-documented clandestine marriages, we must discuss a legal 'grey area' which has not been satisfactorily understood. It is frequently heard that unsolemnised marriages did not create or transfer property rights as effectively as did solemnised marriages. We believe this to be an over-simplification, yet one based on wishful thinking traceable to the civil lawyer Henry Swinburne, writing about 1600.[18]

Swinburne unambiguously asserted that an unsolemnised marriage by spousals brought with it none of the legal consequences of a solemnised one respecting property:[19]

Albeit they that do Contract Spousals *de praesenti*, be very Husband and Wife, in respect of the Knot or Bond of Matrimony . . . yet do not these Spousals produce all the same effects here in *England*, which Matrimony solemnized in the face of the Church doth, whether we respect the Legitimization of their Children, or the Property which the Husband hath in the Wife's Goods, or the Dower which she is to have in his Lands.

Elsewhere Swinburne draws a parallel between the difference in treatment accorded by English ecclesiastical and common law courts to bastards and the treatment by these courts of a *de praesenti*-only marriage. The facts are that common law, which alone had jurisdiction over all real property (land), did not regard a child whose birth preceded the marriage of its parents as legitimate, while the church courts, which had jurisdiction over matrimonial matters, did regard such a child as legitimate. Swinburne believed that the possibility of contrary rules applied by church and common law courts applied also to the rights to property which followed a marriage. These are rights of dower and curtesy, and the consequences of the doctrine of coverture (these rights, as well as bastardy, will be discussed in later chapters). So Swinburne claims that at common law 'no more is [a wife by spousal contract alone] to have any Dower of the same Lands . . . because as yet, she is not his lawful Wife, at least to that effect'.[20]

Whether Swinburne was correct about English common law is open to considerable doubt. He certainly made a very strong case, claiming that although it was formerly held otherwise, in his time an Englishman can make 'a Feoffment' to such a wife which is in common law 'good, as being made, not unto his Wife, but unto a single Woman, and another Person in Law'. Even more strangely, because ecclesiastical law governed married women's chattels (movable property), he continued: 'Concerning Goods, the like may be said of them as hath already be spoken of Lands', stating that this was a difference between 'Civil and Canon Laws' and 'the law of this Realm'. He also alleged that a woman in such a marriage may make her own will (which a *feme covert* could not), but if her husband died intestate she 'cannot obtain the *Administration* of his Goods'.[21]

Such absolute statements have often been summarised in the simple claim that the common law did not recognise a spousal *de praesenti* as a marriage. But these statements should be doubted. As long ago as 1898 Maitland showed the difficulty in testing a proposition that an unsolemnised marriage, although valid, was 'no marriage for purely possessory purposes': to determine this requires evidence which is extremely difficult to obtain because of the problem that 'a marriage might easily exist and yet be unprovable'.[22] Moreover, even if common law courts did show a 'theoretical preference' for solemnised marriages, it is not certain that local manorial courts did the same.[23] There are some early dower and inheritance cases involving land in which a pre-contracted marriage by spousals prevailed over a marriage in the face of the church.[24] The inheritance rights of children of unsolemnised marriages were upheld by Bracton and Glanvill, and in early case law.[25] There is also considerable disagreement among historians and Shakespeare's contemporaries concerning a wife's rights of dower following an unsolemnised marriage, an issue which we will discuss in chapter 9.

The conditions set out in the 1606 statute 3 Jac. I c.5 make unlikely often-heard simplified claims such as that of Lawrence Stone: 'in all matters relating to property, the contract [of a clandestine marriage] had no standing whatever'.[26] Paragraph 13 of the Act disabled clandestinely married women who had been convicted of 'Popish' recusancy from receiving dower, jointure, or any customary widows' portions.[27] Because the Act made conviction for a specific offence a prerequisite for losing dower, it is unlikely that loss of dower was a general disability imposed on all wives who married clandestinely.[28]

In conclusion it seems that Swinburne, perhaps in an attempt to describe a rational structure, overstated the case that common law would not recognise unsolemnised marriages where property was involved. Bess of Hardwick, who worked hard to establish a dynasty, and became the wealthiest woman of the age other than the Queen, would hardly have married without assurance that her property rights on widowhood were secure. And certainly Coke intended to, and indeed did, take Lady Hatton's considerable property when he married her;[29] it is hard to imagine that the greatest common lawyer of his time, who also amassed great personal wealth, would make the mistake of a clandestine marriage if (as Swinburne claimed) such a marriage would not transfer property under coverture. Whether Coke's and Lady Hatton's motives were religious as we have suggested, or were based on aristocratic 'delicacy' about getting married in public followed by traditional ribald celebrations,[30] or on some other cause (for instance, Lady Hatton's pregnancy which receives comment in Aubrey's *Brief Lives*), is unknown.[31]

Another case of clandestine marriage again implies that the husband did enjoy property rights following an unsolemnised union. This was the marriage in about 1600 of Shakespeare's friend, Thomas Russell, first traced through Chancery litigation by Leslie Hotson and since often noted in relation to Shakespeare and marriages made by spousal contracts.[32] Russell deferred the solemnisation of his spousals with the wealthy widow Anne Digges until an arrangement had been reached with Anne's son to minimise the financial loss a remarriage would cause her under the terms of her late husband's will.[33] Next, according to the complaint in Chancery of one William Bamfield, Russell and a confederate arranged a confidence trick that clearly illustrates legal ambiguities over clandestine marriages.[34] Russell's counter-pleadings suggest this ruse was probably the case, and that his motive for 'mak[ing] a praye of' Bamfield was revenge for Bamfield's former mistreatment of him over a debt. Russell's scheme involved a complex sale and exchange of horses, hawks, and cloaks resulting in the 'guilefull trap' wherein Bamfield gave a bond to Russell which would become due on the date of Russell's 'next marriage', if there ever would be one. Bamfield signed the bond after he was invited (or, as Russell insisted, invited himself) to meet the widow Digges, whom Russell said he had 'lately married'. Bamfield claimed that all signs of married life were in evidence at the house at Aldermaston. The confidence trick inflicted on Bamfield hinged on a play on words: although Russell was *married* to Anne Digges, presumably by spousals, they had not had a *marriage*, which would be solemnisation. Payment on the bond eventually was demanded in a common law suit by Russell, with a penalty because Bamfield missed the required payment on the date of the next marriage, although Russell had kept his word not to 'marry another'. An interesting jurisdictional point arises: in his defence Russell stated that he was not compelled by the rules of the court of Chancery to make any answer to the accusations that before the 'marriage' Mrs Digges's children called him father, her servants called him master, and she carried herself at bed and board as his married wife.[35] He claimed these allegations concerned 'some criminal matter not fit to be examined in this honourable court but in some other court', meaning the church courts where he evidently feared little in the way of punishment.[36]

What can we conclude from this farrago, except that Shakespeare's friends actually undertook scams based on 'merry' wordplay exceeding the most wildly mooted premises of a particularly improbable Elizabethan playtext? For one, this affair was based on the anomaly that the laws of the age effectively produced a disjunction between the concepts of 'being married' and having had a 'marriage'. Russell alleged, with what success we do not know, that the church courts alone had to do with marital issues, and the royal courts could not look into these. We do know that even the prerogative Court of High Commission, that did have both competence and power of appeal over ecclesiastical affairs, regularly turned cases regarding the validity of matrimony back to the bishops' courts,[37] and conversely that a bishop's certificate of legitimacy, for instance, would not be accepted in property disputes in the common law courts.[38] So maybe Russell made a legally valid and acceptable point.

Such complexities as those illustrated in the above cases would seem to suggest that the anomalies of clandestine marriage might feature beside those of enforced marriage as a prominent motif in the drama of Shakespeare's age. Yet, even though many clandestine marriages are represented by Shakespeare, the problems of clandestinity are not heavily foregrounded by him. Social toleration and literary convention both may have contributed to this, as will be seen in the following section.

CLANDESTINE MARRIAGE IN SHAKESPEARE'S PLAYS

As we will see in chapter 8 (on divorce), Iago asks Othello a pertinent but difficult question about his runaway marriage: 'Are you fast married?' (*OTH* 1.2.11). Two contrasting answers, both legally plausible for Shakespeare's age, are apparent in *The Merry Wives of Windsor* and *Measure for Measure*. In *Measure for Measure* Claudio says of his Juliet: 'she is fast my wife, / Save that we do the denunciation lack / Of outward order' (1.2.135–7). He is secure she is his wife, but still expresses some misgivings about 'order'. Yet, with no such worries, Fenton in *The Merry Wives* asks a tavern-keeper to 'procure the vicar / To stay for me at church 'twixt twelve and one', not at all doubting that a clandestine ceremony with Anne Page, without banns or publicity, will 'give our hearts united ceremony', and moreover 'in the lawful name of marrying' (4.6.46–50).

Now Claudio, who claims Juliet is 'fast' his wife, most likely meaning unshakeably so,[39] would have been right under English law, although (like Thomas Russell) he has been married without having had a marriage. Yet Claudio is convicted, under a fictional Viennese law mooted in the play, of the capital crime of fornication. Of course, in Shakespeare's England a much lighter punishment would have been applied; laws against fornication of greater severity than those applied in the church courts were repeatedly proposed and rejected before the Commonwealth temporarily brought them in.[40] Under the influence of his conscience (and further prompted by Vincentio) Claudio bitterly regrets his 'sin', and repents. However, Fenton, after only a seemingly clandestine church ceremony of some sort, is convinced that his marriage with Anne Page is wholly 'lawful'. He asserts without any trace of guilt that 'she and I, long since contracted, / Are now so sure that nothing can dissolve us' (*WIV* 5.5.215–16). The paradox is that under English law Fenton's marriage, with no banns read or licence obtained (for Anne is too young to obtain a licence without parental permission), and held in the wholly uncanonical middle of the night, is as clandestine as are Claudio's spousals. Yet the clandestinity of Fenton's marriage counts for little if anything in the play, while that of Claudio's is crucial in his.

An over-ingenious historical speculation might be that Fenton and Anne had purchased a church dispensation.[41] But such dispensations were a topic that Shakespeare did not broach. Various 'dispensations' are mentioned by Shakespeare, literally in *Henry VI, part 1* 5.5.42 and more figuratively in *Love's Labour's Lost* 2.1.87 and *The Rape of Lucrece* 248, and to 'dispense' has similar figurative overtones in several places. But none of these Shakespearian instances suggests a reference to the contentious topic of ecclesiastical dispensations to marry privately, or without licence or banns, or at disallowed times.

Shakespeare's Fenton is not alone in his insouciance; secret or over-hasty clandestine marriages are made in many Shakespeare plays with hardly any comment or importance attached to this. There is certainly no time for banns before the amazed Sebastian is dragged off to a 'chantry' by Olivia to 'plight . . . faith' before a single clergyman as witness, and Olivia herself emphasises the 'haste' and 'conceal[ed]' aspects of these proceedings (*TN* 4.3.22–31). Olivia then attributes a need for the marriage to 'come to note' (be publicised) only to the requirements of a 'celebration . . . / According to my birth', that is, to an (albeit important) social requirement for a 'big wedding',[42] rather than to a religio-legal requirement for solemnisation in the requisite form.[43]

Similarly, further down the social scale, Lucentio and Bianca are married without banns or licence by an 'old priest' at about supper time (*SHR* 4.5.12–16), and the uncanonical hour is emphasised in Biondello's jesting 'I knew a wench married in an afternoon as she went to the garden for parsley to stuff a rabbit, and so may you, sir' (4.5.25–7). Yet the bilked fathers of both

Lucentio and Bianca are almost immediately ready to condone the marriage (after only brief angry sputters, 5.1.126–5, their patriarchal wrath is deflected onto the play's usual lightning-conductors, its witty servants). It is even implied that these fathers will be as financially bounteous to the newlyweds as they would have been had the marriage been made regularly (5.1.126–7). Clandestinity and an over-autonomous choice bring no material penalties to Lucentio, although he suffers from the marriage itself, which turns out to be based on a romantic delusion. There are historical analogies to Lucentio's situation,[44] and even for the case of the 'wench' gathering parsley.[45]

But in higher places clandestine or secret marriages could have great political import. Extraordinary care was taken by Henry VIII to assure the legitimacy of his children with Anne Boleyn; in Shakespeare's play Henry's complex manoeuvres are condensed in an announcement: 'that the Lady Anne / Whom the King hath in secrecy long married, / This day was viewed in open as his queen' (AIT 3.2.403–5). The play ends with the legitimate birth of Princess Elizabeth (her later bastardisation is of course unmentioned).

The marriage of Crown Princess Imogen and plain Posthumus Leonatus is denied validity by King Cymbeline and by his step-son, the first calling Posthumus only a 'minion' (CYM 2.3.39) and the other claiming the contract of marriage 'is no contract, none' (2.3.112). As we will discuss in chapter 8, the marriage of a royal heir carried special requirements. Although late in the play we learn that Posthumus and Imogen had been married in Jupiter's 'temple' (5.5.200), this does not alter the effects of an irregular union.

In comic realms, on the contrary, marriage is a natural process hardly to be restrained by time or conventions. The rhetorical figure *gradatio*, compared in Thomas Wilson's popular manual with 'a paire of staiers',[46] is perfectly exemplified in Rosalind's wonderful description:

There was never anything so sudden but the fight of two rams, and Caesar's thrasonical brag of 'I came, saw, and overcame', for your brother and my sister no sooner met but they looked; no sooner looked but they loved; no sooner loved but they sighed; no sooner sighed but they asked one another the reason; no sooner knew the reason but they sought the remedy; and in these degrees have they made a pair of stairs to marriage, which they will climb incontinent, or else be incontinent before marriage. They are in the very wrath of love, and they will together. Clubs cannot part them. (AYL 5.2.28–39)

Formality and delay are hardly appropriate in such circumstances.

These examples illustrate how some Shakespearian clandestine marriages are problematised, but many others are passed over with more or less impunity, or even silently treated as if solemnised. The disparities are due in part to differing dramatic purposes. For instance, questioning of Fenton's marriage would be inappropriate to the fableland conclusion of *The Merry Wives*; this play involves a final transfer *to* the holiday or 'green' world of Windsor forest *from* the everyday world, not vice versa as in the normal pastoral pattern. This atypical structure demands that Anne and Fenton's marriage be seen as perfectly sound; it is accepted as such by her parents and all others concerned.

Apart from serving literary modes, Shakespeare's dramatic characters' frequent negligence concerning the requirements for marriage solemnisation may have gestured towards the actual outlooks of many Elizabethans. To explain this we may note the interchange when Hermia in *A Midsummer Night's Dream* is faced with the law of Athens that would allow her father to direct her marriage choice. Like many lay Elizabethans (including women) who gained understanding of the law in order to proceed with litigation, the menaced Hermia is bold to enquire into a legal point. She asks Theseus an extremely germane question: 'I beseech your grace that I may know / The worst that may befall me in this case / If I refuse to wed Demetrius' (*MND* 1.1.62–4). She learns that this worst need not be the death penalty as alleged by her father, but could be lifelong celibacy, permanently taking 'the livery of a nun'. Although bad enough in a comedy, this is not death and allows her escape.

Here is the point: Elizabethans contemplating a clandestine marriage may well have considered questions like Hermia's, to the effect of what is 'the worst that [might] befall me in this case . . .' They would have received less frightening answers than she did. The outcome of a willingly undertaken clandestine marriage, where no powerful or political interests were at stake, might well be nothing.[47] The 'worst that [might] befall' was likely to be an order to perform a more or less embarrassing public penance, and such an order was in practice usually commuted to the payment of a fine. Certainly the several recorded cases of clandestinity tried in the early seventeenth-century Stratford-on-Avon bawdy court received light punishments.[48] If a command to appear before a church court was defied, or the order of such a court was flouted, excommunication in the lesser or greater degree, or the milder suspension from the offices of the Church, might be imposed, but these sanctions were also often not much feared.[49] In such circumstances an expensive procedure (never in existing records used at Stratford) could bring the malefactor to the royal courts, or the Court of High Commission could consider stiffer penalties such as imprisonment. But by Magna Carta no courts without juries, that is, none but the king's courts, could impose capital punishment.

So an easy-seeming attitude to the consequences of making a clandestine marriage, as seen often in Shakespeare, is not hard to trace to Shakespeare's world in actuality. Nevertheless great inconvenience, or worse, could arise from secretive and hurried spousals, whether or not they were made before a clergyman.

Even though the traditional sequence of espousal, religious ceremony, and then sexual consummation is seen or implied in all of its stages in *Romeo and Juliet*, thanks to the secrecy of her clandestine marriage Juliet is threatened with being forced into bigamy. Friar Lawrence's original plan had been to conceal Romeo's whereabouts until an opportune moment arises: 'To blaze your marriage, reconcile your friends, / Beg pardon of the Prince, and call thee back' (*ROM* 3.3.150–1). But the threat of an enforced second marriage leads to the Friar's more perilous scheme, which produces Juliet's terrible isolation highlighted in her doubting comment before taking the sleeping potion he has given her:

> What if it be a poison which the friar
> Subtly hath ministered to have me dead,
> Lest in this marriage he should be dishonoured
> Because he married me before to Romeo?
> I fear it is – and yet methinks it should not,
> For he hath still been tried a holy man.
> <div align="right">(<i>ROM</i> 4.3.23–8)</div>

A very young woman has been abandoned by her mother, father, nurse, and possibly the Friar;[50] we see clandestinity leading towards tragedy.

In an alternative pattern, not dire consequences unforeseen, but convenience anticipated, motivates Touchstone's attempt at making a clandestine marriage in *As You Like It*. He explains 'so man hath his desires; . . . so wedlock would be nibbling' (*AYL* 3.3.73–4); bent on seduction, he proposes to marry the 'foul' Audrey saying 'Come, sweet Audrey. / We must be married, or we must live in bawdry' (3.3.86–7). She accepts, and the rogue vicar Sir Oliver Martext agrees to marry them under a tree. Martext's sort of 'calling' (3.3.98), a marrying industry that supported increasingly many mainly unbeneficed clergy until 1753, was a scandal of the age.[51] Amusingly, Martext insists upon a small point in the Prayer Book's marriage rubric, while ignoring its main requirements: 'Truly [Audrey] must be given, or the marriage is not lawful' (3.3.63–4). Jaques volunteers to play this part, but warns that Martext will join them badly. Touchstone then admits: 'I am not in the mind but I were better to be married of him than of another, for he is not like to marry me well, and not being well married, it will be a good excuse for me hereafter to leave my wife' (3.3.81–4). This satirises a seduction scenario seen in many cases that reached the bawdy courts.[52] But, at least according to R. H. Helmholz, irregular marriages deliberately contrived in order to collapse quickly (as Jaques says in 5.4.190, 'but for two months victualled') should not be regarded as common because, for most people if not Touchstone, to take such a cynical step is 'not consistent with human nature'.[53]

In her mental illness, caused by her love for the much-higher-ranking Palamon, the Jailer's daughter of *The Two Noble Kinsmen* enquires about travel to 'th' end o' th' world' (5.4.73). To humour her it is suggested that she might marry her beloved Palamon there, whereupon she comments: ''Tis true – / For there, I will assure you, we shall find / Some blind priest for the purpose that will venture / To marry us, for here they are nice, and foolish' (5.4.77–80). This is surely a satiric reference to the real-world English practice of seeking a technically 'out of this world' venue, such as a liberty or an ecclesiastical peculiar, and a reprobate priest willing to 'turn a blind eye', in order to make a socially unsuitable clandestine marriage.

So we see great variety. In Touchstone's crudity we find the exaggerated image of a social abuse associated with clandestine marriage. Claudio's plight motivates an examination on an 'as-if' mooted basis of the consequences that would follow the harsh application of increased social control of similar abuses. In Shakespeare's representations of marriages like Fenton's in *The Merry Wives*, or Benedick's as proposed in *Much Ado About Nothing* 5.4.29–30, or Sebastian's in *Twelfth Night*, there is no indication of a need for the legally required form for marriage; in these plays' settings this worries no one, and causes no harm.[54] But Romeo marries without banns or publicity in one day (*ROM* 2.2.64), and his city repents for ever.

Most often Shakespeare's stage closely mirrored prevailing Elizabethan attitudes in which mere clandestinity was far more tolerated than the allied issues of rape, abduction, and elopement. These will be considered next.

THE LAW OF RAPE, ABDUCTION, AND ELOPEMENT

We must first offer an explanation. This is not a book about Shakespeare and criminal law, so we do not undertake to investigate the definitions and punishments of sexual offences except where these offences have bearing on the law of marriage.[55] However, it is necessary to discuss the crime of rape because both in law and in available historical evidence rape was often hard to disentangle on the one hand from abduction and ravishment, and on the other from consensual elopements disguised as abductions.

In early modern England the crime of rape was closely linked in its statutory definition with the crime of abduction, and also with elopement. The explanation of these connections lies in the ancient origins of the law of rape, which will be discussed presently, and also in patriarchal models that gave husbands and fathers property-like rights in wives and daughters. In this connection, Holdsworth interpreted a father's common law proprietary rights in his children, wives, or servants as analogous to a lord's rights in wardship.[56] So if a daughter was attacked or carried off, her father had a right to pursue her attacker for financial compensation to be paid to him for the loss of her services, especially if she died or was injured. By the seventeenth century the father's right was seen to lie in the action of trespass, and included damages for his injured feelings. A husband had a stronger claim than a father because of his proprietary interest in his wife's *consortium*, which was lost if his wife was abducted.[57]

Independently of any legal rights that fathers or husbands had, in England women had their own rights of action for rape, for this was a breach of the king's peace. From medieval times rape, like other crimes of violence, had been a felony. Rape was therefore a plea of the crown (an offence heard in the king's courts), but it also appears to have been often treated by local courts as a misdemeanour.

J. M. Carter has examined medieval eyre rolls (which record the pleas heard by itinerant royal justices), and coroner's court and hundred court rolls (which record cases heard in local courts), for several geographical areas, and found that there was no common agreement on the legal status of rape.[58] Carter also found that corporal punishment for felony was only rarely imposed on convicted rapists, so it seems that the local community, acting through the jury, regarded the offence as a misdemeanour meriting only a fine. There is also evidence that women on occasion brought a private prosecution by appeal of trespass in their own names, rather than an appeal of felony, possibly in order to benefit personally if a fine was imposed on the rapist.[59]

A medieval woman who wished to make an appeal of felony for rape had to go through several necessary steps, amounting to a strenuous ordeal. She first had to 'raise the hue and cry' immediately after the attack, then exhibit her torn clothing and injuries to neighbours of good repute, then make her complaint in turn to the reeve of the hundred, the king's serjeant, the coroners, and finally the king's sheriff.[60] It must have been nearly impossible to meet these requirements. In Shakespeare's time the rape victim still had to undergo an ordeal of displaying herself in order to avoid being found guilty of making a false appeal.

As we have mentioned, many difficulties arise for our purposes because clear legal distinctions were not made in medieval and early modern
England between cases of rape and cases involving elopement, runaway
wives, or forcible abduction of women. The law also did not clearly distinguish between abduction for financial motives and abduction for reasons
of sexual assault.[61]

In Roman law a legal distinction between a willing elopement and a
sexual attack developed from the distinction between *raptus*, which involved
abduction and forced intercourse, and *rapine*, which involved theft. But
originally *raptus* was the abduction and sequestration of a woman against
the will of the person under whose authority she lived, and sexual violation
was not a necessary element as long as violence was used in the abduction.
The offence could include theft of property as well as the woman. However,
by the sixth century, Justinian defined *raptus* as a sexual offence meriting the
death penalty and confiscation of the wrongdoer's property.[62] The medieval
canonists held sexual rape to be an *enormis delicta*, and conviction led to
infamia.[63] Yet St Augustine did not include rape as a crime in his scheme of
sexual offences (in which adultery was the most serious);[64] it was probably
for this reason that common law and statute, not canon law, developed
definitions of the offence and its punishment.

After Gratian's medieval revision of Roman law, rape was defined as the
violent abduction of an unwilling woman and unlawful sexual intercourse
with her; although the abduction had to be forcible, it was only necessary
to show, using the 'constant man' test, that the victim feared injury, and
not to show actual grave physical injury. In Gratian's revision the offence
could be mitigated by the subsequent willing marriage of the victim to
the offender. Brundage concludes that this possibility of mitigation, which
applied in England, arose from the incorporation of Germanic tradition.[65]

In the commentator Glanvill's late twelfth-century treatise *On the Laws
and Customs of England* rape is the capital offence of violating a woman by
force. A later marriage would not allow the offender to escape punishment
because this would cause disparagement if men of servile status married
women of good birth, or vice versa.[66] However, Bracton's later treatise *On
the Laws and Customs of England*, c. 1220, holds that if a conviction for rape
was on indictment, the penalty could be mitigated if the woman chose
to marry the accused man.[67] In practice severe punishments were only
handed out for the rape of virgins; for other women an unspecified lesser
scale of punishments applied.[68] For Britton, writing around the end of the
thirteenth century, the punishment for rape was death whether or not the
woman consented after the commission of the felony.[69]

In late medieval and early modern England there were two sequences of statutes, one of which defined the offence of rape and elopement, while the second, known as Abduction Acts, defined the offences of forcibly taking away women who had, or were heirs to, property. Although elopement could be punished under the provisions of either set of statutes, nevertheless it is useful to distinguish the grievances they addressed.

The sequence of statutes dealing with rape and elopement began with the first Statute of Westminster, 3 Edw. I c.13 (1275) and the second Statute of Westminster, 13 Edw. I c.34 (1285). By Westminster I the offence was either to take or to ravish an underage unmarried woman regardless of her consent, or to take or ravish an overage or married woman without her consent. The consequence was either that the victim brought suit within forty days and the king did 'common right', or if not the king could bring suit and punish with two years' imprisonment plus a fine. Westminster II made rape a felony. The offender could be pursued either by appeal of felony brought by the victim herself or her family,[70] or (if no appeal was brought) by indictment by a grand jury. The punishment for the felony was either death by hanging, or mutilation – which could be castration or blinding. In practice sentences of punishment by mutilation do not seem to have been carried out.[71] Felons also had their property confiscated by the crown. The king maintained a right to claim the value of the property taken with an abducted wife, who lost her rights to her dower if she continued to live with her abductor.

Another statute of 1382 (6 Ric. II c.6) extended the right to bring an appeal of rape to fathers, husbands, or next of kin, and treated an eloping couple as dead for the purposes of inheritance. This statute clearly overlaps in its concerns with the Abduction Acts. J. B. Post argues that the statute was enacted following Sir Thomas West's complaint about his daughter's abduction, which included his suspicion that she colluded with her abductor in order to marry him.[72]

Yet, despite the definitions and severe punishments set out in the Statutes of Westminster, until Tudor times rape remained a 'clergyable' offence, which meant that an offender could plead benefit of clergy to avoid capital punishment (see chapter 9 for more detail). By 4 Hen. VII c.18 (1488) clergy could only be claimed once for a conviction for rape and the offender was branded with a T on his thumb. In 1540 (32 Hen. VIII c.12) sanctuary was abolished for those charged with rape. By 18 Eliz. I c.7 (1575) rape became not clergyable. Coke then defined rape as a severe sexual offence, 'unlawfull and carnall knowledge and abuse of any woman above the age of ten years against her will, or a woman child under ten years with her will, or against her will', and stated that the offender could not receive benefit of clergy.[73]

Statutes in a second group, known as Abduction Acts, addressed the patriarchal concerns of fathers and families rather than seeking redress for the assaulted woman. These Acts applied exclusively to women 'having substance, some in Goods movable, and some in Lands and Tenements, and some being heirs apparent to their ancestors'.[74] The first Act, 3 Hen. VII c.2 (1487), made a felony of 'taking away of women against their Wills'. Women included by the Act were 'maidens, widows and wives' who had been stolen by 'Misdoers, contrary to their will' for their 'lucre' and forced into marriage. The Act extended the crime to include those who procured, aided, and abetted the wrongdoer.[75] This was followed by 4 & 5 Ph. & Mary c.8 (1557) which again addressed those who stole heirs and heiresses, punishing with two years' imprisonment and a fine, or five years for taking away, deflowering, or contracting marriage.[76] In 1597 39 Eliz. I c.9 took away benefit of clergy for those convicted under the Act of 3 Hen. VII. It is interesting to note that a Commonwealth Statute of 24 August 1653 defined abduction as stealing, or taking away, any person (regardless of gender) under the age of twenty-one with the intent to marry them. Offenders could be punished with loss of all property, real and personal, and with life imprisonment.[77]

Although rape was a felony, by Shakespeare's time it appears that many cases were non-suited (not pursued), or compromised, or failed before the justices, because of some technical exception to the charge. In some cases this may have been because an agreement for financial compensation had been reached that satisfied the victim's family. Also criminal sanctions were not always applied because appeals of rape could be compromised by subsequent marriage. It is possible that this outcome might sometimes have been intended in advance, suiting the purposes of an eloping woman.

J. B. Post claims that the Statutes of Westminster were interpreted and extended to make the law of rape into a law against elopement and abduction serving 'the interests of [families] who wanted material recompense'.[78] By contrast, a woman's own primary concern may have been to bring her rapist to justice, or in cases of alleged abduction which was really elopement, to marry according to her own wishes or escape from an unwanted arranged marriage.[79]

If some husbands were willing to accept that their wives' abductions were consensual, and their real concern was the recovery of lost property and not of the wives, by contrast in cases concerning the abduction of wards, both male and female, the return of the ward was essential. As we have seen, guardians very often looked to increase their fortunes by arranging a ward's marriage,[80] and the marriages of widows and heiresses were also of great financial interest to families. When an abduction or runaway marriage of a valuable ward took place, as of Walter Aston (a ward of Sir Edward Coke), the main aim would have been to invalidate the marriage, if at all possible.[81] Here the church courts became involved, although they did not usually try cases of rape.

The church courts did have jurisdiction over other sexual offences, such as prostitution, fornication, and adultery. It is probable that some cases nominally treated as fornication or bastardy by these courts were really cases of rape. An example would be a case heard in the church courts alleging sexual coercion that had resulted in the birth of a child.[82]

RAPE, ABDUCTION, AND ELOPEMENT IN SHAKESPEARE

Although the laws of Shakespeare's England did distinguish between the felony of rape and the crime of abduction, as we have seen there were ambiguities and overlap in these laws. In a response to this legal situation and associated social values, or else in accord with his artistic purposes, Shakespeare often presented images of abduction, elopement, and rape that are blurred or overlapping.

The topic of abduction for purposes of marriage appears in the Greek myth of Proserpina seized and carried to the underworld and forced to marry King Dis (or Hades). This 'vegetation' myth is alluded to directly by Shakespeare in *Troilus and Cressida* 2.1.34, *The Winter's Tale* 4.4.116–18, and *The Tempest* 4.1.88–91, and indirectly in his naming of Proserpina's fertility goddess mother Ceres (or Demeter) in *The First Part of the Contention* 1.2.2, *The Tempest* 4.1, and *The Two Noble Kinsmen* 5.1.52. In many versions of the myth the distraction of Proserpina's unhappy mother (while she seeks her daughter or makes strenuous objections to her abduction) causes universal famine. Permanent winter and starvation are alleviated only after Proserpina returns to the earth and to her mother for a seasonal part of each year.

The terror in the abduction of Proserpina is alluded to by Shakespeare (*WT* 4.4.116–18), but this is only indirectly connected with a context of marriage. The closest Shakespeare gets to telling a story of abduction by force leading to marriage is in the two accounts of the military conquest of Hippolyta by Theseus which leads on to a wedding in both *A Midsummer Night's Dream* 1.1.16–17 and *The Two Noble Kinsmen* 1.1.84–5.

While Proserpina's story connects forcible abduction with a forced marriage, another classical myth separates rape from marriage. This is the story of Philomel, who is ravished, mutilated, and eventually metamorphosed into a nightingale. To hide the deed Philomel is not only bereft of her tongue, but also hidden away by her rapist brother-in-law Tereus, so she is abducted, but not for purposes of marriage. Philomel's story is frequently alluded to by Shakespeare (*LUC* 1079 and 1128; *SON* 102; *CYM* 2.2.46; *MND* 2.2.13, 2.2 24; *TIT* 2.3.43, 2.4.38, 2.4.43, 4.1.47, 4.1.52, 5.2.193; *TNK* 5.5.124). It is mentioned twice in Shakespeare's poem on the cruel rape of the chaste matron Lucrece, which concerns a sexual assault unmixed with intentions of either abduction or marriage.[83] Ovid's account of Philomel plays an even greater part in *Titus Andronicus*; as we shall see in that play one sub-plot of an abduction for marriage is contrasted with another concerning the rape and mutilation of a married woman.

In a generally lighter vein, Shakespeare repeatedly portrays the flight of young people who intend to marry as they please despite the opposition of parents or guardians. Several of these elopements, however, damage father figures thwarted and humiliated by the loss of their daughters and their power. Patriarchal laws of Shakespeare's age would have allowed such fathers redress; interestingly, Egeus of *A Midsummer Night's Dream* and Brabantio of *Othello* fail in such attempts at legal redress, and Shylock does not directly attempt it (he is vengefully litigious, but does not sue over the loss of Jessica).

Many of the elopements seen in the drama of Shakespeare's age conform with a revival of the classical theatre's 'New Comedy' in which the erotic intrigues of youth are given a sympathetic slant. Grumio accurately describes a New Comedy pattern as it appears in *The Taming of the Shrew*: 'See, to beguile the old folks, how the young folks lay their heads together' (1.2.136–7). In that play the young wooers of Bianca are aided by witty servants, which is near to the classical pattern, with servants replacing slaves. The use in stage comedy of such motifs accords with what are called in anthropology liminal rituals;[84] these do not indicate that an early modern public wholly approved of conspiratorial clandestine marriages. Liminal rituals, often parts of festivals, temporarily disrupt the social order or hierarchy, but in doing so show where normal limits lie so that they may be reasserted after the festival, holiday, or play is over. Thus the servants (or slaves) of New Comedy are the resourceful abettors and guides of their young masters, or are even disguised as the masters, inverting social order, and the New Comedy is concluded with the triumph of youth over staid, parental figures. In such comedy inversions of the social order-of-things are presented as witty, exciting, daring, or festive. This licensed misrule actually underscores a collective understanding of the 'normal' by displaying its inverse as hilariously transgressive.[85]

Shakespeare makes very original uses of the possibilities of the liminal in comedy, most brilliantly in *The Shrew*. The play starts with an inversion of hierarchy in the temporary ennoblement of Sly, and soon after presents much New Comedy liminal material in the Bianca sub-plot. In the intrigues of that sub-plot the witty servant Tranio exchanges identity with his master, and the master Lucentio gains Bianca in an unauthorised marriage, saying "Twere good, methinks, to steal our marriage, / Which once performed, / let all the world say no, / I'll keep mine own, despite of all the world' (*SHR* 3.3.13–15). In a contrasting main plot, Petruchio directly addresses himself to patriarchal authority to negotiate a marriage with Katherina (the important details of this negotiation will be discussed in chapter 9). However, the description of the church solemnisation that follows is highly subversive, as we have seen in the previous chapter. Moreover, following the farcical ceremony, Petruchio enacts what is virtually an anthropological 'marriage by ritual abduction' of his bride, needlessly proclaiming against any who would assail his marriage (parodying Lucentio): 'They shall not touch thee, Kate. / I'll buckler thee against a million' (3.3.110–11). Although Petruchio does not meet with any opposition except from Katherina herself when he carries her off on horseback, he blusters on comically as if he were opposed, providing an image of abduction.[86]

In all this Shakespeare dazzlingly provokes paradoxes on the uses of liminality, as well as on the themes of elopement and abduction. Christopher Sly arguably shows up the Lord's selfish shallowness far more than the Lord shows up Sly's boorishness, thus inverting the tendency of the liminal to reassert hierarchies. Although the marriage of Lucentio and Bianca is outwardly romantic, runaway, and clandestine, it is also imaged as inwardly mundane and socially appropriate, and it is at last acceptable to the two fathers as in accord with the aims of patriarchy. Thus the play reverses normally expected contrasts between arranged marriages and runaway marriages, a part of its subversion of any fashionable notion that classical New Comedy intrigue should make for more sophisticated kinds of drama than a semi-farcical plot concerning strife and adjustments in an unidealised marital situation.

Shakespeare also undermines romantic conventions when he portrays or alludes to criminal abductions or rapes of young women. Such topics are particularly prevalent in his late plays. *The Winter's Tale* images Proserpina's terror, and *The Tempest* images her mother Ceres' fury. Marina of *Pericles* is abducted by pirates and threatened with rape by brothel customers and a brothel-keeper. Imogen of *Cymbeline*, an unprotected runaway bride, only narrowly avoids rape by a rejected suitor. In these plays flight or abduction is imaged more as a desperate than a romantic motif.[87] Hence, perhaps, a patriarchal model of a father's protection and confinement of young women is given a positive valuation, although the fathers Prince Pericles and King Cymbeline are deficient in being either absent or wrong-headed.

Although there is never any explicit Shakespearian approval of fathers forcing unwanted bridegrooms on daughters, runaway daughters are shown at risk of being traded as objects in *The Two Gentlemen of Verona*. Silvia willingly elopes, but is hardly any safer from rape in the forest outside Milan (*TGV* 5.3–5.4) than kidnapped Marina is in the brothel of Mytilene (*PER* s.19). But neither Silvia nor Marina are assaulted by the professional ruffians they encounter in their adventures; the pirates of *Pericles* are too mercenary to spoil a virginity which has a market value, and the outlaws of *The Two Gentlemen* have been taught by Valentine not to commit 'uncivil outrages' (5.4.17). Both these heroines meet challenges to their virginity rather only from 'gentlemen' they encounter in unprotected circumstances. In *Pericles* s.19 Marina is up for sale to Lysimachus, the Governor of Mytilene, and some of the 'Gentlemen' of his city, at a brothel. Silvia, when rescued from outlaws by the 'gentleman' Proteus, must resist first his dishonourable wooing, and then his threatened rape (*TGV* 5.4.19–59). Silvia is rescued by her beloved Valentine, but within a few lines Valentine is willing to forgive Proteus his trespass against himself (the assault on Silvia is unmentioned), and then to hand Silvia over to Proteus out of sheer friendship (5.4.77–83). This weird development could be attributed to the breakneck pace of this the play's concluding scene, but it surely also images the vulnerability of women who follow young men into forests and forgo the protection of fathers and civility.[88] Next, Silvia's father, the Duke of Milan, and her suitor Thurio are captured by the outlaw band, and Valentine wins the rights Thurio has in Silvia by means of a martial challenge. Again an unprotected woman is bandied about as a prize of masculine force; the Duke himself approves of Valentine's bold 'spirit' and he hands Silvia over from Thurio to Valentine. Only the men speak in the last fifty lines of the play; Silvia is never asked if the lover who has just offered to give her as a gift to his friend (her would-be rapist) merits her continuing consent to marry.

Elopement then forces the two heroines of *The Two Gentlemen* into a position where they must marry men whom they have no reasonably based motive to respect or love. The continuing affection of another eloping girl, Jessica of *The Merchant of Venice*, is also severely challenged following

her irreversible flight with a feckless husband.[89] Running away from the
protection of parents is unsafe for many Shakespearian heroines.

In a play laden with scepticism, and built around the vicissitudes of sexual desire, Paris of Troy debates that his abduction of Helen (a collusive
abduction or 'fair rape') should be defended to protect Troy's honour (*TRO*
2.2.147–61). He argues that the 'soil of her fair rape' can be 'Wiped off in
honourable keeping her' (2.2.147–8), proposing that valour can counterpoise adultery and abduction. Although we are given perspectives from
which we may doubt all positions taken in this play, Shakespeare's general
contempt for rape and lust gives a particular reason to mistrust a 'fair rape'
backed by military honour.

When we turn from his comedies or problem plays with very dark aspects
to his outright tragedies we encounter Shakespeare's portrayals of violent
sexual rape, and disastrous abductions or elopements. The word 'rape' when
used by Shakespeare always images the horrible and degrading; it is used,
for instance, in a metaphor for an ultimate political misdeed in *King John*
2.1.97–8, while Tarquin's soliloquy in *Lucrece* emphasises that rape degrades
the perpetrator (197–210). In his calumny in *All's Well That Ends Well* 4.3.255
Parolles alleges that Dumaine 'parallels Nessus' in his numerous 'rapes and
ravishments'. Indeed male incontinence is always deplored by Shakespeare,
and especially when seen in heads of state such as Edward IV in *Richard,
Duke of York* 3.2.69–81, Angelo in *Measure for Measure*, and Malcolm in his
(falsely) confessed 'voluptuousness' of *Macbeth* 4.3.61–6.

The complications of what 'rape' meant for Shakespeare's age can perhaps
be best seen in relation to the sadistic rape of Lavinia in *Titus Andronicus*.[90]
For, in fact, the first time the word 'rape' is heard in the play (*TIT* 1.1.401),
it refers to the abduction of Lavinia as a wholly willing woman, which
allows her happy marriage, and not the later violent sexual assault upon
her. A clarification of the term 'rape' by legal writers and the increasingly
stringent criminal sanctions applied to rapists up to Shakespeare's time may
correspond with the outrage shown against the use of 'rape' in this dramatic
context; thus Lavinia's husband Bassianus says '"Rape" call you it, my lord,
to seize my own – / My true betrothed love, and now my wife?' Indeed,
as Bassianus considers that he was betrothed to Lavinia before a dynastic
match was contrived by Titus, he invokes the protection of 'the laws of
Rome' against Titus' plan (1.1.402–4).

Bassianus' idea of legal protection for individual rights is in drastic contrast with the actions and ideals of Titus; Bassianus' abduction of Lavinia
appears in the same long scene as the hewing to pieces of the eldest son of
Tamora by Titus and Lucius, and the slaying by Titus of his own youngest

son Mutius. So while Bassianus calls on law to protect faithfulness and love, Roman men of power slaughter in the name of 'honour', glory, and pride.

Tamora, whose pleas for her son's life were dismissed by Titus, becomes Empress instead of Lavinia, and plans a devious revenge (1.1.447–52). Her lover Aaron dissuades Tamora's two remaining sons from battling over Lavinia's love, and persuades them to join forces to rape her (2.1.60–136). This rape of Lavinia, intending maximum degradation and driven by spite and revenge, starkly contrasts with her earlier consensual abduction called a 'rape'.[91]

The mental and physical brutalising of Lavinia is nearly identical to that planned by the vengeful Cloten of *Cymbeline*, who out of sheer spite intends to rape Imogen in a manner adding extra 'torment to her contempt' (3.5.137–45). Just before the wife's rape the death of her husband 'in her eyes', as Cloten puts it, is planned in both plays. This plan is achieved in *Titus*, where the corpse of Lavinia's husband is used as 'pillow to [the rapists'] lust' (2.3.130). The coward Cloten's idea of a further refinement is that he plans to be dressed in Posthumus' clothes when he rapes Imogen (*CYM* 3.5.137–43). An intent to degrade the husband through the rape of the wife is clear in both plays; consistent with this, in both plays the intent is not to abduct the wife or hide her away, but rather to expose her sufferings to the world. Here a rape used to dishonour a man unable to protect his wife recurs identically at both ends of Shakespeare's career.

Finally, the ill-fated elopements of Romeo and Juliet, and of Othello and Desdemona, may be placed within the range of Shakespearian treatments of elopement/abduction/rape. A necessary qualification of romantic presumptions is well expressed by Bruce W. Young, who suggests that an appropriate audience response to Romeo and Juliet's elopement is 'a combination of sympathy and concern', adding:[92]

Shakespeare is calling forth from audiences a complex response, one suited by its inner contrasts and tensions for drama and one adequate (as simple responses will not be) to the complexities of life, whether in the Renaissance or in any other period. The play's references to haste and wildness make it hard to imagine that Shakespeare is simply celebrating a young couple's violation of social norms. On the other hand, he portrays the pathos of their situation and the beauty of their love so effectively as to make it impossible to think of him as simply condemning them.

We would add that, although Young emphasises the extreme youth of the protagonists and the 'too rash, too unadvised, too sudden' marriage contract anxiously described by the inexperienced Juliet (*ROM* 2.1.160), it is not youth alone that brings her disaster. Othello of course is mature in years, and Desdemona seems wholly mature in her remark 'I saw Othello's visage in his mind' (*OTH* 1.3.252). But, tragically, once married Desdemona fails to 'see' Othello's mind in his visage, and he does not in hers. A runaway marriage following a highly charged romantic experience of an idealised other, be it in extreme youth as is Romeo and Juliet's, or not as is Othello and Desdemona's, is dramatised as producing disastrous misunderstanding (the child couple's mistakes are error, the older couple's are obtuseness). Surely there is some suggestion in this that those who betray or ignore the collective knowledge of marriage embodied in the views of communities and families, and ignore the guidance of laws, customs, and traditions, place themselves in positions of considerable danger. As married women in particular had only their husbands to look to for support (for legal reasons to be investigated in the next chapter), they were the especially vulnerable half of eloping couples. As seen in *Othello* 1.3.234–44, and in *Romeo and Juliet* 5.3.160–9, some women in Shakespeare who marry as they wish finally have nowhere to go except their graves.

The early modern legal status and positions of married couples will be our next concern.

CHAPTER 7

The effects of marriage on legal status

PATRIARCHY AND THE SOCIAL ORDER

During the past century the legal status conferred by marriage on a man and woman has been increasingly attenuated and the traditional common law rights and obligations of married people towards each other have been reconsidered and much reduced.[1] In Shakespeare's time, by contrast, a family unified under its head (the husband/father) was considered to be of primary importance for 'social order and political authority',[2] and the legal autonomy of individuals within the family was subordinated to this.

The patriarchal ideal of a well-ordered family was widely used as an analogy for a well-ordered wider society. William Gouge, for instance, considered the family was the seminary of the Church and the commonwealth: the family is 'a Bee-hive, in which is the stoake, and out of which are sent many swarmes of Bees: for in families are all sorts of people bred and brought up and out of families are they sent into the Church and commonwealth'.[3] In accord with its greater social importance, the early modern marriage was subject to greater outside scrutiny than today. The domestic relations between man and wife were watched over by the community for instance through the agency of the constables, the Poor Law and the church courts.[4]

Marriage was accorded much attention in many contemporary texts, including conduct books, printed sermons, and legal treatises,[5] and Parliament ordered the printing of *An Homilie of the State of Matrimonie* to be read out in church. The Elizabethan *Homilie* states at the outset that matrimony 'is instituted of God, to the intent that man and woman should live lawfully in a perpetuall friendship'.[6] Such formulations are used by those who argue that in early modern England the Protestant Reformation brought about a change in relations between husband and wife within a new model of 'companionate marriage'.[7] These relations within companionate marriage have been characterised as being analogous with all-three-at-once of a business partnership between near-equals, the 'compact' between

God and His Church, and the relations between a loving king and his subjects.[8]

The suggestion has been made that this reconceiving of marriage in terms of a partnership, compact, or social compact was a move away from earlier fixed notions of the predetermined status of the husband and wife, and towards individual contractual relations. This would be a move away from teachings that stressed the husband's role as governor in the house, likening it to the status of a king.[9] Such a move would be temptingly reminiscent of Henry Maine's thesis that English history reveals generally a movement from status to contract.[10] But this thesis needs to be investigated in detail rather than applied as a *vade mecum* to the history of social, personal, or economic relations. In the case of marriage, a contractual model for marriage formation had been dominant from the twelfth century.

Legal status within marriage remained significant, complex, and far-reaching in its consequences in early modern England. So we will first review the changes in the husband's and wife's status brought about by marriage in some detail, and then seek their reflections on the Shakespearian stage.

THE DOCTRINE OF COVERTURE

Immediately on entering into a valid contract of marriage an early modern man and woman acquired a changed legal status. For the new wife the most startling change must have been the effect on her of the imposition of far-reaching legal disabilities.

Before she married a woman's legal status was that of a *feme sole*, and as an unmarried woman she could purchase, hold and alienate (sell or give away) property, and enter into contracts in her own name. But once married a woman became a *feme covert*, which had consequences on her contractual relations, her liability in criminal law, and her rights to hold property. A married woman could no longer enter into contracts in her own name (although she was able to enter into contracts if she acted as the agent of her husband). She could not sue or be sued in her own name. She could not devise, or alienate, or own property.

The classic definition of coverture was made in the eighteenth century by William Blackstone:[11]

By marriage, the husband and wife are one person in law: that is, the very being or legal existence of the woman is suspended during the marriage, or at least is incorporated and consolidated into that of the husband: under whose wing, protection, and *cover*, she performs everything; and is therefore called in our law-french a *feme-covert*.

The nature and content of the doctrine of unity of person has been closely identified with that of the Church's doctrine of 'one flesh', which signified that on marriage husband and wife were joined together as one body; an early seventeenth-century commentary says, 'the common Law here shaketh hand with Divinitie'.[12] But really these two theories, of one flesh and of unity of person, address different considerations, and remain separate. The religious doctrine of one flesh is derived from St Paul's Letter to the Ephesians which advised women to submit to their husbands,[13] and this was considered important enough to be read out in church during the legally required Prayer Book marriage solemnisation.[14] St Paul's Letter addressed the nature and purposes of marriage, whereas in contrast the doctrine of unity of person was a legal fiction which described the legal relations between husband and wife and summed up the legal disabilities of the married woman.

In legal theory the husband and wife were simply unequal. Church theory differed from legal theory because in the medieval scholastic synthesis between Christian theology and Aristotelian philosophy a distinction had been drawn between the equality of men and women's immortal souls and the earthly inequality of women.[15]

Returning to Blackstone, we find his assumption is that the doctrine of coverture with its concomitant suppression of married women's legal rights rests on the legal fiction of the doctrine of unity of person in marriage. Blackstone's description of a married woman's legal status summed up the definition that was widely accepted in the early seventeenth century. It was even held then that a husband could not make gifts to or contract with his wife, because that would be considered as making a gift to or contracting with himself.[16] *The Lawes Resolutions of Womens Rights*, a commentary or guidebook rather than an ultimate authority, states that 'this conglutination of person in Baron and feme, forbiddeth all manner of feoffing or giving by the one to the other, for a man cannot give anything unto himselfe . . . But a gift to a plaine Concubine is good enough.'[17] This treatise adds that 'Wedlock is a locking together: it is true that Man and Wife are one person',[18] but also qualifies:[19]

A married woman perhaps may either doubt whether she bee either none or no more than halfe a person. But let her bee of good cheare . . . though . . . they bee by intent and wise fiction of Law, one person, yet in nature & in some other cases by the Law of God and man, they remaine divers.

Whatever the theory, the notion of husband and wife becoming 'one person' was never applied completely consistently in law.[20] The church courts, which had jurisdiction over many matters concerning marriage, probate, defamation, and sexual behaviour, 'unlike the courts of common law . . . did not observe the doctrine of coverture'.[21] The local courts of urban boroughs and rural manors (although in steady decline during Shakespeare's age) continued to offer customary rights that sometimes favoured women, and particularly widows, more than the common law would have done.[22] The central equity courts gave audience to married women, sometimes even allowing them to sue husbands. These courts upheld a number of rights for women that helped to overcome some of the restrictions of coverture.[23]

There were also a number of specific limitations to the doctrine of coverture in the common law. A woman was not liable for her husband's debts. However, a husband could be liable for his wife's debts; at common law a man had a duty to maintain his wife, which meant providing her with food, shelter, and clothing, so if a wife purchased food or goods on credit, then the vendors could pursue the husband for payment on the basis that her purchases had been necessary for maintaining family life and therefore were made with his express or implied consent.[24] Neither was a wife liable for her husband's crimes. A husband was not liable for crimes committed by his wife because in criminal law a woman's capacity to commit any crime and her liability to be punished for it were unaffected by coverture. But because it was understood that a wife was susceptible to her husband's authority the courts would apply the presumption that the wife had been coerced by the husband if it could be argued that her crimes were committed at his command. This legal presumption played an important role in the time when courts could not allow a woman (unlike a man) to plead benefit of clergy, a legal fiction used to mitigate a mandatory death sentence (clergyable offences will be further discussed in chapter 9).[25]

During her coverture a wife was deprived of her capacity to sue at civil law, but in criminal law she could bring criminal appeals of felony for rape or for the alleged murder of her husband.[26] An appeal of felony was a private prosecution which was available to a victim of a crime and was an alternative to the indictment that could be brought against an offender by the community. At the trial of an appeal the appellee (the defendant) had the right to claim trial by battle. A battle, or fight, was then supposed to take place in the public lists between appellee and appellor or their hired champions. Although women could bring an appeal they were not allowed to take part in judicial battle.[27] In fact, very few trials ended in battle in medieval England, and probably none in Tudor England,[28] because the judiciary disliked the appeal process and severely restricted the occasions when judicial combat would be allowed. Nevertheless, appeals continued to be brought and there is evidence that courts assisted appellors who were women.[29]

Married women were also sometimes allowed by the justices to bring appeals for the killing of a son or brother, or even for robbery. Here possibly is evidence of the continuing force of the ancient belief that it was the duty of the victim or their family to pursue the wrongdoer.[30] When women did bring an appeal it was usually non-suited (abandoned), probably because most of these cases were settled before trial after financial compensation was paid.[31]

Despite coverture, married women frequently were the initiators of in-stance litigation in the church courts of Shakespeare's period. Moreover, women often testified in such cases. In a survey of 5,371 consistory court cases between 1572 and 1640, Laura Gowing found that in marriage cases (sued half the time by women) 36 per cent of the witnesses were women, while in defamation cases, 46 per cent of the witnesses were women, and in those cases fought between women, 60 per cent of the witnesses were women.[32] This presents a contrast with the survey by Tim Stretton of Elizabethan cases brought from Somerset to the central equity court of Requests. Stretton found that, of the 290 Somerset Requests actions that survive Elizabeth's reign, about 39 per cent involved at least one woman litigant, and of these he estimates that 70–80 cases involved disputes over customary law governing a copyhold widow's estate.[33] Yet in a sample of 50 such cases Stretton found that only '9 out of 211 deponents who testi-fied [as to what was customary] were female. The custody of custom was apparently seen as a male preserve and the majority of litigants in Requests preferred to call men as witnesses to describe the experiences of widows, rather than calling the widows themselves.'[34]

Early modern authors of conduct literature are 'adamant' that women should avoid going to court because to appear and speak publicly would compromise their honour.[35] But Shakespeare's Hermia, Quickly, Isabella, Desdemona, Hermione, and many other Shakespearian women who speak up in the prerogative courts of king in council (as well as many other dramatised women litigants or defendants of the age) seem not to heed that propaganda.

In certain circumstances vestiges of feudal law operated to diminish the status of a married woman to her great detriment. If a wife killed her husband she was guilty of the serious felony of petty treason because in feudal theory she was subject to her husband's guardianship and authority and he was her *baron* or lord.[36] For this the punishment was burning to death,[37] a most cruel and terrible punishment, whereas if a man killed his wife then the lesser penalty of hanging for murder applied.

Although the different treatment accorded to married women in criminal law was important, it is particularly in property law that the most disabling effect of the doctrine of unity of person was evident. There was no concept of common ownership of property between husband and wife in Shakespeare's England, although such a system of community property did exist in some other parts of Western Europe (and may have existed to a certain extent in England before the Norman Conquest). Although the legal status of a married woman differed from that of an unmarried woman, and she had no legal interest in any family property, the married woman was not dead in law like a member of a religious order. She did not suffer from a general lack of legal capacity, but she did lack the capacity to own property in her own name. In principle, a wife could not own any personal property and did not have the right to make a will (there were some exceptions to restrictions on wills that we will consider in chapter 9). Any personal property she owned before marriage or acquired during marriage vested absolutely in her husband, and he could deal with it as he wished. This included livestock, money, household effects, furniture, jewellery, and even her clothing. This theory went so far as taking no note of chattels a married woman might own if she was convicted of a felony (for the purposes of forfeiture) because she was presumed to own none.[38]

Marriage agreements entered into before marriage often specified the amount of personal spending money, by the seventeenth century popularly known as 'pin money', that a husband would allow his wife as an annual payment. This money was a married woman's own separate property, for her to use to buy clothing, purchase gifts, give as charity, or spend as she needed. It could take the form of a trust of real or personal property or an annuity. But if she used the money for purposes or purchases other than clothing or such necessities then under coverture the property became her husband's. Although at the beginning of the century there was some doubt that pin money could be a legally enforceable contract debt owed by a husband to his wife, by the end of the seventeenth century the equity court of Chancery acted to allow a wife who saved up her pin money to keep her savings for her own use.[39] As Susan Staves has remarked, pin money reflected an increasing tendency to construe marriage as contractual.[40] By the nineteenth century an agreement for pin money in a marriage settlement represented an agreement to pay a wife only small sums of money for minor expenses, but in the seventeenth century pin money or separate estate could involve an agreement to pay very large sums of money, as much as 1,000 pounds per annum.[41]

The regime for a woman's personal property was also subject to exceptions in certain parts of the country, where borough customs could allow a wife to hold personal property and to leave it by will. The customs of London, for instance, treated a woman married to a merchant as a '*feme sole* merchant', which allowed her to hold property and trade in her own name, provided she practised a different trade from that of her husband.[42] But where there is evidence that the guilds and companies which regulated trading in cities did allow women to become members, this membership ceased on marriage. It is unclear who these women livery company members were: perhaps they were widows continuing their husbands' business for an allowed period of time.[43] Married women were also traditionally recognised as *feme sole* merchants when they acted as small-scale retailers selling agricultural produce, bread, and other goods from market stalls in town and country. But in general a married woman's earnings were her husband's property. This meant a deserted wife who worked to support her family might lose all her savings to her husband if he chose to take them.[44]

Coverture had an important effect on a woman's right to own real property, or land. If a wife brought her own land into her marriage then this also vested in her husband during marriage, but unlike personal property a wife's real property did not vest in her husband absolutely. During the marriage he had 'seisin' (the right to possession) and was entitled to all profits from the property, but he was not able to alienate (sell or give away) the wife's land without her consent. If he did then the widow or her heir had the right to recover it after the husband's death.

Because her real property vested in her husband, a wife could not alienate her own land during marriage without his consent. If the husband and wife agreed to sell her land, this could be accomplished successfully if they together levied a 'fine' in the Court of Common Pleas, which was a settlement of fictitious suit at law. The agreement was recorded in court as a 'final concord'.[45] In such cases the judge was supposed to question the wife away from her husband on her own to ensure her agreement to alienate was genuine and not forced on her by her husband. This process was also effective to bar her dower on the alienated land because she would be asked in court if by her own free will she resigned her rights to dower in the land sold.[46] Whether these safeguards used by the courts to protect a married woman's interests were really adequate seems open to question.

Even a woman as wealthy, and presumably as well advised, as Lady Margaret Hoby did not succeed in ensuring that her property would be inherited by her relatives. In 1632 she transferred her extensive lands to her husband, apparently on the legally non-enforceable understanding that if she died first then he would leave instructions in his will that some of the land formerly hers would be sold to provide legacies for her relatives. If she had not done this then on her death Lady Margaret's blood relatives and not her husband or his family would have inherited all her real property.[47] But after Margaret Hoby's death Sir Thomas failed to carry out her requests for making gifts of money to her relatives, and when he died his own family inherited all his property, including that brought into the marriage by his wife.[48] Lady Margaret's biographer reports on the disturbing local rumour that Sir Thomas hastened her death 'by kicking her downstairs', but discounts the story as unlikely as the grieving Sir Thomas later built and endowed a chapel in his wife's memory.[49]

By Shakespeare's time marriage settlements arranged in advance of marriage were utilised by property owners to achieve various purposes including preserving a wife's separate estate (we have glanced at these in chapter 4). These could take several forms. The entailed estate (which should be distinguished from the strict settlement, developed after 1640) was in the process of developing.[50] This ensured that real property devolved (usually) in the male line, and so 'reinforced the practice of primogeniture'; such agreements were usually prepared in advance of an eldest son's marriage.[51] Shakespeare himself alluded to entails and other subtleties of land law.[52] Alternatively, a marriage settlement could be drawn up before a daughter's marriage to safeguard her separate property by means of a trust. In addition, many other matters were commonly arranged in marriage agreements. In defiance of the doctrine of coverture, model forms for settlements made before marriage found in published manuals show that wives were offered, in addition to the more usual pin money or jointures, agreements that they could make wills, arrange the marriages of the children of their former marriages, give dowries for such marriages, and preserve property from a former marriage.[53]

Agreements allowing property to be held in trust for a woman's own separate use were upheld by the equity court of Chancery. Chancery had upheld uses in favour of married women since the end of the middle ages, and after the Statute of Uses of 1536 Chancery upheld similar devices called 'trusts' protecting wives' separate property. However, such an arrangement was always vulnerable to the danger that a wife might be prevailed upon to agree to alienate her trust property, either to her husband or to someone else for his benefit. Therefore a clause known as a 'restraint on anticipation' was often inserted in deeds settling property on married women which prevented them from alienating. This worked by postponing a wife's absolute interest in the property until such time as she was widowed. If she attempted to alienate before that time the estate was forfeited, which would act as a deterrent to an attempt at sale. But although such clauses were common after 1800 it is not known how much they were in use before then.

The increase in all sorts of agreements in advance of marriage for a wife's separate estate during the seventeenth century has been attributed to the increasing importance of personal property relative to real property, because as we have seen a wife's personal property became her husband's absolutely on marriage (unless protected) while real property did not.[54]

The Lawes Resolutions of Womens Rights argues that despite 'whatever Bracton say' it was indeed possible to enfeoff (transfer property to) a wife, and so argues that a man can leave property to his wife in a will, or 'a feoffment, fine, or recovery may be made, acknowledged or suffered, to the use of her and her heyres which is wife to the feoffer'. Also one man can enfeoff another man on the condition he enfeoff his wife 'and the condition is good'.[55] But the examples given do not allow a wife to hold property in her own name. They are rather devices to enable a man to pass property to trustees for the benefit of his wife. Only a use (trust) upheld by equity in the court of Chancery would achieve this, and such safeguards for a wife's separate property were mostly only available to wives of the nobility, gentry, or wealthy merchants.

SHAKESPEARE AND THE EFFECTS OF MARRIED STATUS

As we have seen, the idea of the husband as the monarch or lord in his family had a peculiar reflection in the criminal law of petty treason. Unlike contemporary playwrights, Shakespeare does not portray wives killing, conspiring to kill, or even injuring, husbands.[56] In one partial exception, King Cymbeline's unnamed wicked Queen dies confessing her plans to poison the King in order to usurp the throne for her son (*CYM* 5.6.49–61), but her intent at regicide was high treason, not petty treason nor murder (the law of criminal intent to murder was not well developed in Shakespeare's age, but such intent directed against a King was certainly treasonous).[57]

Although Shakespeare mainly avoided the topic of husband-murder, a number of Shakespeare critics have investigated the law of petty treason.[58] That law does have the interest of embodying a conceptual equivalencing of any husband in his household with a king in his realm. The analogy underlying the (partial) equivalence of petty treason with high treason is made explicit in Kate's now-notorious speech:

> Such duty as the subject owes the prince,
> Even such a woman oweth to her husband,
> And when she is froward, peevish, sullen, sour,
> And not obedient to his honest will,
> What is she but a foul contending rebel,
> And graceless traitor to her loving lord?
>
> (*SHR* 5.2.160–5)

Here Kate seems to express wholly orthodox doctrines, but a key phrase to notice may be 'his honest will'.[59] Many conduct books taught that wives should bear with patience even the most unjust (e.g. dishonest) ill-treatment by husbands.[60] An analogous doctrine, that subjects must never oppose a ruler, even if tyrannical, was also often expressed in Shakespeare's time, but this view too had its opponents;[61] a range of positions on this crucial constitutional issue is implicit within Shakespeare's history plays, especially *Richard III* and *Richard II*.[62] Interpretation of Kate's speech is also complicated because its register has been much debated by critics. There is no general agreement about whether it shows a caricature of received doctrines, or her participation in a conspiracy with Petruchio, or her submission to brain-washing or to sheer violence, or even her eventual triumph and vindication.[63]

We move from disputed ideologies to a mirroring of legal and economic realities when we consider Shakespearian reflections of the full economic subordination of a wife to her husband embodied in the doctrine of coverture. This doctrine is made crystal clear when Portia contracts marriage with Bassanio, yet again using the image of the husband as a king:

> But the full sum of me
> Is sum of something which, to term in gross,
> Is an unlessoned girl, unschooled, unpractised,
> Happy in this, she is not yet so old
> But she may learn; happier than this,
> She is not bred so dull but she can learn;
> Happiest of all is that her gentle spirit
> Commits itself to yours to be directed
> As from her lord, her governor, her king.
> Myself and what is mine to you and yours
> Is now converted. But now I was the lord
> Of this fair mansion, master of my servants,
> Queen o'er myself; and even now, but now,
> This house, these servants, and this same myself
> Are yours, my lord's. I give them with this ring.
>
> (*MV* 3.2.157–71)

However, almost immediately after this willing acceptance of subordination, a wife's capacity to gain an advantage from insubordinate scolding is teasingly made clear as well; thus Portia sets the condition that her ring must be protected absolutely or else it will 'be my vantage to exclaim on you'. As she will scheme to overturn Bassanio's pledge to keep the ring, it is uncertain just how 'unschooled' she will prove. As seems true in many Shakespeare plays, particularly *The Merry Wives of Windsor*, the legal personality of married women may be subsumed in their husbands', but not all their personality.[64]

Despite the various legalistic or fantastical merry tricks featured in the play, including Portia's and Nerissa's elaborate stratagems over the oaths taken concerning their rings, at the moment of Portia and Bassanio's spousal contract (called in *The Merchant of Venice* 3.2.193 'the bargain of [their] faith') the transfer of her extensive property is absolutely to her husband without limit. There are no dowry or other pre-marital negotiations, unlike those seen for instance in *The Taming of the Shrew*, *King John*, *All's Well That Ends Well*, and *Henry V*; once the contract is sealed with the gift of a ring, and perhaps the scroll's suggested 'loving kiss' (*MV* 3.2.138), Portia tells Bassanio that he is lord of all that she possesses. This immediate unconditional all-giving (atypical for the well-propertied) may be a poetic feature of fabulous romantic Belmont. But the fabulation here still recognises the legal reality that mutual spousals (without further ceremony or any sexual consummation) conferred on husbands the full property rights of *baron* over a *feme covert*, despite Swinburne's demurs discussed in chapter 6.

And yet, just after giving him her all in making her spousal contract, Portia demands to know in detail the contents of a new-arrived private letter that upsets Bassanio and concerns his affairs:

> With leave, Bassanio, I am half yourself,
> And I must freely have the half of anything
> That this same paper brings you.
> (*MV* 3.2.246–8)

Here she expresses a notion that the doctrine of 'one person' in a marriage means that the wife must share in all her husband's concerns and business. This notion belongs to a 'companionate' model of marriage, which as we have said may have roots quite distinct from the patriarchal principle of coverture.

A similar notion of a right to share in all her husband's affairs, reflecting a companionate model of married relations, recurs when another Shakespearian Portia, the wife of Brutus in *Julius Caesar*, argues that she

must be told about what troubles her husband by claiming they are 'incorporated' and 'one':

> You have some sick offence within your mind,
> Which by the right and virtue of my place
> I ought to know of. And upon my knees,
> I charm you by my once-commended beauty,
> By all your vows of love, and that great vow
> Which did incorporate and make us one,
> That you unfold to me, your self, your half,
> Why you are heavy, and what men tonight
> Have had resort to you – for here have been
> Some six or seven, who did hide their faces
> Even from darkness . . .
> Within the bond of marriage, tell me, Brutus,
> Is it excepted I should know no secrets
> That appertain to you? Am I your self
> But as it were in sort or limitation?
> To keep with you at meals, comfort your bed,
> And talk to you sometimes? Dwell I but in the suburbs
> Of your good pleasure? If it be no more,
> Portia is Brutus' harlot, not his wife.   (*JC* 2.1.267–86)

The burden of a similar plea is implicitly denied in Macbeth's brushing aside his wife with 'Be innocent of the knowledge, dearest chuck' (*MAC* 3.2.46) when he arranges the murder of Banquo and Fleance; arguably, this gesture occasions a great turning point of the play after which this husband and wife can never again be 'one'.

These interactions are among a wide range of ways in which a companionate model of marriage may be reflected in Shakespeare's plays. Before raising some more examples, we may consider a representative sampling of the numerous positions that have been taken on Shakespeare and companionate marriage. John Bean argues that friendship rather than passion was emphasised in sixteenth-century matrimonial handbooks, and finds this reflected in Shakespeare's plays.[65] Irene Dash agrees with the startling proposal that Shakespeare 'created a new ideal: the love marriage'.[66] Diane Dreher does not find Shakespeare so much the originator, but holds that his 'depiction of young love was progressive, his portrayal of marriage influenced by the Puritans and humanist reformers of his age'.[67] Joseph Boone similarly finds Shakespeare instrumental 'in giving literary articulation to the emerging ethos of marriage as a lasting love union', and adds the debatable view that 'One cannot stress too greatly the importance of the historical shift from Catholicism to Protestantism in helping to shape the English attitude towards connubial relationship.'[68] Showing admirable historical and critical tact, Jean Hagstrum describes a gradual progression over several centuries towards 'the potential for friendship in marriage' culminating in Shakespeare's age, during which the 'opportunity for man–woman love to grow in both intimate vitality and companionable maturity' was reflected in his plays.[69]

Many critics have found deep and serious reflections of companionate marriage in Shakespeare's plays.[70] But the doctrine of 'one person' in marriage is also spoofed or parodied in other Shakespearian contexts. The familiar idea that a marriage creates one person, and the husband is the head,[71] underlies Pompey's quibbling reply to the Provost's 'Can you cut off a man's head?' This is: 'If the man be a bachelor, sir, I can; but if he be a married man, he's his wife's head, and I can never cut off a woman's head' (*MM* 4.2.1–5). The doctrine of 'one person' is more passionately, if no less bizarrely, expressed when Adriana insists:

> How comes it now, my husband, O how comes it
> That thou art then estranged from thyself? –
> Thy 'self' I call it, being strange to me
> That, undividable, incorporate,
> Am better than thy dear self's better part.
> Ah, do not tear away thyself from me;
> For know, my love, as easy mayst thou fall
> A drop of water in the breaking gulf,
> And take unmingled thence that drop again
> Without addition or diminishing,
> As take from me thyself, and not me too.
> (*ERR* 2.2.122–32)

With absurd logic following from an over-literally mooted premise this leads on to her claim that his (supposed) adultery makes him a cuckold, for as she is 'one' with him, his adultery must be her adultery also.[72]

DOMESTIC VIOLENCE AND EARLY MODERN LAW

Reports of violence within a family in early modern England are familiar from a variety of sources, ranging from court reports to popular ballads. While historians have argued over the general levels of violence in early modern society,[73] within the family allowed violence was part of a husband's prerogative in the exercise of his patriarchal power.[74] In Shakespeare's period wife-beating was not considered a criminal assault, provided excessive force was not used.

It is not easy to find any clear legal authority for the existence of a right for husbands to beat their wives.[75] There are reports of a right to beat wives under ancient Welsh common law which specified the number of strokes (three) and the thickness and length of the stick, and other reports of similar Irish customary law.[76] In England there is evidence for the existence of such a right in a manual of procedure for lawyers, Fitzherbert's *The New Natura Brevium*. This included a *pro forma* writ of *Securitate Pacis* or *supplicavit*, available to litigants from the court of Chancery or King's Bench, which instructed local Justices of the Peace to take surety for good behaviour from an alleged assailant.[77] Fitzherbert clearly considered that *supplicavit* was available to assaulted wives because he declared that 'if the Wife be in feare, or doubt that her Husband will beat her, or kill her, she may sue a *Supplicavit* in Chancery against her husband, to find Sureties'.[78] The *pro forma* set out a form of words to be used in such a writ seeking relief from threat and violence, but crucially added the proviso that relief was asked from 'any damage or evil to the [wife] in her body, otherwise then to her husband because of rule, and chastisement of his wife lawfully and reasonably belongeth he shall not do, nor procure to be done in any wise'.[79]

Another sixteenth-century legal text, *Eirenarcha*, written by William Lambard as a manual for the use of Justices of the Peace, specified that men have the right to exercise authority over (beat) others by either natural or civil rights. For example, a parent had a natural right over a child, while a man had a civil right to exercise authority over his servants.[80] However, Lambard also holds, citing Fitzherbert, that 'The wife if she be threatened to be killed, or to be outrageously chastised by her husband, may with good reason demand the Peace against him . . . And I do not doubt, but a Justice may (in such a case) command it upon his owne discretion.'[81]

These legal texts and others suggest that in Shakespeare's age there was popular acceptance of the idea that a husband had a right to beat his wife, but that this beating was not to be excessive and his right was never considered to be unlimited. By the late eighteenth century the 'rule of thumb' allowed a wife to be beaten as the legitimate exercise of a husband's authority provided the stick used to beat her was no thicker than a man's thumb. It has been said that the appearance of this rule (which operated to define acceptable violence without any limitations of the frequency or severity of beatings) is evidence of an increase in a husband's power, because in the seventeenth century no such rule existed allowing the unlimited

exercise of patriarchal authority.[82] Keith Wrightson comments that none
of the contemporary early modern diaries known to him provide evidence
of wife-beating taking place 'as a response to domestic conflict' among
'the middling sort' of people,[83] and urges caution in accepting too readily
the common assumption that it was a characteristic solution to resolving
domestic tensions for the poor.

Although cases in assize courts provide evidence of battered, even mur-
dered, wives this does not mean that such activities were popularly condoned. On the contrary the cases and commentaries provide evidence that
assaulting wives met with much public condemnation and disapproval.[84]
Wife-beating that exceeded common notions of appropriate behaviour was
often dealt with unofficially by the community itself through the intervention of neighbours, churchwardens, parish priests, or local dignitaries.[85] In
the prevailing theory a man's role in public and private life was to govern
his household peaceably and well. This meant controlling the actions of
his wife and children and servants by the use of physical force if necessary.
But use of excessive force and violence was regarded as evidence of failure
to govern well, and shaming to him.[86] While the early modern local community engaged in rituals called riding skimmington and rough music to
shame men who failed to control unruly wives,[87] other public rituals were
enacted to shame the wife-beater.[88]

Conduct books and legal commentaries provide evidence of both rights
to beat wives and condemnation on those who do. *The Lawes Resolutions
of Womens Rights* assumes a husband may beat his wife, much the same
as he may beat a traitor, a pagan, or a villein, because all these lack legal
rights of action against the assault. But the author concludes with 'God
send Gentlewomen better sport, or better companie.'[89]

Some contemporaries argued to endorse a legal right to beat wives. In
1608 William Gouger gave a public lecture in Oxford, a preached theology
thesis called an 'Act'. The subject matter of his dissertation was the existence of a man's legal right to beat his wife, a right which Gouger approved
of and supported.[90] This lecture provoked an angry reply in a small book
by William Heale of Exeter College.[91] Heale began by describing a companionate 'heaven of government, the husband intent on his businesse, the
wife imploied in her house' which existed if husband and wife 'make up
the sweet harmonie of mutual love, in a reciprocal content and union'.[92]
Heale launches his attack on Gouger by arguing that the 'rigour & severity
of . . . lawes against women' are the result not of hate, but of ignorance, because the lawgivers were canonists, 'single and unmarried' men who knew
nothing of marriage and ranked a wife as a 'man's best servant'.[93] But even

while acknowledging that men have a power over their wives, Heale cannot find any authority in canon, civil, or common law for beating a wife.[94]

In general the writers of conduct books urged husbands to treat their wives with moderation, while accepting that the husband had legitimate authority over them. The official *An Homilie of the State of Matrimonie* also declared that beating a wife brought shame on a husband.[95] In 1613 Sir Edward Coke, as Chief Justice, went so far as to deny in court that a husband had the right to 'correct' his wife, although his was a minority opinion.[96]

There were several ways in which an abused wife could seek a remedy from the courts. Wives who were misused, or their families on their account, were able to apply to local Justices of the Peace at assize sessions for their husbands to be made to enter into a recognisance to keep the peace. Other, probably wealthier, women applied to the court of Chancery or King's Bench which took recognisances from abusive husbands (see above on the writ of *supplicavit*). There is evidence that the levels of surety demanded for good behaviour from an abusive husband were set at a level sufficiently high to act as a real deterrent, and also evidence that wives did make frequent use of the court's procedures.[97]

It was also possible for an abused wife to go to the church courts which had disciplinary and supervisory jurisdiction over moral behaviour.[98] In such cases the records indicate that allegations of physical assault and cruelty were more likely to be made during an application for a separation or a complaint about desertion than as an unrelated complaint about a violent spouse.[99] The church courts' powers did not include binding over for good behaviour, and while punishments such as penance or excommunication were sometimes severe in their effect, they did not provide an immediate remedy.

The legal right of husbands to beat their wives was closely tied to their right to physically confine them.[100] The right to confine a wife, which could mean abducting her and locking her up, was seen as enforcing the matrimonial duty to cohabit and therefore as a proper exercise of a husband's authority. By the seventeenth century the husband's most likely motive for confining a wife was not to curb her extravagance or misbehaviour, but to force her to come to an arrangement with him over disputed property.[101]

SHAKESPEARE AND DOMESTIC VIOLENCE

On the Shakespearian stage the mistaken or diseased fantasy of jealous husbands impels Othello's murder of Desdemona, Leontes' unjust attempt to execute Hermione, and Posthumus' intent to murder Imogen by proxy. Iago, who is also sexually jealous, wounds his wife fatally because she does not heed his commands in the culminating (finally physical) act of his villainy.

These cases of Shakespearian wife-murder, or attempts at murder, would have fallen under the sway of criminal law, not family law.[102] Despite the surprising fact that murder was very rare in Shakespeare's England,[103] between 1590 and 1610 there was a run of popular English stage plays based on contemporary domestic murder cases linked with marital issues such as wardship or adultery.[104] But there are no parallel Shakespearian exemplars based on contemporary murders in the English family.

As close as Shakespeare gets is in the deliberately exotic story of the murder of Desdemona, and in this story there is also a sole Shakespearian instance of on-stage wife-beating.[105] In a kind of parodic rehearsal for his later private, wholly self-convincedly 'rational', murder of Desdemona, Othello strikes his wife both publicly and irrationally, in the grip of an obscure impulse.[106] This act amazes for several reasons. It contradicts the premise of the heroically 'companionate' love-match that has caused Desdemona to become estranged from her father and removed from her native surroundings; this is the premise that Othello will always be her protector and friend, and will love her absolutely.[107] It also radically contradicts Othello's long-established social identity as an immensely dignified and impressive leader of men. The savagery of a public wife-beater is inconsistent, for instance, with the cool presence and towering authority that we have seen halting a street fight with no more than a touch of silver words: 'Keep up your bright swords, for the dew will rust 'em' (*OTH* 1.2.60). The ease with which Othello obtains obedience to his commands is implicitly equal to the ease with which he masters himself: now he not only loses self-control, but is visibly subject to incomprehensible vagaries. So it is no wonder that, witnessing the wild flailing of a jealous husband break out in Othello, Lodovico comments: 'My lord, this would not be believed in Venice, / Though I should swear I saw 't' (4.1.242–3). The abnormality of the event is its hallmark; it dishonours Othello, stuns Desdemona, and appals the witness.

Because they are shameful even to behold, physical assaults on wives are not seen serving the farcical or other dramatic purposes that physical abuse or threatened chastisement of servants serves in many of Shakespeare's plays.[108] The particular shamefulness of wife-beating emphasised in texts like *An Homilie of the State of Matrimonie* seemingly mirrored contemporary attitudes. A man's honour as the governor of the household was, as we have said, compromised if he was violent. But a condemnation of violence is not the only reason why misogynistic jealousy is not approved of by Shakespeare. Ford, for instance, makes himself publicly ridiculous in his intrusive jealousy of his wife, saying to his neighbours: 'If I find not what I seek, show no colour for my extremity; let me for ever be your table-sport; let them say of me, "As jealous as Ford, that searched a hollow walnut for his wife's leman". Satisfy me once more; once more search with me' (*WIV* 4.2.148–52). Yet Ford beats only Falstaff, as the witch of Brentford, not his wife.[109] Strikingly, even while he is still convinced that Imogen was guilty of adultery, Posthumus comes to feel intense guilt for having (he thinks) killed a wife 'better than [him]self' for no sufficient cause, but for only 'Wrying but a little' (*CYM* 5.1.2–33).[110]

Nevertheless, that attacks on wives were familiar in his age is reflected by Shakespeare. So, in defending wives who cuckold their husbands, Emilia cites in their justification:

> But I do think it is their husbands' faults
> If wives do fall. Say that they slack their duties,
> And pour our treasures into foreign laps,
> Or else break out in peevish jealousies,
> Throwing restraint upon us; or say they strike us,
> Or scant our former having in despite:
> Why, we have galls; and though we have some grace,
> Yet have we some revenge. Let husbands know
> Their wives have sense like them. They see, and smell,
> And have their palates both for sweet and sour,
> As husbands have. What is it that they do
> When they change us for others? Is it sport?
> I think it is. And doth affection breed it?
> I think it doth. Is 't frailty that thus errs?
> It is so, too. And have not we affections,
> Desires for sport, and frailty, as men have?
> Then let them use us well, else let them know
> The ills we do, their ills instruct us so.
>
> (*OTH* 4.3.85–102)

Her logic of tit-for-tat is very similar to Shylock's when he defends his own motivation for revenge. However, the 'higher' sense of vision alluded to in 'Hath not a Jew eyes?' (*MV* 3.1.54) is joined here in Emilia's redaction with the lower faculties of smelling and tasting (for her all equalling lust). The equation here made by Emilia between female sexual desires and male sexual desires, in line with the argument in Montaigne's essay 'Upon some Verses of Virgil',[111] is in distinct opposition to a misogynistic ideology of evilly rampant female sexuality that has often been alleged to be the stance of Shakespeare's age. We may well remain dubious of Shylock's and Emilia's arguments that suffering a wrong justifies the taking of revenge in kind. Nevertheless there is no doubt that the actual oppression of Shylock is depicted as despicable, and the structural parallel suggests we are expected also to view Emilia's husbands who '[Throw] restraint upon' or 'strike' their wives with disapproval and distaste.

We may wonder if there is any less condemnation implicit in the use in *Henry IV, part 2* of a metaphor of 'provoked' wife-beating. The metaphor is used by the Archbishop of York in a hopeful explanation of why, peace once being offered, King Henry will not seek further to punish rebellion:[112]

> No, no, my lord; note this. The King is weary
> Of dainty and such picking grievances,
> For he hath found to end one doubt by death
> Revives two greater in the heirs of life;
> And therefore will he wipe his tables clean,
> And keep no tell-tale to his memory
> That may repeat and history his loss
> To new remembrance; for full well he knows
> He cannot so precisely weed this land
> As his misdoubts present occasion.
> His foes are so enrooted with his friends
> That, plucking to unfix an enemy,
> He doth unfasten so and shake a friend;
> So that this land, like an offensive wife
> That hath enraged him on to offer strokes,
> As he is striking, holds his infant up,
> And hangs resolved correction in the arm
> That was upreared to execution.
>
> (*2H4* 4.1.195–212)

The context of these remarks, a conference in Gaultree forest, makes them highly ironic. Just after the conference, in the same scene, Prince John accepts the truce offered by the Archbishop using tones of seemingly genuine good will. But then John immediately reneges on his offer of 'restored love and amity', arrests as capital traitors the Archbishop and the other rebel leaders, and kills them and as many as he can of their peacefully retiring forces (4.1.291–349). John's calculating cunning and logic-chopping replace his delusive tones of forgiveness and harmony. In the next scene Falstaff famously attributes Prince John's cold disposition to a lack of drinking sherry sack (4.2.83–121). After this we hear only a little more of Prince John, whose behaviour is isolated in the play from Prince Hal. But we should note that his dishonourable deed of cold policy is imagistically connected with merciless wife-beating.

The most offensive Shakespeare play, for many critics, is *The Shrew*, for this is claimed by them to countenance male domestic violence. The farcical assumptions that apply in certain parts of the play (assumptions that stage puppets, when struck, like Punch and Judy have only wooden heads) do not pertain in the relations of Petruchio and Kate, nor in the 'taming' sub-plot, although this may at first seem otherwise. On his first appearance Petruchio physically assaults his manservant Grumio in a bit of stage business involving crude and zany humour, dependent on misunderstanding of the Elizabethan dative 'knock me' meaning 'knock for me' (*SHR* 1.2.1–18). Symmetrically, on her first appearance Kate is seen tying up and physically abusing her sister Bianca out of spite and jealousy (2.1.1–22). Expectations are thus aroused that we will see a rough and tumble relationship between Petruchio and Kate, and in some film and stage versions this is duly seen on stage. But the Shakespeare text says otherwise.

In their first encounter there is plenty of verbal sparring between Kate and Petruchio, but only one (and the play's only) instance of on-stage physical violence between them. The violence is Kate's against Petruchio (the stage direction in italics is from the First Folio, tln 1096):

PETR Good Kate, I am a gentleman.
KATE   That I'll try. *she strikes him*
PETR I swear I'll cuff you if you strike again.
KATE So may you lose your arms.
    If you strike me you are no gentleman,
    And if no gentleman, why then, no arms. (*SHR* 2.1.217–21)[113]

To repeat, here we *see* the only blow struck between these two in the play. In accord with the principles of masculine honour that we have outlined, Kate is safe in her assumption that Petruchio, a 'gentleman' bearing heraldic arms, will not strike a woman, although he replies that if he is struck again he will reply in kind.

Although Kate suffers physical abuse in the events following her madcap marriage, this is always reported as either accidental or in odd ways indirect.[114] The grasp 'about the neck' and resounding kiss she receives in the church (part of the subversion of the marriage ceremony that we have discussed in chapter 5), and her horse falling on her in heavy mud (and then it seems that Petruchio's falls also), are farcical events revealed only in report (3.3.50–3, 4.1.47–75). When her horse falls the servant Grumio receives a beating 'because her horse stumbled'. (This may seem typically madcap and unjust, but did Katherina's horse fall because 'her bridle was burst' (4.1.72), a matter of Grumio's responsibility?)[115] Likewise when the food, the cap, the gown, the bed, and all other comforts are deemed insufficient for Kate by Petruchio, it is the servants and providers who are assaulted by him, while Kate pleads for him to desist.[116]

Of course Kate is a victim. During her mad honeymoon she is deprived of all the comforts she needs or wants, on the pretext that they are not good enough for her. This ploy, worsening the deprivation, rankles: 'And that which spites me more than all these wants, / He does it under name of perfect love' (4.3.11–12).

Kate is also unwillingly abducted from her own wedding feast, and constrained to remain in Petruchio's household against her will. The two forms of Kate's abuse by her overbearing husband, her deprivations within the household and her confinement there, need to be distinguished from one another, as they are dealt with in different registers, serve different functions in the play, and bear very different relations to the assumptions and values of Shakespeare's society.

The matter of just-married Kate's deprivation of all comforts and goods because they are not 'good enough' for her supplies a crucial element to the imaginary economy of the play. Petruchio's scheme to pretend 'That all is done in reverent care of her' (4.1.190) relates to a central theme of education in the play. One of us has proposed, on the basis of a special thematic use of language in the play, that this is a mutual education involving the self-education of Petruchio as well, and that as a result Shakespeare subverts the conventions of a 'taming' farce.[117] This view links to arguments made by a number of critics that this play is centrally concerned with female education.[118] Certainly the formal education of the Minola sisters included Latin and Greek as well as music and poetry. The education of Katherina may be implied to go beyond her sister's training in such accomplishments; Randall Martin argues persuasively that Petruchio's ploys have the humanist and Neo-platonic objective of a 'companionate pursuit of higher values'.[119]

But certainly, when it comes to Kate's forcible confinement amounting to imprisonment, the play mirrors conventional and legally sanctioned violence against women. Kate's abduction is passed over without any other character's comment than the wildly farcical claims of Petruchio, who carries her off before the wedding feast ranting:

> She is my goods, my chattels. She is my house,
> My household-stuff, my field, my barn,
> My horse, my ox, my ass, my anything,
> And here she stands, touch her whoever dare.

I'll bring mine action on the proudest he
That stops my way in Padua. Grumio,
Draw forth thy weapon, we are beset with thieves.
Rescue thy mistress if thou be a man.
Fear not, sweet wench. They shall not touch thee, Kate.

(*SHR* 3.3.102–10)

As has been noted in chapter 6, no one attempts any such thing, and that absence of the wish to keep Kate is the main drollery of this climax to an absurd wedding. Kate is deprived of her big day, and will have no chance to shine in public again until she returns to deliver her now-notorious speech on obedience. There is another irony too; Petruchio's miscellany of real property and chattels, house, household stuff, fields, oxen, in fact received different treatments in both property and marriage law. Petruchio's preposterous muddling of all together seems done deliberately in order to underline a claim to complete ownership of his wife as property. Petruchio's words 'I'll bring mine action . . .' may draw attention to his deliberately exaggerated swaggering, for by including 'chattels' and landed property in his list he makes a nonsense any threat to bring a legal action, leaving only a threat of physical 'action'. Here a failure to mirror legal reality (or a great exaggeration of the doctrine of coverture) underscores the violence, or at least violence in pretence, in Petruchio's demonstration of how married status reduces women's rights.

Christopher Sly, after brief objections, has no wish to escape from the situation he is thrust into when abducted by the Lord of the Induction. Kate by contrast is willing to agree to any proposition, no matter how absurd, in order to go 'forward' towards her father's comfortable establishment and not return to the deprivations of Petruchio's house. She agrees the sun is a moon, and that an old man is a budding virgin, and also agrees to reverse these views just as suddenly (4.6.1–50). It may be noted, however, that she does this with some spirit, and is called 'merry' by an unbiased if astounded witness (4.6.54).

Be that as it may, the assumption is tacitly adopted in the play that a husband has the absolute right to compel his wife to live with him where and when and in what style he chooses, and this does mirror both the legal and the social assumptions of Shakespeare's age.

CHAPTER 8

Marriage breakdown: separation, divorce, illegitimacy

EARLY MODERN SEPARATION AND DIVORCE

In early modern England once a man and woman were validly married they remained bound to each other for as long as they lived, for better or worse, because divorce in its modern sense was not available. If a marriage failed the church courts were sometimes able to grant an order for one of two kinds of divorce, but neither corresponds to the modern law of divorce. Firstly, the church courts could grant a divorce *a vinculo matrimoni*. Here a marriage was annulled if the courts found a 'dirimentary impediment' making the marriage void *ab initio* – it had never existed. The parties could then be free to marry again.[1] Secondly, the church courts could make an order for a divorce *a mensa et thoro*. Here husband and wife were freed from their legal duty to cohabit, but they were not free to remarry.[2] This kind of divorce more nearly corresponds to modern judicial separation.

By Shakespeare's age these were the only forms of divorce allowed in England, but this had not always been the position in Europe. The early Church in the centuries following Christ's death had allowed divorce for certain matrimonial offences including adultery, and even in Anglo-Saxon England divorce and remarriage had been available. In the early middle ages the Church had not been able to make clear distinctions between marriage and concubinage. One reason for this must have been that, as we have seen, no universally agreed formula for contracting a valid marriage existed. Because of the evidence of continuing concubinage, lack of Church regulation of marriage and very few records of divorce some historians have argued that in practice divorce was readily available even later in medieval England, for many people took matters into their own hands and divorced and remarried as they chose without recourse to church courts.[3]

All this can lead to the conclusion that marriage during the middle ages was unstable and insecure: it was always possible to find some way to terminate an unsatisfactory union. But such a conclusion is not universally accepted because the very same scarcity of records of divorce litigation in medieval church courts that leads some historians to believe informal divorce was common, leads others to conclude on the contrary that divorce was rare.[4] Be that as it may, by Shakespeare's time although the post-Reformation English Church held that matrimony was not a sacrament, but an honorable estate, it still held that a marriage could not be ended by the will of either party, but only by the death of one of them.

The church courts would grant a divorce *a vinculo matrimoni* if a dirimentary impediment could be proved, but such a divorce brought with it very serious consequences, particularly for a wife and children. A wife was barred from the widow's rights to dower (see chapter 9) she would otherwise have claimed, and could be impoverished. Any children born during the marriage might become illegitimate (see below).

The dirimentary impediments acceptable as grounds for annulling a marriage were lack of capacity to contract marriage, affinity, consanguinity, duress, impotence, mistake of person, the existence of a pre-contract, a religious vow of celibacy, difference of cult, and unknowing marriage to someone of servile status.[5] A lack of capacity for a marriage arose if either party was unable to give valid consent, for example because of insanity or infancy. In a contract *per verba de praesenti* young people were unable to consent until they reached the age of puberty, taken to be twelve years for women and fourteen for men. The age of consent for a pre-contract *per verba de futuro* was only seven years, but when the child reached puberty the marriage could be avoided as long as consummation had not taken place. Swinburne also mentions the incapacity to give valid consent occasioned by furore and drunkenness.[6] In chapter 2 we saw that a lack of capacity to consent to marriage could be cited to prevent a marriage taking place if it could be proved that duress was used to coerce the parties. Claims of a lack of capacity due to duress were also cited in actions for divorce.[7]

The most significant impediments to marriage were those due to affinity and consanguinity. The impediment of affinity came into existence if a pre-existing relationship between the parties had been created by a former marriage or even by a carnal relationship outside marriage.[8] Affinity extended to the first, second, and third cousins of a spouse or a person with whom one had had sexual intercourse, and was also created by 'spiritual connections', such as those with god-parents or god-parents' relations and prospective marriage partners.

Consanguinity was created by a blood relationship between the parties within the prohibited four degrees. This meant, approximately, that all people descended from a common great-great-grandfather were barred from marriage with each other. The law of consanguinity was complex. During Henry VIII's reign there were several statutory changes, in particular the Marriage Act 32 Hen. VIII c.38 (1540) which set out simplified prohibited degrees of relationship based on Leviticus. In 1563 Archbishop Parker's *Admonition to All Such as Intend to Marry*, a book containing a table of prohibited relationships, was ordered to be placed in every parish church for people to consult before marriage. Nevertheless the complexity of the law meant that marriages inadvertently falling within the prohibited degrees were probably not uncommon. In 1599 Lady Margaret Hoby wrote in her diary of a conversation 'wth a woman that was to be diuorsed from Hir Husbande with whome she liued inceasteously'.[9] We may wonder if this was a divorce sought by the woman or her husband, or if it followed a report made to the church courts by a parish official or neighbour.

The legal historian F. W. Maitland once suggested that the complexities of the impediments of affinity and of consanguinity meant that divorce was nearly always possible because 'spouses who had quarrelled [and] began to investigate their pedigrees . . . were unlucky if they could discover no impedimentum dirimens'.[10] But recently this 'hoary tradition in English historiography' has been doubted.[11] Helmholz suggests that the reason for the lack of divorce cases based on impediments is that such marriages were rare because popular opinion held that any marriage contracted within the prohibited degrees would fail to prosper.[12] But the requirements of strict rules of proof coupled with the difficulty of proving distant relationships in an age without many written records must also contribute to the scarcity of recorded cases. The nobility and the gentry, who often intermarried and whose pedigrees were well documented, were more likely to claim the impediments of affinity and consanguinity than other people. Certainly Henry VIII famously made great use of arguments of impediments of affinity to achieve his aim of divorcing several of his wives.[13]

Other impediments to marriage which could be used in a suit for a divorce included proof of the existence of a pre-existing marriage contract with a third party, and the impediment of 'crime'. This latter prevented a married man who had committed adultery with a woman from marrying that woman after the death of his wife. The woman was said to be 'polluted by the adultery' and the impediment to their marriage was permanent, although it does seem likely that this prohibition on marriage was ignored in practice because of difficulties of proof:[14] the second marriage must have been contracted *de futuro* during the life of the first wife.

Sexual frigidity (impotence) too could prevent a valid marriage being contracted, the problem being again one of proof. The lawyer Ariosto of

John Webster's *The Devil's Law-Case* fulminates against 'Wicked divorces, or your vicious cause / Of *plus quam satis*', hilariously parodying the legal tag '*nunquam satis*' (by no means enough) used in such suits for annulment.[15] Although the divorce action brought by Frances Howard against the Earl of Essex in 1613 on the grounds of his impotence caused widespread and often ribald astonishment,[16] this sort of action was not unprecedented in earlier English cases.[17] Canon law distinguished between different causes of impotence, ranging from physical deformity to natural frigidity. Helmholz's investigations into Canterbury and York cases find all to have been brought by wives against husbands, and gives details of the remarkable hands-on methods ordered by the courts to establish their claims. Helmholz comments that these methods were not recommended by the Church of Rome or any canonists and so were most likely practical local innovations.[18]

The second kind of divorce available from the church courts, a divorce *a mensa et thoro*, ended the duty to cohabit owed by all married people, a duty which was enforced by the church courts. Once granted a husband and wife were able to live apart from each other but they were not free to remarry. This form of divorce was available in cases of adultery, sodomy, 'spiritual fornication' (by which was meant apostasy or heresy), and cruelty or fear of future injury.[19] A reconciliation following the adultery or cruelty which appeared to condone the wrong done acted as a bar to the future grant of such an order. It is uncertain whether or not the grant of a divorce *a mensa et thoro* absolved a husband from his legal obligation to maintain his wife but fathers have always had a duty to maintain their children (whether or not legitimate).[20]

When a marriage broke down many people made their own private arrangements to live apart or turned to unofficial arbitration for their marital disputes, which could explain the lack of many recorded cases for divorce *a mensa et thoro*. The risk with following this course of action was that the church courts refused to recognise private agreements to separate, and would instead uphold the duty to cohabit. When cases of divorce *a mensa et thoro* did reach church courts the judge often assumed the role of a mediator between the husband and wife, attempting to reconcile them and acting as 'a rather heavy-handed marriage counsellor'.[21]

In an age when physical abuse of wives was both socially tolerated and not unlawful (within certain limits, as we saw in chapter 7), when most women had no financial independence, and when the duty to cohabit was upheld by parents, local community, and church, the church court's intervention (sometimes initiated *ex officio*) must have offered some degree of protection from domestic violence. In the church courts, as in cases brought before the

Justices of the Peace, violent husbands were often ordered to offer sureties for future good behaviour in return for resumed cohabitation, and where an order for divorce *a mensa et thoro* was made the court could order payment of alimony.

When the marriages of politically powerful men and women failed even a sovereign would intervene, or supply an arbitrator. In 1584 Queen Elizabeth instructed Leicester to act as mediator between Bess of Hardwick, Countess of Shrewsbury and her fourth husband George Talbot, 6th Earl of Shrewsbury, who was at the time acting as the reluctant jailer of Mary Queen of Scots. Leicester was unsuccessful and the Queen then appointed a Commission of Enquiry composed of the Lord Chancellor and two Chief Justices who ordered Bess and Shrewsbury to appoint counsel and submit evidence about their differences.[22] Relations between Sir Edward Coke and his wife Lady Hatton were so poor that King James tried to intervene, but Lady Hatton refused to sit at table with Coke.[23]

Henry VIII's notorious marital problems illustrate the difficulties and limitations of the canon law of divorce in early modern England. In 1509 he married Katherine of Aragon, the widow of his deceased elder brother Arthur. The marriage was *prima facie* void, but Pope Julius II granted a dispensation from the impediment of affinity which allowed the marriage to go ahead. That dispensation appears to have been incorrect because if, as was claimed, Arthur's marriage was unconsummated, arguably no impediment of affinity should have arisen between Katherine and Henry. However, the impediment of 'public honesty', which prohibited marriage between people related through a pre-contract, might have.[24] No one queried Henry's marriage to Katherine until many years later when he determined to divorce Katherine in order to marry Anne Boleyn. Henry became immersed in the details of canon law in an attempt to uncover arguments favourable to his cause. In 1528 Pope Clement VII sent Cardinal Campeggio to England to preside over a special legatine court convened in 1529 to consider and conclude the King's 'great matter'. Henry apparently intended to argue that the Pope's dispensation had been invalid because the marriage between Katherine and Arthur had indeed been consummated. Katherine then complicated matters greatly by producing a copy of a second papal bull, in the form of a brief, which appeared to grant the dispensation necessary for her marriage with Henry to take place whether or not her marriage to Arthur had been consummated. Cardinal Wolsey was probably correct to conclude that the problem was that both bulls had been very badly drafted, but this did not advance the King's cause. Henry argued instead that he had been twelve years of age and therefore too young to consent when the marriage with

Katherine had been arranged, and later had protested against the marriage. He also argued that the marriage was part of a plan supposed to ensure peace between England and Spain, but by the time it actually took place peace was not in issue and therefore not a valid reason to grant a papal dispensation. Finally, Henry went ahead and married Anne Boleyn privately, and the newly appointed Archbishop of Canterbury, Thomas Cranmer, announced the marriage to Katherine void for reasons of affinity.

The long-defunct possibility of a divorce for adultery allowing remarriage was proposed anew by Cranmer,[25] who considered that a divorce *a mensa et thoro* offended against the duty to cohabit insisted on by the Church. He drafted a new marriage code which allowed divorce followed by remarriage for marital misconduct such as adultery, cruelty, desertion, or 'bitter enmity'. But these proposals came to nothing (although for a while there was some uncertainty about the effect of a divorce *a mensa et thoro*).[26] In 1548 the Marquis of Northampton divorced his wife *a mensa et thoro* and then remarried, his second marriage being confirmed by a 1552 Act of Parliament (repealed in 1553). The validity of such a remarriage was overruled by Star Chamber in Rye v Fuljambe, 1602 (Moore K. B. 683, 72 English Reports 838). After this, divorce by private Act of Parliament for a wife's adultery (not for the adultery of a husband) did not become a possibility again until 1670 when Lord Roos divorced by this means and remarried.[27]

SHAKESPEARE AND DIVORCE

i Mainly divorce 'a mensa et thoro'

Although divorce in the modern sense was not available in his England, the word 'divorce' was used by Shakespeare in nearly half of his works, mostly in family contexts, and typically to describe 'hateful', frightening, or violent events. Even where it has no legal overtones the word usually has dire implications in Shakespeare: for instance, in *The Comedy of Errors* 1.1.104 'this unjust divorce of us' refers to the long separation (following a shipwreck) of all the members of a family.

Divorce, however, may sometimes have been sought by one or both parties to a marriage in Shakespeare's age. Although officially disallowed unless sanctioned by church courts, self-proclaimed or *de facto* separations *a mensa et thoro* were not uncommon; this appears to have been particularly so among the upper classes, amongst whom husbands and wives sometimes occupied separate households. According to Lawrence Stone 'about a third' of 'older peers' were estranged from their wives between 1595 and 1620.[28] Perhaps mirroring customs in which aristocratic married couples not infrequently lived apart, Gloucester proclaims a divorce *a mensa et thoro* from his ambitious duchess Eleanor in *The First Part of the Contention* 2.1.209–11: 'I banish her my bed and company, / And give her as a prey to law and shame / That hath dishonoured Gloucester's honest name.' But this self-proclaimed separation does not protect him from the taint of her offence of witchcraft; here a husband is destroyed politically by the scandal of his wife's behaviour despite the legal principle that husbands and wives are not responsible for one another's crimes (see chapter 7).

Again without any apparent Church sanction, Shakespeare's strong-minded Queen Margaret proclaims her 'divorce' *a mensa et thoro* from King Henry VI:

> But thou preferr'st thy life before thine honour.
> And seeing thou dost, I here divorce myself
> Both from thy table, Henry, and thy bed,
> Until that act of Parliament be repealed
> Whereby my son is disinherited.
> (*RDY* 1.1.247–51)

Henry's submission to this is, among other things, an indication of his weakness as a king.

In a more equivocal Shakespearian instance of a weak king, the fact that Bushy and Green have caused 'a divorce betwixt his queen and [King Richard II]' is viewed by Bolingbroke as treasonous. So 'to wash your blood / From off my hands' before executing (or murdering) these courtiers, Bolingbroke explains:

> You have misled a prince, a royal king,
> A happy gentleman in blood and lineaments,
> By you unhappied and disfigured clean.
> You have, in manner, with your sinful hours
> Made a divorce betwixt his queen and him,
> Broke the possession of a royal bed,
> And stained the beauty of a fair queen's cheeks
> With tears drawn from her eyes by your foul wrongs.
> (*R2* 3.1.8–15)

Yet, ironically, once having usurped the crown, Bolingbroke himself forces the separation of Richard from his Queen; in a scene filled with their sorrows, Richard says: 'Doubly divorced! Bad men, you violate / A twofold marriage: 'twixt my crown and me, / And then betwixt me and my married wife' (5.1.71–3). Here the often-heard analogy of the husband in the house-hold and the king in the realm is explicitly expressed in Richard's 'Doubly divorced!'

The legal requirement for married couples to cohabit is tested in aber-rant circumstances by the highly contrived plot of *All's Well That Ends Well*. Although in chapter 3 we have examined a mirror-like treatment of Bertram's and Helena's wardship in this play, other elements of its plot sub-ject matrimonial law to a series of fantastic mootings. In particular, young Count Bertram effectively self-proclaims a divorce *a mensa et thoro* after marrying the non-aristocratic Helena when he declares 'Although before the solemn priest I have sworn . . . I'll to the Tuscan wars and never bed her' (*AWW* 2.3.266–70). The legal aspects of his refusal to consummate his marriage or cohabit with his wife (whom he sends back to his mother) have been much discussed, but often with confusion.[29] For instance, some critics suppose that the non-consummation of their marriage could have supplied *prima facie* grounds to dissolve it, but this is not true. In accord with many actual Elizabethan marriages of reluctant wards, it is also unlikely that an impediment of duress could have been argued against the validity of the marriage. Rather, Helena and Bertram are indissolubly married by the 'con-tract' named in the play (2.3.179), which is sealed by public handfasting (2.3.177), and solemnised in an off-stage church 'ceremony' (2.3.179–81). Only the sequel to this dramatic 'set-up' becomes fantastic: in this patient-Griselda type of fable Helena becomes with child by Bertram and obtains his ring, both without his knowledge. Because she had apparently fulfilled his wholly extra-legal conditions (contrived so as to be impossible (3.2.57–61)), Bertram says to the King: 'If she, my liege, can make me know this clearly / I'll love her dearly, ever ever dearly' (5.3.317–18). Helena's reply is 'If it appear not plain and prove untrue, / Deadly divorce step between me and you' (5.3.319–20). Behind the paired 'if – then' conditional state-ments in these two rhyming couplets lie two as-it-were twined legal and social positions. One was that church courts would uphold a marriage 'if intercourse had taken place [even after a] forced exchange of promises to marry'.[30] The other was that divorce would be indeed 'deadly' to Helena's life and reputation once she had publicised her pregnancy and use of the dubious bed trick.[31]

In fact Bertram's free consent is not indicated by the sexual relations in the bed trick (no more than is Angelo's in *Measure for Measure*). As we have seen, at least according to Swinburne, such a lack of willing consent would have negated a sexual connection as a basis for completing a *de futuro* marriage contract (had there been one). Yet, despite Helena's grave risk, and despite Bertram's induction into a settled marriage through what might seem trickery and a contrived public humiliation (not much different from the gulling of Parolles), it is suggested that all will 'end well' by Lafeu's reaction to the outcome: 'Mine eyes smell onions, I shall weep anon' (*AWW* 5.3.322).[32]

In Shakespeare's time, on lower social levels than Count Bertram's, many angry or injured wives refused to live with their husbands, as may be seen in church court actions brought by husbands seeking to enforce rights to cohabitation. Physical injury was a common reason for these separations, but infidelity or other misbehaviour also played a part. In *The Comedy of Errors*, which is set in a fabulated and comic ancient Ephesus, a self-proclaimed divorce for reasons of adultery is imaged when jealous Adriana berates her seeming husband:

> How dearly would it touch thee to the quick
> Shouldst thou but hear I were licentious,
> And that this body, consecrate to thee,
> By ruffian lust should be contaminate?
> Wouldst thou not spit at me, and spurn at me,
> And hurl the name of husband in my face,
> And tear the stained skin off my harlot brow,
> And from my false hand cut the wedding ring,
> And break it with a deep-divorcing vow?
>
> (*ERR* 2.2.133–41)

She then adds, following the doctrine of 'one flesh' to its illogical limit, that his adultery would make her adulterous, and therefore he must abstain from sexual infidelity or else be a cuckold:

> I am possessed with an adulterate blot;
> My blood is mingled with the crime of lust.
> For if we two be one, and thou play false,
> I do digest the poison of thy flesh,
> Being strumpeted by thy contagion.
> Keep then fair league and truce with thy true bed,
> I live unstained, thou undishonoured.
>
> (*ERR* 2.2.143–9)

The comic twist to her enterprising argument is that she furiously berates not her husband as she thinks, but rather his bemused twin brother.

In another fabulated and pre-Christian setting King Lear also alludes to a kind of divorce for reasons of adultery when he states that if Regan were to fail, as Goneril has done, to welcome him as he would wish, she must be a bastard: 'If thou shouldst not be glad / I would divorce me from thy mother's shrine, / Sepulchring an adultress' (*LRF* 2.2.302–4 / *LRQ* s.7.292–4). In their vehemence both Adriana and Lear may image the ancient world's allowance of a full divorce for adultery, which was proposed again in Henry VIII's time, and may well have been remembered in Shakespeare's day.

Shakespeare and his audiences certainly knew that a full divorce allowing remarriage had long been unavailable on grounds of adultery.[33] Yet there was one way in which the consequences of a wife's adultery could allow remarriage; this was when an adulterous queen was executed for high treason, ending a royal marriage.

Such deaths had been the fate of two of Henry VIII's wives, Anne Boleyn and Katherine Howard. A distinction between the handling of these two treasonous queens throws an interesting light on the manner in which King Leontes of *The Winter's Tale* insists that his offspring with Queen Hermione are bastards. Because Henry VIII had had no children with Katherine Howard he executed her for treason but had no need to, and did not, divorce her. But, in order to bastardise Princess Elizabeth, Henry had Archbishop Cranmer proclaim that his marriage with Anne Boleyn had been void from the outset.[34] In Shakespeare's fiction, the 'indictment' of Queen Hermione for high treason alleges adultery and conspiracy (*WT* 3.2.11–20), but there is apparently no legal move made to dissolve the marriage and legally bastardise the children. Rather, even more cruelly than in the practice of Henry VIII, Hermione's children are publicly proclaimed illegitimate without proof, and then one is exposed to die and the other dies of grief.

Only later in *The Winter's Tale* is an actual 'divorce' named. This is in circumstances that moot complicated legal matters. The disguised King Polixenes unmasks himself to interrupt the public celebration of the handfasting of his son and heir, saying 'Mark your divorce, young sir' (4.4.417). Divorce may well be an apposite word here. It seems that Perdita and Florizel are indeed married at that point, having joined hands when the Shepherd said 'Take hands, a bargain; / And, friends unknown, you shall bear witness to 't' (4.4.381–2); they have by gestures shown present willing consent, as is necessary for a *de praesenti* spousal.

The problem is that, as even Polixenes acknowledges, a father's consent was not normally required for marriage, although his advice would normally be sought: 'Reason my son / Should choose himself a wife, but as good reason / The father, all whose joy is nothing else / But fair posterity, should hold some counsel / In such a business' (4.4.406–10).

Also, normally, once a couple married by mutual consent an outraged parent could not 'divorce' them at will. So it would seem that the King's words, paralleling his following cruel threats to Perdita, are tyrannous. However, the marriage of a royal heir-apparent did (and still does) occupy a special position in law. Indeed, when Lord Hardwicke's Marriage Act at last reformed English marriage law in 1753, it specifically excluded from its regulations the marriages of royalty, Jews, and Quakers.

Yet, in storytelling, royal heirs – especially when visiting the pastoral world – repeatedly ignored the marital restrictions placed on them by their rank. One of Shakespeare's aims in using this motif may have been the exploration in extreme circumstances of the notion of a right to autonomy in matrimonial choice. A particularly apt example of that may arise in the instance of Princess Imogen's unapproved heterogamic marriage in *Cymbeline*, and this is a marriage which also raises complex legal questions.

Even for a Shakespearian Romance, the plot of *Cymbeline* is extraordinarily complicated, and the play straddles exceptionally many boundaries of genre, setting in time and place, and tone.[35] And yet, with all that, it is still a play that mirrors many of the values and concerns of Shakespeare's own England. Some of these are reflected in enigmas about Imogen's marriage. For instance, it is uncertain if that marriage is based on irrevocable *de praesenti* spousals, or on a *de futuro* contract, and this distinction is highly significant because in 2.5.9–13 Posthumus indicates the marriage has not been consummated. Anne Barton has in fact very persuasively argued that the uncertainties over the marriage in *Cymbeline* pointedly reflect early modern confusions over the validity of marriages by spousals.[36]

If we observe the language of the play we find contradictions concerning the status of the marriage. Imogen, Posthumus himself, and others, repeatedly describe Posthumus as Imogen's 'husband' (1.1.8, 1.1.86, 1.1.97, 1.6.3, 2.1.60, 3.4.14, 3.4.55, 3.4.131), while Posthumus, even in anger, refers to Imogen as his 'wife' (1.1.114–18, 2.5.7). Moreover Imogen herself calls Cloten 'A foolish suitor to a wedded lady' (1.6.2). Yet King Cymbeline, Imogen's father, wishes to separate her from his erstwhile ward Posthumus, whom he calls merely 'her minion' (2.3.39).

The vexed question of the status of the marriage in *Cymbeline* may be not so much one of who is right, as of whose competing social values or legal principles should be applied. For instance, in pursuit of his own marriage with Imogen, Imogen's step-brother Cloten derides her adherence to her marriage 'contract'. Cloten's position is based on an assumed aristocratic superiority to plebeian practices:

> The contract you pretend with that base wretch,
> One bred of alms and fostered with cold dishes,
> With scraps o' th' court, it is no contract, none.
> And though it be allowed in meaner parties –
> Yet who than he more mean? – to knit their souls,
> On whom there is no more dependency
> But brats and beggary, in self-figured knot,
> Yet you are curbed from that enlargement by
> The consequence o' th' crown, and must not foil
> The precious note of it with a base slave,
> A hilding for a livery, a squire's cloth,
> A pantler – not so eminent.   (*CYM* 2.3.110–21)

Cloten displays here, as he usually does, despicable pretentious arrogance. Does his readiness to proclaim an *ad hoc* divorce allowing remarriage reflect the waning aristocratic mores of Shakespeare's age? It certainly occasions Imogen's fury. Also, a matter of 'class' distinctions arises. Like Webster's Duchess of Malfi, Princess Imogen seemingly claims a right to a 'companionate' style of marriage based on liking and love, a style viewed by Cloten as appropriate only to 'meaner parties', and yet one championed in Shakespeare's age by the rising 'middling classes'.

Yet might Cloten be right in claiming that Imogen's marriage to Posthumus is invalidated by what he calls 'The consequence o' th' crown'?[37] The answer to that might be observed in a near parallel to Posthumus' and Imogen's situation which arose in Thomas Howard's actual unauthorised marriage with Lady Margaret Douglas, Lady Margaret being second in line to the crown. Howard was attainted for treason and executed as a result, and 'an addendum to his attainder [made] it high treason in future to espouse or marry the king's children (and those commonly reputed or taken for his children), his sisters or aunts, or children of his brother or sisters without a licence under the Great Seal' (28 Hen. VIII c.18). Commenting on this, E. J. Carlson notes that here, even after the English Reformation, we see 'the ultimate admission that the principles of papal law were still accepted: even the king, the Supreme Head, could not terminate a marriage by words of present consent without killing the parties'. Carlson then offers the witty if macabre formulation: 'The statute did not alter ecclesiastical law by declaring such marriages void, but could only impose the ultimate penance.'[38]

So we may conclude that in Shakespeare's age royal birth did not invalidate a marriage by (even unauthorised) *de praesenti* spousals, nor was it an impediment allowing divorce *a vinculo matrimoni*, but it could result in an execution. The question of Imogen's possible remarriage is thus a question of what sort of divorces the play implies were possible in her situation. The play's Italian-Renaissance-style villain Iachimo, gossiping over Posthumus' 'banishment' following his 'marrying his king's daughter', remarks on his 'lamentable divorce' (1.4.13–19), which would seem to be a separation *a mensa et thoro*. Yet a 'horrid act' of 'divorce' *a vinculo*, allowing the remarriage of Imogen with Cloten, is feared by an unnamed English Lord (2.1.60–1). Such a 'horrid act' would mirror full divorces obtained on the basis of great power doing as it pleased; historians have said such divorces were indulged in by the gentry of the Roman Empire and by medieval European royalty.[39]

Historically, although powerful families did sometimes sorely oppress their children's spouses, they could not legally impose divorces (a brutal English medieval case in which such a forced divorce was prevented by the Pope is recounted by Christopher Brooke).[40] Yet several Shakespearian contexts portray patriarchal power (like Cymbeline's) attempting to force the divorces or separations of validly married children; fathers in *The Winter's Tale*, *A Midsummer Night's Dream*, *Romeo and Juliet*, *Cymbeline*, and *Othello* attempt just that.

Brabantio attempts to use law to inflict a punishment on his son-in-law Othello that would have an effect equivalent to that of a divorce. Of course it was possible for married couples to be separated on account of imprisonment or other punishments. Those are the circumstances of Shakespeare's Posthumus and Imogen, and Richard II and his Queen, and were the actual circumstances of John Donne and Ann More (see chapter 6). With such a pattern in mind, Iago warns the newly married Othello that Brabantio's influence is so great:

> He will divorce you,
> Or put upon you what restraint or grievance
> The law, with all his might to enforce it on,
> Will give him cable.   (*OTH* 1.2.14–17)

That Brabantio does not succeed in his accusations against Othello (for erotic witchcraft) seems due more to the wartime pragmatism of the Venetian Senate than to the law.

Later in the same play Desdemona, suspected of adultery, asks Iago's help and advice, averring that she 'ever did, / And ever will – though he do shake me off / To beggarly divorcement – love him dearly' (4.2.160–2). Isolated from all she had known, with no family to return to, cast out like 'patient Griselda', Desdemona still sees divorce as her worst possible fate.

ii Mainly divorce 'a vinculo'

In the Shakespearian instances so far examined 'divorce' is often seen as a terrible fate, even when it does not result in the full annulment of a marriage. The grounds that *would* allow an annulment or divorce *a vinculo* were dirimentary impediments. Impediments to a marriage are mentioned, but without any legal precision, in Shakespeare's sonnet 116: 'Let me not to the marriage of true minds / Admit impediments. Love is not love / Which alters when it alteration finds, / Or bends with the remover to remove.' As is usual in Shakespeare's poetry, law terms are used here figuratively with an at best oblique relation to legal complexities.

However, the term 'impediment' is used quite literally when an 'impediment' due to unchastity between spousal and the marriage ceremony is allegedly 'discovered' in *Much Ado About Nothing* (3.2.83). When planning to 'cross' Claudio's intended marriage, Don John says 'Any bar, any cross, any impediment will be medicinable to me' (2.2.3–7). Don John then alleges Hero's sexual dishonour when he is asked by Claudio 'If there be any impediment, I pray you discover it' (3.2.83–4). At the start of the marriage ceremony Hero and Claudio are asked 'If either of you know any inward impediment why you should not be conjoined, I charge you on your souls to utter it', and Claudio tries Hero's conscience with the sarcastic 'Know you any, Hero?' (4.1.12–15). He then refuses to marry Hero on the grounds of a valid impediment, since following spousals *per verba de futuro* if one party has sexual relations with a third person then the other party is free to dissolve the contract.[41] Here the law is not misapplied, but it is used unnecessarily brutally (so much so that Hero apparently dies), and the alleged facts are incorrect.

The counterfeiting of a sexual transgression, used in *Much Ado* in an attempt to destroy a marriage, was seen in actual church court records.[42] Conversely, concubinage was sometimes covered up to allow marriages to take place. In accord with this, in Shakespeare's *Antony and Cleopatra* a possible impediment to a dynastic marriage between Antony and Octavia is raised obliquely when Cleopatra is named scandalously by Octavius Caesar. Antony replies 'I am not married, Caesar' (*ANT* 2.2.126–9), and when concluding the marriage agreement he says 'May I never / To this good purpose, that so fairly shows, / Dream of impediment!' (2.2.151–3).[43]

Even messier matrimonial arrangements arise in *Hamlet*, in which Claudius and Gertrude marry despite having been brother-in-law and sister-in-law, and perhaps also adulterous lovers. In accord with Leviticus 18.16 and 20.21, Hamlet is strictly correct in calling his mother's marriage with his uncle 'incestuous' (*HAM* 1.2.157).[44] Old Hamlet's Ghost calls Claudius moreover 'that incestuous, that adulterate beast' (1.5.42), adding 'beast' because he supposes that Claudius had seduced Gertrude during her first marriage.

Indeed Hamlet (whose opinions need not have been Shakespeare's, nor his age's) seems convinced along with the Player Queen and Player King that any woman's remarriage is depraved (3.2.170–6, 205–6). But actually the remarriage of Elizabethan widows was not at all universally despised (this will be discussed in chapter 9). Convinced furthermore that his father was killed by Claudius, Hamlet hopes for revenge when his uncle 'is drunk asleep, or in his rage, / Or in th' incestuous pleasure of his bed' (3.3.89– 90), and kills him at last as 'thou incestuous, murd'rous, damned Dane' (5.2.276).

The famous issue of incest in relation to *Hamlet* connects – at least in terms of the laws of marriage – with questions of the impediments of affinity that applied to in-laws. In fact, according to Christopher Brooke, questions of remote affinity or consanguinity became less important to Church authorities from the twelfth century onward. From that time the authorities became less concerned about obscure forms of incest used to dissolve marriages, and more concerned to support the stability of marriages.[45] However, a brother's wife or widow was so well within the prohibited degrees of affinity that a marriage with her remained sinful until the twentieth century.

Different dirimentary impediments, due to the existence of a prior marriage contract, are wilfully ignored or simply defied by several Shakespeare characters. This is most consequential in the cases of two Shakespearian kings. When Henry VI asks the Lord Protector, Gloucester, to 'give consent / That Marg'ret may be England's royal queen', the reply is dusty:

> So should I give consent to flatter sin.
> You know, my lord, your highness is betrothed
> Unto another lady of esteem.
> How shall we then dispense with that contract
> And not deface your honour with reproach?
>
> (*1H6* 5.7.25–9)

However, Suffolk, Margaret's champion, counsels Henry to ignore his precontract with the daughter of the Earl of Armagnac on the cynical grounds that 'A poor earl's daughter is unequal odds, / And therefore may be broke without offence' (5.7.34–5). Henry, in his weakness, accepts the advice, and the results (as discussed in chapters 1 and 2) are disastrous.

In *Richard III* 3.7.4–5 Richard colludes with Buckingham to allege that one or more similar impediments of pre-contract have invalidated the marriage of Edward IV, and have therefore bastardised Edward V. In an ensuing charade dramatising Richard's mock-reluctance to reign, Buckingham pretends to have to persuade Richard to take the throne thus:

> You say that Edward is your brother's son;
> So say we, too – but not by Edward's wife.
> For first was he contract to Lady Lucy –
> Your mother lives a witness to his vow –
> And afterward, by substitute, betrothed
> To Bona, sister to the King of France.
> These both put off, a poor petitioner,
> A care-crazed mother to a many sons,
> A beauty-waning and distressed widow
> Even in the afternoon of her best days,
> Made prize and purchase of his wanton eye,
> Seduced the pitch and height of his degree
> To base declension and loathed bigamy.
> By her in his unlawful bed he got
> This Edward, whom our manners call the Prince.
>
> (*R3* 3.7.167–81)

Therefore, Buckingham urges, Richard must take the throne, 'If not to bless us and the land withal, / Yet to draw forth your noble ancestry / From the corruption of abusing times, / Unto a lineal, true-derived course' (3.7.187–90). The story of the pre-contract with Lady Lucy, in More's *History of King Richard III*, has no other Shakespearian expression. But as described by Shakespeare, the sequence in Edward IV's marriage negotiations with Princess Bona comprises Warwick's embassy to France to woo her arranged in *Richard, Duke of York* 2.6.89–90, then the 'bluntest' wooing of Lady Elizabeth Grey in 3.2.69–81, then the acceptance of Edward's proposal by Lady Bona immediately followed by the arrival of news of his new marriage to Lady Grey in 3.3.139–66. This sequence is complicated by delays due to messengers, an incalculable time scale, and conflicts between personal and dynastic reasons to marry, making the truth of Richard's (albeit cynical) allegations of bigamy and bastardy due to pre-contract uncertain.

Without any similar ambiguity (or dynastic consequence), *Henry V* 2.1.16–18 reveals that Pistol has married Nell Quickly despite the existence of an impediment in Nym's prior 'troth-plight to her'. Irregular marriage practices among the age's tavern-haunting set were possibly only slightly less rife in reality than as satirised by Shakespeare. Also, as in the play, in reality resulting multi-party disputes often may have been settled privately, not in church courts; such likely practices would have left gaps in records that may now be deceptive.

In a less mirror-like setting, and at a higher social level, an impediment due to Isabella's impending religious vows is overlooked by Duke Vincentio when he twice proposes marriage to her in *Measure for Measure* 5.1. Although Isabella is 'yet unsworn' (*MM* 1.4.9), and still only a 'novice' sister of Saint Clare (1.4.19), in a pre-Reformation case outlined by Christopher Brooke, the mere intent of the bride, Christina of Markyate, to follow a religious life was enough to give rise to an annulment. Brooke reports that in this case the husband was willing to support Christina's demand for a divorce *a vinculo* after he had become convinced that she was 'radically opposed to consummating the marriage'.[46] Some important critical readings and stage interpretations have suggested that congruent attitudes may be implied in the silence of Isabella in *Measure for Measure* 5.1 when she is asked to marry.[47]

In further twists of the complexly mooted matrimonial complications of *All's Well* (discussed above and in chapters 1, 3, and 4), there are implicit questions over impediments to Bertram's offers to marry Diana, and later Maudlin, after his forced marriage to Helena. Bertram's first offer, part of an attempted seduction, is to marry Diana after Helena's future death (revealed in *All's Well* 4.2.72–3 and 5.3.266–7). Because this conditional spousal contract *per verba de futuro* is made void by the impediment of 'crime', Bertram's later willingness to a match with Maudlin (5.3.77) is not technically disallowed by the impediment of a pre-contract with Diana. His willingness to marry Maudlin is not prohibited by the impediment of bigamy either, for it follows his sincere belief that Helena is dead (4.3.54–67 and 4.3.91). But the bed trick, in which Helena substitutes for Diana, disrupts all of this tangled logic.

Exceeding the contrived mooting in *All's Well*, and moving into territories of outlandish satire, Albany's bitter remarks on marriage contracts in *King Lear* (Folio) 5.3.68–82 present a wild set of propositions about affinity and bigamy. Albany's aim is to underscore, by sarcastically 'legally' analysing it, the sensational situation in which Edmund has promised to marry two sisters, both of whom are already married. Albany reveals his knowledge of this situation immediately after widowed Regan (not yet aware that she has been poisoned by the jealous Goneril) publicly says to Edmund:

> Take thou my soldiers, prisoners, patrimony.
> Dispose of them, of me. The walls is thine.
> Witness the world that I create thee here
> My lord and master.   (*LRF* 5.3.68–71)

Regan's offer in the present tense only needs to be matched by Edmund's words of present consent to make a valid marriage by spousals, but Albany steps in to prevent that. He arrests Edmund 'on capital treason', and, in the Folio text, also impeaches Regan for treason,[48] proclaiming:

> For your claim, fair sister,
> I bar it in the interest of my wife.
> 'Tis she is subcontracted to this lord,
> And I, her husband, contradict your banns.
> If you will marry, make your loves to me.
> My lady is bespoke.   (*LRF* 5.3.77–82)

Here Albany's invention of the legalistic neologism 'subcontracted', indicating a (preposterous) impediment of prior contract, shows his knowledge of Edmund's prior promise of marriage to his (Albany's) own wife. Yet, under that sardonic premise, Albany in a sense properly shows impediments to the spousals of Regan and Edmund, on the grounds of a pre-contract (with Goneril), and also affinity. To cap his mock-legal analysis, Albany sarcastically suggests that his sister-in-law Regan might approach him for a marriage, which of course would be bigamous, adulterous, and incestuous: Albany's explanation, 'My lady is bespoke', recalls the rules of marriage impediments in order to indicate that he knows of the affair between his wife and Edmund.

We will consider finally Shakespeare's portrayal in *All Is True* of an only slightly less scandalous historical reality, the divorce of Queen Katherine and Henry VIII.[49] An accurate and subtle legal point is raised in the play when Katherine refuses to accept Cardinal Wolsey as her judge because of his lack of impartiality (2.4.73–82), using the form *recusatio* that was allowed in church courts.[50] In his treatment of the divorce Shakespeare generally follows his sources closely, is diplomatic to all parties, and makes no reference to the non-consummation of Arthur's marriage.[51]

Shakespeare also, of course, makes no mention of the future bastardisation of Princess Elizabeth, who is born to Anne and is the occasion of great rejoicing at the end of *All Is True*. However, in the age of Shakespeare, because some divorces nullified marriages *ab initio*, bastardisation could be an outcome of marriage breakdown. Bastardy, like marriage, was a legal status which had its effect on many aspects of economic, social, and civil life, and these we will consider next.

Under canon law the parents of an illegitimate child were considered to have sinned because they had conceived a child outside a marriage. Therefore the parents should be punished and inevitably the child was punished too because bastardy was a status which brought with it certain civil disabilities. For example, a bastard could not be ordained as a priest unless a dispensation was granted.[52]

By contrast, apart from disabilities on their rights of inheritance bastards had the same rights at common law as any free person.[53] By a legal fiction of common law an illegitimate child was *filius nullius*, the child of no one. In the twelfth century Glanvill wrote that this meant he or she could not inherit real property (land) from either parent, and bastards themselves had no heirs except those born of their body. This meant that they could have no collateral heirs and even brothers or sisters could not inherit from them.

A mother wanting financial support orders from an alleged father could apply to the church courts. Cases were also brought to the church courts by means of *ex officio* prosecutions for fornication or adultery. There is evidence that the church courts used 'both conciliation and penal sanction' when making support orders against a man.[54] Both parents could be punished and ordered to do penance.[55] To prove paternity the court relied on evidence of opportunity and mostly reputation, the 'common fame' of the community.

Public disgrace and shame were clearly considered to be part of the punishment for unmarried mothers, a reflection of both moral condemnation and also seventeenth-century secular concern about the economic costs to the local community of abandoned illegitimate children and children of single mothers. After the Elizabethan Poor Law 18 Eliz. I c.3 (1576) responsibility for punishing unmarried mothers and for providing material support for their illegitimate children was increasingly seen as resting with the community through the agency of Justice of the Peace and parish rates. Fathers, if identified, could be ordered to support their illegitimate offspring.[56] Mothers also could be punished, for instance under the Act 7 Jac. I c.4 ch. 7&8 (1609) specifying the incarceration for one year of women who had a bastard chargeable to the parish, but Osborne shows the inability of some Justices of the Peace to enforce this.[57] Other punishments included public shaming by being ordered to stand in the market place for a certain number of days or by public whipping.

In theory jurisdictional reciprocity (see Introduction) existed between church and common law courts in cases of bastardy. Disputes about the validity of a marriage, and the punishment of marital and sexual offences, were heard in the church courts, but any disputed inheritance of real property had to be determined by the common law courts. So determination of legitimacy or otherwise was referred to the church courts for a bishop's certificate of legitimacy which should have then been passed to the common law courts who would decide the dispute about the real property. However, church and common law courts came into conflict about the criteria to be used to determine a child's legitimacy.[58]

The problem was that the common law and canon law applied different rules to determine illegitimate status. The main difference concerned cases of 'special bastardy' where a child had been born to parents who subsequently married. Under canon law this subsequent marriage legitimised the child, but at common law it did not (until 1926).[59] To avoid the problem of having to accept the bishop's certificate, in the thirteenth century the common law courts decided not to ask the church courts whether or not the child was legitimate but instead to certify that the child had been born after marriage.[60] From this time until the Legitimacy Act 1926 the common law courts did not accept that a certificate of legitimacy provided by a church court was conclusive as to legitimacy, although they would accept as conclusive a bishop's certification of illegitimacy.

There were other differences between the canon and common law findings of illegitimacy. Canon law bastardised children born from an adulterous relationship, but the common law had a strong presumption against a finding of illegitimacy for a child born to a married woman. So at common law, for example, if a husband was in France at the time when conception might have taken place then the child was *prima facie* presumed to be legitimate (the husband could have sailed home at night).[61] This evolved into the 'four seas' test which held that as long as the husband was not impotent and could have been in the kingdom at any time at all during the pregnancy then the child was presumed legitimate.[62] The rule was quaintly expressed in a case reported in a Year Book in 1406 as 'Whoso bulleth my cow, the calf is mine.'[63] Amazingly, the four seas test was used until 1732.

In another divergence, at canon law children born into marriages that had been made in good faith were not always bastardised if their parents' marriage was later annulled. An example would be the discovery of a previously unknown impediment. The English common law courts did not agree, and held that while divorce for the impediments of consanguinity and affinity did not make a child illegitimate, divorce on account of prior spousals did.

As a result, if a question of legitimacy and inheritance was before the king's court, and the cause of possible illegitimacy was a prior spousal contract, then the king's court would issue the writ asking the church court to determine the legitimacy, knowing the result would be decided in the same way in both jurisdictions. But if the cause was consanguinity or affinity, then the king's court refused to refer to the church court.

Perhaps surprisingly, in some circumstances a finding of bastardy could bring a positive advantage to an illegitimate child. Because such a child was a *filius nullius* he could not inherit the status of his father, for he had none. So the illegitimate child of a villein gained a free status.[64] J. H. Baker reports that some bishops were quite happy to oblige an applicant by conferring this privilege of bastardy in their church courts even where it was not strictly merited.[65]

BASTARDY IN SHAKESPEARE'S PLAYS

Illegitimate birth is referred to in nearly every one of Shakespeare's plays, and in those of many of his contemporaries.[66] Insults such as 'whoreson', 'half blooded fellow', 'bastard blood . . . / Contaminated, base, / And misbegotten blood' (*1H6* 4.6.20–2) are flung about liberally in most of Shakespeare's plays, and such epithets, together with plain 'bastard', were used by Shakespeare in mainly derogatory contexts.

There are, however, several more or less oblique Shakespearian exceptions to disapprobation of illegitimacy. Scurrilous Thersites actually revels in his 'bastard' birth, mind, valour, and learning (*TRO* 5.8.8–10).[67] There are also several strong if amoral Shakespearian characters who express themselves as defiantly pleased to be illegitimate, including Joan la Pucelle (*1H6* 5.6.7–9), Philip Faulconbridge (*JN* 1.1.205–13), and Edmund (*LRF* 1.2.6–22).

Bastardy is very important thematically in several Shakespeare plays. In accord with some contemporary ideas about a special vitality conferred by bastardy,[68] Edmund of *King Lear* claims a personal superiority (*LRF* 1.2.1–15), and becomes a powerful, self-directed amoral force.[69] In reply to Perdita's rejection of hybrid 'bastard' flowers, King Polixenes in *The Winter's Tale* 4.4.92–7 may express similar notions of special vitality in horticultural metaphors. Yet bastardy's conferring of social and economic disabilities seems to motivate also unscrupulous and/or envious scheming in Faulconbridge, Edmund, and Don John (as revealed in *King John* 2.1.562–99, *King Lear* (Folio) 1.2.1–22, and *Much Ado* 1.3.10–34).[70] Moreover, one among many of Shakespeare's 'humorous' references to the bawdry leading to bastardy, which might seem merely tasteless, may actually have had crucial wider overtones; there is a possible connection between Launcelot Gobbo's excuse for 'the getting up of the Negro's belly' in *The Merchant of Venice* 3.5.36–40 and an obscure and repulsive English law against Jewish/Christian miscegenation, and from thence to a theme of prejudice central to the play.[71]

The legal status of a bastard as a *filius nullius* is reflected in bantering puns bounced between the clowns Speed and Launce, in which the former alleges 'she hath many nameless virtues', and the latter says 'That's as much as to say "bastard virtues"' (*TGV* 3.1.310–11). It is seen also in Charmian's bantering 'belike my children shall have no names' (*ANT* 1.2.31).

More subtle legal issues are mirrored in the reply made in *1H6* by the Shepherd, her father, to Joan la Pucelle's proud claim to being not his child but rather a higher figure's bastard. Joan had earlier claimed shepherd ancestry (*1H6* 1.3.51), but at her trial she denies her father with: 'Decrepit miser, base ignoble wretch, / I am descended of a gentler blood. / Thou art no father nor no friend of mine' (5.6.7–9). The Shepherd replies just as an ecclesiastical court would require: "tis not so. / I did beget her, all the parish knows. / Her mother liveth yet, can testify' (5.6.10–12). The Shepherd's reply, however, is not fully in accord with the presumption in favour of marriage in English common law, which looked no further to determine legitimacy than to the married status of the mother and to the father's presence within the kingdom during any portion of the time of pregnancy.

Just such issues arise in the law case involving the legitimacy and therefore the inheritance of Philip Faulconbridge in *King John* 1.1.[72] King John in his council, acting as a judge as he may, settles this case between the brothers Philip and Robert Faulconbridge. At issue is their father's attempt to disinherit the elder son Philip using a deathbed will. The younger brother Robert explains:

> large lengths of seas and shores
> Between my father and my mother lay,
> As I have heard my father speak himself,
> When this same lusty gentleman was got.
> Upon his deathbed he by will bequeathed
> His lands to me, and took it on his death
> That this my mother's son was none of his;
> And if he were, he came into the world
> Full fourteen weeks before the course of time.
> (*JN* 1.1.105–13)

But, according to English common law, no note can be taken of the 'four seas' rule, since the father had not been abroad during all of his wife's pregnancy. Hence King John replies correctly in reciting the common law rule that married women cannot bear bastards:

> Sirrah, your brother is legitimate.
> Your father's wife did after wedlock bear him,
> And if she did play false, the fault was hers,
> Which fault lies on the hazards of all husbands
> That marry wives. Tell me, how if my brother,
> Who, as you say, took pains to get this son,
> Had of your father claimed this son for his?
> In sooth, good friend, your father might have kept
> This calf, bred from his cow, from all the world;
> In sooth he might. Then if he were my brother's,
> My brother might not claim him, nor your father,
> Being none of his, refuse him. This concludes:
> My mother's son did get your father's heir;
> Your father's heir must have your father's land.
>
> (*JN* 1.1.116–29)

But, as Philip Faulconbridge physically resembles Richard Coeur-de-lion, he is offered an alternative in which he will 'bequeath' the Faulconbridge lands to Robert, accept a knighthood, and be renamed 'Sir Richard and Plantagenet' (1.1.160–2). He accepts because an offer of royal favour makes him glad to be landless and known as a bastard (1.1.164–6).

Similar gladness to be an illegitimate son of a king is also heard when the Trojan warrior 'bastard Margareton' boasts himself 'A bastard son of Priam's' (*TRO* 5.5.7 and 5.8.7). A converse gladness to have fathered a well-favoured bastard is seen when the clown Costard compliments the witty page Moth with: 'O, an the heavens were so pleased that thou wert but my bastard, what a joyful father wouldst thou make me!' (*LLL* 5.1.71–3).

Acknowledgment is, however, mixed with wryness when in *King Lear* Gloucester admits fathering his bastard son Edmund: 'I have so often blushed to acknowledge him that now I am brazed to 't' (*LRF* 1.1.8–10). Gloucester's blushes place him, although in ancient Britain, also in contemporary Shakespearian mirrorland, or at least halfway there. For concubinage and attendant bastardy remained widespread in Europe generally up to the sixteenth century when attempts at vigorous regulation began, although those were not very successful until the early seventeenth century.[73] Shakespeare's Gloucester on the one hand is boastful of the 'good sport at [Edmund's] making', leaving noble Kent to side-step this gross remark and be gracious about Edmund's good bearing (*LRF* 1.1.12–24). But on the other hand Gloucester's embarrassment reflects a new social attitude of

c. 1606 concerning bastard-bearing. Not long before then, according to many social historians, especially high-born fathers did not blush to acknowledge their bastards, but typically acknowledged them openly with pride.[74] Several historians have speculated that more austere attitudes, and with these a rapid fall in the rate of illegitimacy, may be attributable to advancing Puritanism, or to the Elizabethan Poor Laws.[75] But the sole importance of the ideology of Puritanism has been widely questioned.[76] Indeed, according to Flandrin, Catholic as well as Protestant Europe in the period saw the final decline of a widespread medieval toleration for concubinage; by the early seventeenth century those living in open concubinage 'had virtually disappeared from sight: only the kings and the most powerful lords still reared their bastards in public'.[77]

In this connection it is interesting to observe the disapproval of free-and-easy royal marriage customs expressed by Elizabeth, the exiled Winter Queen of Bohemia. Elizabeth had been raised in her father James I's court, and in 1613 the King's Men had performed fourteen or more plays, at least four by Shakespeare, for her marriage festivities.[78] Did she express the values of her youth when in 1657 her own son, the Elector Palatine Carl Ludwig, declared his marriage void because he was dissatisfied with his wife? Carl Ludwig then 'entered into a morganatic union with . . . one of his wife's ladies in waiting' (she was to bear him thirteen children), whereupon Elizabeth wrote in English:[79]

Your open keeping of that wench does no small dishonor to all persons of all conditions. If everybody would quit their husbands and wives for their ill humours, there would be no small disorder in the world; it is against both God's law and Man's law for though you be a sovereign, yet God's law is above you.

Writing on the cusp of such changes, Shakespeare shows Gloucester at first ashamed of Edmund, keeping him from the court for nine years and intending 'away he shall again' (*LRF* 1.1.32). But Edmund, publicly called by his father a 'whoreson' (1.1.23), compensates for his status so effectively that he even overcomes the legal disability of a bastard to be an heir, persuading Gloucester to seek means to make him 'capable' to inherit 'land' (2.1.82–4).

There are multiple hints in *The Winter's Tale* of Perdita's bastardy, and also that this status might make her available to become Prince Florizel's concubine.[80] Baby Perdita's illegitimacy is not only alleged by her deluded father; her exceptional beauty causes even the good old Shepherd to suppose her the product of an illicit court-intrigue: 'Though I am not bookish, yet I can read "waiting-gentlewoman" in the scape' (*WT* 3.3.70–1). Her bastardy is also surmised by Antigonus (3.3.42–5), and later Polixenes (4.4.156–9) and Camillo (4.4.578–9) presume it likely that she has had higher parentage than her station. Perdita's awareness of such perceptions may mesh with her worries lest Florizel 'wooed me the false way' (4.4.151), and makes more poignant her shunning of hybrid flowers 'Which some call nature's bastards' (4.4.83).[81]

That Perdita's worries may be justified is borne out by remarks in other Shakespeare plays suggesting that female bastards are actually raised to be employed in prostitution. Speaking of her 'conscience', the Bawd of Mytilene speaks of 'bringing up of poor bastards – as I think I have brought up some eleven', but Boult replies 'Ay, to eleven, and brought them down again' (*PER* s.16.13–15). Similarly, Mistress Overdone says ominously of Kate Keepdown's one-year-old illegitimate child 'I have kept it myself' (*MM* 3.1.461).

The complex legal status of bastardy, with its differing effects on women and men at various social levels, is portrayed comically or seriously, with little or with great import, and with sympathy or scabrously, in many varied Shakespearian settings. But its constant reappearance in Shakespeare's works relates to the centrality of the family, inheritance, and birth in Shakespeare's world. Next we will consider the breakdown of family relations that resulted from death.

CHAPTER 9

'Til death us do part

OVERVIEW

The title of this chapter, taken from the Prayer Book marriage service, was a phrase sadly apposite to family life in Shakespeare's England. The demographic facts meant that children were often orphaned and that widows and widowers were familiar figures, as were step-parents and step-brothers and step-sisters.[1]

The emotional impact of the early deaths of many early modern parents and children has been much debated by historians.[2] But, whatever can be concluded about the emotional effects on families of deaths, it is certain that the death of a wife or husband had very considerable legal implications for the surviving spouse and any children. These implications fall into three main categories, which are changes of status, inheritance, and provisions for widowhood.

Changes in survivors' legal status following the end of a marriage include that under certain circumstances male or female children who lost a father might have become wards, as we have seen in chapter 3. In this present chapter our chief concern will be with the changed status of surviving male or female spouses.

We will then consider the effects of the ending of a marriage in death on matters of money or property, first in the operation of the laws of inheritance and wills,[3] and then in the consequences of curtesy, dower, or jointure rights.

Legal and social issues arising from death in families had a significant impact on the structures and the meanings of a wide range of Shakespeare's plays. As we shall see, in some cases articulating the legal and social ramifications of death as the final termination of marriage will not only reorient, but may even overturn, widely accepted critical views.

WIDOWERS' STATUS AND REMARRIAGE IN SHAKESPEARE'S
TIME AND IN HIS PLAYS

When his wife died an English widower could become a tenant by 'curtesy' in all of his late wife's real property. This meant that he acquired a life interest in all her land, but after his death this land would devolve on her heirs.[4] The right of curtesy was available to a man provided a child of the marriage had been born alive, even if the child did not live long after birth, and such a right continued even if he remarried. Here, as always, the distinction of real property (land) from personal property (movables) was significant; in accord with the doctrine of coverture (discussed in chapter 7) a widower was entitled to all of his wife's personal property absolutely.

Statistics show that in Shakespeare's world a widowed husband's remarriage was very common, or even nearly ubiquitous.[5] Yet there may have been some ethical or religious scruples felt over male remarriage, perhaps because of allocating spouses on the Day of Judgment – see Matthew 22:30, Mark 12:25, Luke 20:34–6, and *Hamlet* 3.1.150–2.[6] Also, earlier Tudor law may have implied some doubts about the acceptability of male remarriage, or perhaps adumbrated some lingering sense of a preference for celibacy over marriage, especially for clergy. For until the statute 1 Edw. VI c.12 (1547) a legal distinction was made between men who married for the first time with women who married for the first time, and men who married either as widowers or who married widows. This distinction discriminated against those who remarried or married widows, for these were denied the mitigation called 'benefit of clergy' of a sentence of capital punishment following conviction for certain felonies.[7] This mitigation was available because certain wrongdoers were allowed to make fictitious claims of being in clerical orders, and of therefore not being subject to the jurisdiction of the king's courts. Even a married man could claim benefit of clergy because clerics below the rank of subdeacon could marry as long as they were not bigamous. Bigamy in this context was taken to include marrying again after a first wife's death, or marrying a widow.[8]

Literalism in that respect was curious, for the fictitious nature of benefit of clergy is highlighted by a number of Tudor statutes modifying its scope. As we have mentioned in chapter 6, women's interests were advanced by 4 Hen. VII c.18 (1488) which made rape clergyable once only, and by 18 Eliz. I c.7 (1575) which removed all benefit of clergy for rape.[9] Benefit of clergy was also offered or withdrawn to make fine distinctions between various offences;[10] from 1547 it was generally extended to remarried widowers, and in the statutes 21 Jac. I c.6 (1624) it was partly, and in 3 Will. &

Mary c.9 (1691) fully, extended to women. And so the fiction of being in clerical orders became entirely divorced from reality.

Shakespeare's plays present many men whose wives are said to have died, or who have apparently been married but have no wife in evidence. Curiously (and possibly in accord with the prejudices adumbrated above) most of these Shakespearian widowers remain unmarried. The few male remarriages to be noted in Shakespeare's plays include the personally and politically damaging remarriages of Antony and of King Cymbeline, and the nearly bigamous mistake of Bertram in *All's Well That Ends Well*.[11]

Statistics concerning death in Shakespeare's time show also that fathers were more likely than mothers to die first, and that it was very common for children to have lost at least one parent by the time that they themselves married.[12] In addition it has been shown that early modern Englishwomen did not die as frequently in childbirth as often supposed.[13] Therefore the prevalence in Shakespeare's imaginary worlds of male single parents of marriageable children over female ones was not in accord with the actual facts of his age. The frequent appearance of a Shakespearian son or daughter with only a father and no mother has sometimes been seen to present a tendency to either a deliberate, or unconscious, 'erasure' of mothers. Due to a parallel anomaly of un-remarried Shakespearian widowers, there is certainly some tendency in Shakespeare's plays to the erasure of the step-mothers of grown children.

Rather than seek new wives, some widowed Shakespearian fathers plan to spend their declining years being cared for by their daughters (these include King Lear and the Duke of Milan in *The Two Gentlemen of Verona*, as has been mentioned in chapter 4). A similar arrangement applied in the real-life situation of Brian Annesley, whose youngest unmarried daughter Cordell Annesley had to seek legal protection in 1603–4 to retain care of him and guard him from an elder sister and her rapacious husband.[14] However, conduct books and popular sentiment opposed the co-residence of widows with married children,[15] and in general the co-residence of generations was not common.[16]

Conflicts between widowed, or apparently widowed, fathers and their grown children are very common in Shakespeare's plays (Egeus of *A Mid-summer Night's Dream*, the Duke of Milan of *The Two Gentlemen*, Baptista Minola of *The Taming of the Shrew*, Shylock of *The Merchant of Venice*, Brabantio of *Othello*, Lear and Gloucester). One might wonder if the ab-sence of mothers has something to do with this. However, even where objecting mothers are present several patriarchal fathers in Shakespeare are not deterred from heavy-handed interference in the lives of their children (the Duke of York in *Richard II*, Capulet in *Romeo and Juliet*, Page in *The Merry Wives of Windsor*).

It is often said that in early modern England the widow's position in law was enviable compared with that of a married woman who was subject to the legal disabilities of the doctrine of coverture. Certainly, when she became a widow a woman's legal personality revived and she was once more able to hold property, to bring lawsuits in her own name,[17] to enter into contracts in her own name, and to earn money and keep it.

A widow was able to recover to her own use and possession all the real property that she had brought with her into the marriage, and also any property she had been given or inherited after marriage. Although during her marriage all of a wife's property was held by her husband in his name, and he was entitled to all the profits from it, if her husband had alienated her real property the widow was able to recover it from the third party. But any personal property a wife brought into the marriage became her husband's absolutely. Therefore, if on widowhood nothing of her personal property remained, the widow had no rights and could not pursue anyone now in possession of what had once been hers. The widow had claims only to any specific legacy of personal property made to her in her husband's will, and to her 'paraphernalia', by which was meant personal clothing and jewellery. However, the latter was subject to claims against the husband's estate from creditors.

The remark that a widow's position was enviable needs more careful examination, for many remarried and so resumed coverture.[18] In late Elizabethan London, in particular, wealthy widows or widows of the very poor seldom remarried, but widows from craft and trade backgrounds frequently did so, within an interval of often less than one year; younger widows were more likely to remarry bachelors (rather than widowers), and overall a pattern emerges of widows marrying men younger than themselves.[19]

Sometimes an English town widow chose not to remarry, but to manage her deceased husband's trade on her own account. This appears to have been most possible to achieve for the wives of London craftsmen and tradesmen. But such a choice was hampered by the 'forces of patriarchalism and fraternalism institutionalised in the household and . . . in about eighty London companies which held a jurisdiction over virtually all trades and a myriad of craft specialities'.[20] Possibly for this reason married women and widows appear infrequently in registers of apprentices or of freedom of companies.[21]

Widows of high social standing or wealth were not much more free in marriage choices than were unmarried girls of the same ranking.[22] The Coronation Charter of Henry I in 1100 confirmed the rights of the widows of his barons not to be forced to remarry, but this was not honoured, and notoriously high fines were extracted from widows in return for remaining unmarried. As a result of the barons' dissatisfaction, Magna Carta and its variously amended reissues of 1215, 1217, and 1225 reconfirmed a widow's right to choose not to remarry.[23] But even in Tudor times the rights of the marriage of widows continued to be a valuable commodity, particularly if the widows were in royal control. These rights were administered, alongside the rights of controlling the property of wards and of lunatics in royal custody, by the Court of Wards and Liveries.

WIDOWS' REMARRIAGE IN SHAKESPEARE

According to *OED*, the appellation 'dowager' was first applied to Henry VIII's sister, Mary Tudor, Dowager of France. So it was a quite new title when applied by Henry to his wife Katherine of Aragon, as represented in *All Is True*. The questioning in *All Is True* by Henry VIII of 'this our marriage with the dowager, / Sometimes our brother's wife' (*AIT* 2.4.177–8) presages Henry's first divorce. Cranmer's machinations are reported by Suffolk:

> Shortly, I believe,
> His second marriage shall be published, and
> Her coronation. Katherine no more
> Shall be called 'Queen', but 'Princess Dowager',
> And 'widow to Prince Arthur'.   (*AIT* 3.2.67–71)

The result is that the marriage of widowed Katherine to Henry is annulled, and her royal status changed from Queen to Princess Dowager.

Usually Shakespeare's plays reflect disapproval of remarriages of widows (in an exception, Mariana's chances for a second marriage are encouraged after the condemnation of Angelo in *Measure for Measure* 5.1.421–2). How closely this mirrored contemporary social attitudes is open to question. Jennifer Panek has recently argued that Jacobean drama reflected a social climate in which remarriage 'was widely tolerated and even encouraged for both sexes'.[24] However, Vivian Brodsky held that male dramatists reflected disapproval, which contrasted with popular practice.[25] Elizabeth Foyster notes that widowers remarried more often and sooner than widows, and that many men, especially of the middling ranks, chose to marry widows. But she adds that 'while remarriage was frequent, it was also subject to suspicion and disapproval'. She explains that the image of remarriage contradicted the companionate model of marriage, for marriage with a widow especially was typically assumed to be for sex or money, not affection: 'the stereotypical remarrying couple were portrayed as disparate in wealth and age'.[26] Such attitudes are often expressed either wryly or bitterly in Shakespeare's plays (*MM* 2.1.190–6, *ANT* 2.1.35–8, *TIM* 4.3.38–42).

Although Foyster agrees with others' findings that a marriage with an English widow was often desired,[27] she adduces reasons for anxiety about it:[28]

The experience which women had gained managing their legal and financial affairs during their widowhood, however short, meant that in men's eyes they could make formidably assertive marriage partners. Within their new marriages widows could unsettle the dynamics of power which had traditionally given men the upper hand.

Possibly in accord with such fears, widows conspicuously make bad wives in Shakespeare's *Titus Andronicus*, *The Shrew*, and *Cymbeline*. In the first of these plays, the widow Tamora is lustful, unfaithful, and hideously vengeful, but these villainies are perhaps more excusable than those of the odious Saturninus whom she marries. Disappointed in romantic love, Hortensio in *The Shrew* resolves to marry a widow mistakenly hoping for 'Kindness in women' if 'not their beauteous looks' (4.2.41). What he gets, however, is a practised shrew: when Tranio says 'he'll have a lusty widow now, / That shall be wooed and wedded in a day' Bianca comments ominously 'God give him joy' (4.2.50–2). The mother of Cloten, wife to King Cymbeline, does not even merit a name, and only ever-worsening evil comes of this 'widow / That late he married' (*CYM* 1.1.5–6).[29]

In addition to carrying possible reflections of social censure, Shakespeare's portrayals of the remarriages of widows often carry implications of illegality and immorality. The lust-driven marriage of King Edward IV to the widowed Lady Grey seen in *Richard, Duke of York*, which will be analysed presently, both violates the law of impediments by pre-contract and has dire political consequences.

Nell Quickly styles herself 'a poor widow of Eastcheap' in *Henry IV, Part 2* 2.1.71, at the same time as forcefully threatening legal and physical action against Falstaff. In her self-description she lampoons a longstanding legal view that a widow is a weak, defenceless, *miserabilis persona* deserving of special sympathy and protection.[30] She also parodies a style of self-presentation, sometimes self-serving and dubious, typical among the numerous widows who brought lawsuits in the courts of Shakespeare's age.[31] Then in *Henry V* 2.1 we learn that Nell has married the absurd Pistol, despite her prior trothplight with Nym. This remarrying widow thus mirrors a contemporary counter-stereotype of widows' lustful immorality; indeed her irregular marriage is wholly invalid on account of the impediment of pre-contract.

As we have seen, the rapid remarriage of widowed Queen Gertrude in *Hamlet* is also invalid, in her case by the impediments of affinity and possibly 'crime'. Her particular 'incest' inspires Hamlet's disgust, but he is also opposed generally to remarriage of widows. Thus when he hears the Player Queen's conventionally virtuous 'Both here and hence pursue me lasting strife / If, once a widow, ever I be wife', he comments 'If she should break it now!' (*HAM* 3.2.211–13). This vehemence falls short, though, of the apparent aberration behind Hamlet's rant 'I say we will have no more marriages' (3.1.150). Whether his mania is real, feigned, 'north-north-west', misogynistic, seriously in favour of celibacy, pathological, or cunning has been endless debated. But, unless written by Hamlet, the final couplet of the Player Queen's sententious:

> The instances that second marriage move
> Are base respects of thrift, but none of love.
> A second time I kill my husband dead
> When second husband kisses me in bed.
> (*HAM* 3.2.173–6)

does imply in its proverbial tone that Hamlet's sexual disgust concerning his mother is in accord with certain accustomed values.

However, Akiko Kusunoki very interestingly argues that Hamlet's own attitude is only one of a number of attitudes to remarriage in Elizabethan society, that these included newer attitudes favourable to both women's agency and women's sexuality (and so were sympathetic to a widow's choice to remarry), and that the newer attitudes as well as the older ones are represented in the play.[32]

INHERITANCE

Many of the laws for inheritance of property that applied in Shakespeare's age had their origins in the feudal structure of society imposed at the time of the Norman Conquest. Although that structure was no longer socially or militarily relevant, land law retained the doctrines of tenures and estates, and the patriarchal rules associated with inheritance of land, including in particular primogeniture and wardship.

Different legal rules were applied for the inheritance of real property (land) and chattels (personal property). In the case of personal property, during the middle ages customary rules of descent had allowed a limited degree of free testation for a man, but gave priority to family claims.[33] Because under coverture married women could not own property in their own name, these rules did not apply to them. In theory they could not make wills at all, but the church courts encouraged them to do so for the good of their souls.[34] The church courts accepted and administered such wills (unless an objection was made by the widower) because of the importance placed by Church teaching on gifts of alms, particularly the virtue of making a final gift of alms.[35] Unmarried women, however, were able to bequeath their personal property as they wished. If they died intestate then the same rules applied to them as to intestate men.[36] There is much difficulty in judging if single or widowed women who were eligible to do so were less or more likely to make a will than were men.[37]

The inheritance of real property (land) was subject to various customary laws, and the right to devise land (leave land by will) evolved over a period of time. There were 'strong traditions' at the time of the Norman Conquest that land should be divided equally between sons.[38] It was also traditional that an ancestor could nominate his own heir, which certainly benefited Kings William I, William II, Stephen, and John, all of whom were crowned despite the existence of closer claimants.[39] There was another regional custom found in Wales, Kent, and East Anglia known as 'gavelkind', which was the equal division of land between sons.[40] The custom known as 'borough English' or 'ultimogeniture', in which the youngest son inherited all the land, was found in some areas. Copyhold lands descended to widows in varying proportions in accord with manorial customs known as freebench. However, in most of England by the twelfth century the common law rule for descent of most land was primogeniture.

Primogeniture and the laws of intestate descent rested on patriarchal principles. For women the rules of inheritance depended on whether they had any brothers alive capable of inheriting. If so, daughters' rights to inherit were deferred to their brothers' rights.[41] Only if there were no sons did daughters inherit, in which case all sisters would take equally as 'coparcenors' (unless they were royal).[42]

After the 1540 Statute of Wills (32 Hen. VIII c.1) these customary rules of inheritance of real property could in most cases be excluded by a will. The exception was land held by military tenure, knight service, where only two-thirds of the land could be devised by will. Additionally, the widow's rights of 'dower' and widower's rights of 'curtesy' produced customary rules that could still limit free testation of land in Shakespeare's time, as we shall see presently.

WIDOWS AND INHERITANCE

A man was able to make specific gifts to his wife in his will, and so a widow could benefit from property left to her and dispose of it as she wanted. Widows sometimes appear in literature and in recent social historical studies as powerful rich old ladies who prevent (male) heirs from enjoying their inheritance for decades, sometimes inconveniently outliving them.[43] But it has been argued that this perspective tacitly assumes the superior claim of primogeniture, ignoring the claims of a wife or younger sons and daughters. In practice a husband often wanted to provide for his widow and younger sons or daughters.[44] To lay excessive stress on patrilineal descent also overlooks the fact that many wealthy dowagers had been heiresses in their own right before marriage, and on widowhood once more gained control of their own property.[45]

When husbands failed to specify in their wills what houses or adequate funds were to be available to their widows, but left the widows' living arrangements to the heirs' discretion, the results could be unfortunate. Emmison gives examples of pious admonitions and moral injunctions to sons to care for their mothers expressed in husbands' wills which were not legally enforceable and which left some widows in dire poverty.[46] This was sufficiently a scandal of the time for it to receive comment in conduct literature.[47] Not only heirs, of course, but also other interested parties (such as those having claims on late husbands' property or business interests) sometimes tried to limit or to contest widows' inheritance of property; many widows applied for relief to various jurisdictions, including but not exclusively the equity courts, and had varying degrees of success.[48]

Most London widows acted as the sole executors of their husbands' estates,[49] and according to Brodsky this implies that many citizens formed with their wives their 'deepest affective bonds'.[50] On the other hand, many husbands' wills reveal clauses preventing a widow's remarriage by stipulating that this event would result in a forfeiture of property. This brings into question the supposed freedom and economic power of widows in early modern England.

There were other constraints placed on the inheritance rights of widows in special circumstances. Despite the fact that a husband and wife were not held responsible for each other's crimes, her own lands, lands devised to her by her husband, and lands that would automatically become hers by rights of dower (discussed below) might be lost by a widow if her husband was convicted of a serious crime. For instance, the widow of a traitor needed an Act of Parliament to retain lands which she had held either in her own right or jointly with her husband.[51] Sometimes the crown exempted the traitor's family from part of this penalty, or made grants or annuities to destitute widows and children. But because of religious, political, and civil upheavals many Tudor women of the ruling classes faced difficulties. Lists of traitors' widows and families were found among Thomas Cromwell's papers after his death, and it appears he personally decided on whether they should retain any property or not.

Similarly, an old 'idea that "corruption of the blood" should follow conviction of a serious crime' meant that the children and wives of felons were disinherited,[52] although this was mitigated by some statutes which specifically removed this punishment from certain felonies.[53] The widows of men who had abjured the realm were also deprived of their property, but they were free to remarry immediately because at law their husbands were considered dead.[54] Abjuring by sanctuary men was prohibited by Henry VIII (in 22 Hen. VIII c.14, 28 Hen. VIII c.1, 32 Hen. VIII c.3).[55] But 35 Eliz. I c.1 (1592–3) demanded abjuration of unrepentant religious nonconformists, an act which was aimed at Roman Catholic recusants.

WIDOWS AND INHERITANCE IN SHAKESPEARE

We have mentioned a supposed resentment by the younger generation of some widows' control of extensive property. However, a rich widowed aunt is noted without resentment in Lysander's: 'I have a widow aunt, a dowager / Of great revenue, and she hath no child, / And she respects me as her only son' (*MND* 1.1.157–9). But, as often, Shakespeare exposes two sides of the same issue. At the start of the same play Theseus images youthful frustration in a comment on the slowness of the passage of four days between his spousal and the solemnisation of his marriage thus: '. . . but O, methinks how slow / This old moon wanes! She lingers my desires / Like to a stepdame or a dowager / Long withering out a young man's revenue' (1.1.3–6).

There are many Shakespearian references to attainture or corruption of a blood line.[56] At least one instance makes explicit the consequence of this in a widow's deprivation. Lady Elizabeth Grey and her children have lost their inheritance after her husband died fighting on the Yorkist side of the civil wars (*RDY* 3.2.1–7). The lustful King Edward IV agrees to her request to restore the lost lands to her children and what Lady Grey calls her 'dower', but he demands a sexual payment. Edward well deserves to be called 'the bluntest wooer in Christendom' (3.2.83) when he sets out this condition:

> KING EDWARD To tell thee plain, I aim to lie with thee.
> LADY GREY To tell you plain, I had rather lie in prison.
> KING EDWARD Why, then, thou shalt not have thy husband's lands.
> LADY GREY Why, then, mine honesty shall be my dower;
>   For by that loss I will not purchase them.
> KING EDWARD Therein thou wrong'st thy children mightily.
> LADY GREY Herein your highness wrongs both them and me.
>   But, mighty lord, this merry inclination
>   Accords not with the sadness of my suit.
>   Please you dismiss me either with ay or no.
> KING EDWARD Ay, if thou wilt say 'ay' to my request;
>   No, if thou dost say 'no' to my demand.
> LADY GREY Then, no, my lord – my suit is at an end.
>   (*RDY* 3.2.69–81)

Thus the widow resists becoming a royal 'concubine' (3.2.98), and in consequence Edward marries her, despite his possible pre-contract with Princess Bona of France. Richard III later makes political use of this irregularity (*R3* 3.7.174–81).

Another Shakespearian example, that of Mariana in *Measure for Measure*, may also indicate that a felon's goods were confiscated and her inheritance and dower were lost to his widow. Yet Clarkson and Warren are sceptical that such matters relate to Mariana's situation following Angelo's condemnation in 5.1.419–22. They argue the technical point that since from 1551 dower was allowed to the widows of some felons, Mariana would not lose dower.[57] If one wanted to be overly technical, however, confiscation as well as the death penalty would apply to Angelo for the crime of treason, which did still bar dower in Shakespeare's time. Both to protect Mariana from the scandal of an illicit but not illegal marriage, and to assure her attractiveness for remarriage, Duke Vincentio orders her to be publicly married to Angelo just before his execution:

> Consenting to the safeguard of your honour,
> I thought your marriage fit; else imputation,
> For that he knew you, might reproach your life,
> And choke your good to come. For his possessions,
> Although by confiscation they are ours,
> We do enstate and widow you with all,
> To buy you a better husband.   (*MM* 5.1.416–22)

The rare use here of the verb 'to widow', meaning to grant a widow rights to her late husband's property, suggests that Vincentio's is a special act of granting that which would normally be confiscated. We do not know why the usually astute Clarkson and Warren demur.

ENGLISH WIDOWS' DOWER RIGHTS, AND THE MUTUAL EXCLUSIVENESS OF JOINTURE AND DOWER

The term 'dower' originally indicated the gift of property made by the husband to the wife on marriage, which would become available to her on widowhood. In England this endowment in time became a right not dependent on the husband's gift, and by the twelfth century an English widow's rights to dower were binding at common law.

Both Church and common law developed rules regulating a widow's rights to dower. However, while questions of the validity of a marriage remained the preserve of the English church courts, questions of real property (land) were not. The Church accepted the common law's right to determine disputes about land between husband and wife, and following on from this questions of dower were seen as the concern of the common law from the early middle ages.[58]

There is disagreement among historians about whether some formal ceremony was needed before a widow could claim dower, although many literary commentators take note of only one side of this debate.[59] Following Bracton, some historians hold that the common law demanded that a right to dower was dependent on the prior endowment of the bride by her husband at the church door.[60] Others suggest that dower was a widow's right at common law whether or not this ceremony had taken place.[61]

In a celebrated case of 1225 dower was denied to the long-term concubine of James de Carduville who married him privately just before he died.[62] The court refused dower because by entering into a deathbed agreement James de Carduville had 'acted for the salvation of his soul and in peril of death'. Clearly the court doubted the sincerity of de Carduville's consent to be married, and without sincere consent there could be no valid marriage. But that decision on its own cannot mean that the common law would not recognise an unsolemnised marriage, or that endowment at the church door was essential for the award of dower. It has been pointed out that all the cases cited in the classic account by Pollock and Maitland of 'disputed dower in "death-bed" marriages' involved problems about lack of evidence of consent rather than any principle of law.[63]

The question of whether church solemnisation was needed to secure property rights in marriage is not easy to resolve. Eventually, endowment became part of the sacramental liturgy of church marriage. In the Tudor Prayer Books endowment is moved from the traditional church door to the body of the church. Nevertheless, in Shakespeare's time a valid marriage could still be made without church solemnisation or endowment, and, it can be argued, such a marriage did result in the transfer of property rights. In the early sixteenth century Fitzherbert wrote:[64] 'And a woman married in a Chamber shall not have Dower by Common Law ... *Quare* of marriages made in Chappels not consecrated, &c for many are by Licence of the Bishop married in Chappels, &c. And it seemeth reasonable, That in such cases she shall have Dower.' As we have seen, the marriage of Sir Edward Coke with Lady Elizabeth Hatton was unsolemnised, yet the great and very acquisitive lawyer would hardly have missed his chance to acquire rights to his wife's extensive property. Indeed Coke himself wrote a detailed discussion of forms of dower.[65]

The technicalities of dower were long established by Shakespeare's time. By the end of the thirteenth century the common law accepted that dower was to be calculated as a freehold life estate in one-third of the deceased husband's real property. If it was greater, the heir was allowed to reduce the widow's share to this amount by the Writ of Admeasurement.[66]

The rights of dower were extensive. Dower continued beyond any re-marriage. On the husband's death even lands sold or disposed of during the marriage were subject to dower. If real property (land) had been alienated (sold) by the husband after the marriage, or by the heir after the death, then the widow could use her rights at common law to recover it.[67] Yet dower was not part of the feudal order because it was not a form of tenure; the widow did not hold her land from her husband's lord, and did not owe services for it. Dower was rather 'an internal arrangement within the inheritance'.[68] The widow held from her deceased husband's heir, and he owed the feudal services for it. So to enter her dower the widow would sue out a writ in the heir's court to obtain it from him.[69] Similarly, if the property was in the hands of a third party, then she would have to join the heir to sue.[70]

Widows' rights to dower could set up tensions within an inheritance, conflict with a lord's right to wardship, and cause grave difficulties in the conveyancing of land. For these and other reasons, including the possibility that a widow would remarry, landed husbands or their families often took steps to bar rights of dower.

Dower rights in land could also be barred by agreement with the wife in a collusive court action which was then recorded as a legal 'fine'.[71] Such agreements to bar dower in order to alienate land were frequent. There was also another way to bar dower that was very commonly used before 1536. Before that date lands held in use (in trusts) were not subject to dower. From the fourteenth century uses were very frequently employed to bar dower, and by 1535 the majority of land in England was actually held in use.[72] But in 1536 Henry VIII forced his momentous Statute of Uses through Parliament. This Act 'executed' most uses, so that the beneficiary of the trust was treated in law as the legal owner of the land. In consequence, lands held in use would have been subject again to dower. To prevent this happening a special clause (27 Hen. VIII c.104) was inserted to provide that an agreement made before the marriage for payment of a jointure to a widow would act as a bar to widow's rights of dower. The provision that the jointure had to be negotiated before the marriage was probably included to protect wives from compulsion to accept less valuable jointures after marriage. The Act provided that if a jointure was agreed after the marriage a widow could elect whether to accept it or instead take up her right to dower.

Despite this minor protection, Eileen Spring argues that the dower-barring clause of the Statute was a 'husband's charter', and that the Statute could have been written in other ways so as to avoid the problems of a sudden great transfer of lands, while the preamble of the Statute, which claimed it executed uses in order to eliminate fraud on widows, was the very opposite of the truth.[73]

Unlike the dower which it barred, the amount and conditions of a jointure were not regulated by law, but were negotiated and arranged by private contract. A jointure was originally a joint estate in land for husband and wife which devolved on the widow, but it came to be a life estate in property limited to the wife which came into being immediately on the husband's death, with no intermediaries such as executors or trustees. By the sixteenth century a jointure could also take the form of an annuity based on a rent-charge on the property granted to the widow. An agreement to provide a jointure was very often contingent upon the payment by the bride's father of a marriage portion or dowry. It was usual practice for the cost of the jointure to be met by the property transferred with her at marriage. There is evidence that throughout the early modern period the cost of join-tures rose steeply.[74] The ratio between portion and jointure is said to have risen from 5:1 to 10:1 during the seventeenth century.[75] By the eighteenth century draft agreements set out in precedent books, used by lawyers and interested parties, presupposed a ratio of 10:1 between portion and jointure, and they provide examples of both jointures for life and jointures limited to widowhood.[76] Spring comments that a rising ratio between the cost of

the bride portion and the value of the widow's jointure indicates a decline
in the bargaining power of women.[77]

While the rise to the 10:1 ratio applied in families of the aristocracy,
Chancery records indicate that gentry families and merchant families did
not see such a dramatic rise in the cost of portions. Erickson considers that
this could be explained by the different use made of portions.[78] Families
of peers were more likely to use a cash portion to purchase land to provide
income from rents or to purchase an annuity for the widow. Land prices
were sharply rising at the time. Gentry, merchant, and yeoman families
were not so likely to purchase land. Instead evidence from the probate of
wills of married yeomen indicates that their marriage agreements provided
the widow with a cash sum, or bonds secured by a double penalty, which
matched in value the portion that she brought into the marriage.[79] Even the
wills of those below the level of yeomen reveal they had marriage agreements
which left small sums for a widow.

SHAKESPEARE AND WIDOWS' RIGHTS

Despite widespread practices used to limit them, it was believed that a
widow's rights were sacred. In accord with the Church's teaching that widows deserved universal charity and protection, Constance in *King John*, for
instance, relies for support on the Duke of Austria and the King of France
(see *JN* 2.1.32 and 2.1.549), and Theseus in *The Two Noble Kinsmen* relieves
three foreign widows, delaying his own marriage.

When it comes to particular rights for widows' maintenance, confusingly
Shakespeare uses the word 'dower' in three different ways. One use, in
which the term is interchangeable with the 'dowry' discussed in chapter 4,
indicates the marriage portion given by the woman's family to the man upon
marriage. Another use of 'dower' is in contexts where 'jointure' would be
the technically correct term; these will be discussed in the next section of
this chapter. Here we will discuss Shakespeare's third and technically correct
usage of the term 'dower'.

We have already seen that the recovery of her dower rights was the
motive of Lady Grey's beseeching King Edward in *Richard, Duke of York*.
She correctly names her rights in her husband's lands as her 'dower' (3.2.72),
but the property rights offered in *Measure for Measure* to Mariana on her
widowhood (discussed above), or in *The Shrew* to Katherina Minola on
hers (discussed below), are also dower (as their husbands do not arrange
jointures).

We will come to the important technicalities of these cases presently. First we should mention the great importance in theory of widows' property rights. Depriving widows of their customary rights is listed by Salisbury among heavy sins that cannot be excused even by the commitment of taking an honourable oath:

> It is great sin to swear unto a sin,
> But greater sin to keep a sinful oath.
> Who can be bound by any solemn vow
> To do a murd'rous deed, to rob a man,
> To force a spotless virgin's chastity,
> To reave the orphan of his patrimony,
> To wring the widow from her customed right,
> And have no other reason for this wrong
> But that he was bound by a solemn oath?
>
> (*CYL* 5.1.180–8)

The 'customed right' referred to could have been the common law dower of one-third of the husband's real property, or could be half as in some borough customs, or one-third, half, or even all, as was customary with copyhold or villein tenure.[80]

SHAKESPEARE AND JOINTURE

Shakespeare and his world were very well aware that a jointure arranged before the marriage would bar a widow's common law rights to dower. They also knew that negotiations over dowry and jointure could be complex if the parties involved were landed aristocracy, gentry, or wealthy merchants.[81]

Shakespearian contexts that are concerned with jointures often adopt a mirrorland mode. For instance, written 'articles' are drawn up 'Touching the jointure' King Edward will make to Bona 'Which with her dowry shall be counterpoised' (*RDY* 3.3.136–7). Jesting, Rosalind notes that houses were often part of jointure agreements in *As You Like It* 4.1.48–58. In exchange for her own inheritance from a grandfather,[82] and an expected dowry, Shallow offers to Anne Page on Slender's behalf a 'hundred and fifty pounds jointure' in *The Merry Wives* 3.4.47–8.[83]

Less simply, taking due note of the legal interactions of dower and jointure may contribute new perspectives to the long-running debate over the marriage of Petruchio and Katherina in *The Shrew*.

A great many alternative readings of Kate's treatment by her husband have been offered, interpreting the play's 'taming' as either farce (simply enjoyable, or male triumphalist and cruel, or female triumphalist and sub-versive), or else as an educative, humanising, and finally collaborative ef-fort towards the creation of a 'good marriage' founded on respect and mutuality.[84] We believe that a careful reconsideration of the complex fi-nancial negotiations preceding the marriages of the two Minola daughters in *The Shrew* may in fact illuminate such debates concerning the several marriages in the play.

Indeed the dowry and widowhood arrangements seen negotiated in *The Shrew* have been mentioned as mirroring social norms of Shakespeare's England, yet criticism to date has not correctly identified how closely they mirror the relevant legal features of these norms.[85] We will attempt to do this.

Petruchio, who frankly seeks a large marriage settlement, presents himself as being in the same rank of wealth as the wealthy dowry that he seeks. So he avers: 'Crowns in my purse I have, and goods at home, / And so am come abroad to see the world' (*SHR* 1.2.56–7) and 'My father dead, his fortune lives for me' (1.2.190). At the start of dowry negotiations he introduces himself as 'Antonio's son, / A man well known throughout all Italy' (2.1.68–9), and additionally tells Baptista 'You knew my father well, and in him me, / Left solely heir to all his lands and goods, / Which I have bettered rather than decreased' (2.1.116–18). All these claims establish Petruchio as both well placed financially, and autonomous. A good dowry befits such a condition – it is anachronistic to condemn Petruchio as a 'fortune-hunting rascal, supported by [Kate's] fine dowry'.[86] We might note also that an impoverished fortune-hunter in the Elizabethan style, one who like Bassanio would borrow heavily to give new-minted servants 'rare new liveries' (*MV* 2.2.103–4),[87] would never like Petruchio come to his wedding dressed in the eccentric and debased attire of a tramp.[88] Neither would such a dowry-seeker arrive late to the church, ride on a jade, molest the priest and sexton, or depart with the bride in as roaring a manner as Petruchio did.

The eccentricity of wealthy Petruchio goes much further than his choice of wedding attire, or his mode of celebration during and after the church ceremony. It is most interestingly seen in his bargaining over provision for Kate's widowhood in exchange for her very large dowry. Petruchio is offered half of Baptista's lands on his death, and an immediate 25,000 crowns (*SHR* 2.1.121–2). The sums are large, but the terms are realistic. As we have said, under English law from the time of Henry I, when a father like Baptista died leaving no sons his daughters would share equally in his lands as 'coparcenors' (whom Antigonus calls his 'co-heirs' in *The Winter's Tale* 2.1.150). So if Baptista followed customary practices in his will, or died intestate, and did not remarry or change his will, Katherina would indeed inherit half his lands, and these would become Petruchio's under the rules of coverture. As we have also seen above, in England after 1540 'free testation' allowed a father to change the disposition of his lands at any time before his death, yet expectations of future inheritances did feature in mirrorland dramatic representations of pre-marital negotiations (as in *Timon of Athens* 1.1.140–5).

Various suggestions have been made concerning the crucial moment when Petruchio makes his counter-offer in reply to Baptista Minola's offer of this rich dowry, but none of these have avoided confusions. In fact, several particularly ahistorical readings of this moment were justly critiqued by Cook in 1991.[89] But Cook also to some degree confused the issues involved, for, in common with other critics, she did not sufficiently note the important distinctions of a jointure from dower.[90] Indeed a 1981 article by Cook seems to use 'dower' and 'jointure' as synonyms,[91] and that is not fully corrected in the later book. This article also alleges that Petruchio's courtship follows a 'highly conventional procedure', and then minutely describes the jointure he makes:[92]

he sets up a jointure that goes to her only if he dies first and only for her lifetime . . . No future husband or children of any future marriage can share in more than the income during Kate's lifetime.

Although not atypical, these were not the only conditions that were typically negotiated for jointures (these included a condition that a widow's remarriage would terminate the jointure); more importantly, there is no reason at all to suppose they are Petruchio's conditions. In Cook's later book the identification of a 'jointure' by name is removed, but the conditions of a jointure are still described very similarly in relation to Petruchio's 'splendid bargain'.[93]

On the contrary, and most significantly, Petruchio's actual words in the play indicate that no jointure is offered by him at all. If his actual words are analysed we see that instead of a typically bargained-over fixed jointure (funded by her dowry), Petruchio offers for the support of Katherina, if she survives him, unimpeded rights to her widow's dower, which will be a proportion of all his real property. That is to say, his offer is to allow her the default dower rights which were due to widows by common law, despite the fact that prior to most wealthy marriages such rights to dower were barred by readily available legal means. Petruchio offers to do this in exchange for the good dowry that has been offered by Baptista: 'And for that dowry I'll assure her of / Her widowhood, be it that she survive me, / In all my lands and leases whatsoever' (SHR 2.1.123–5).

To clarify, well-propertied Petruchio does not offer a fixed jointure for Katherina in widowhood on any terms at all, but rather agrees not to bar her from her widow's share in all of his 'lands and leases whatsoever', exactly as in common law dower. It is interesting to consider whether propertied husbands were often as generous as that to wives, or if this is rather an instance of a wild Shakespearian mooting as unlikely to mirror reality as Petruchio's other eccentricities. In any case, undoubtedly an Elizabethan audience would have understood the great significance of Petruchio's offer.

Certainly no similar offer is repeated by any of Bianca's more conventionally inclined wooers. Although Baptista says that he 'That can assure my daughter greatest dower / Shall have my Bianca's love' (SHR 2.1.339–40), the very fact that he calls for negotiation over promised sums shows that he uses the term 'dower' imprecisely. For, as we have seen, dower was set by law in England to be a life interest in a third of the husband's total estate (including that acquired after marriage), and so it could not be varied nor even fully known in advance of marriage. Therefore the marriage settlements proposed by Bianca's suitors were offers of 'her jointure', as one indeed says.

First old Gremio boasts of his wealthy household, implying untruly that a wife as a *feme covert* would share in its possession (2.1.342–58).[94] Then Lucentio's proxy Tranio proposes a more precisely arranged 'jointure' for Bianca:

> I'll leave her houses three or four as good,
> Within rich Pisa walls, as any one
> Old Signor Gremio has in Padua,
> Besides two thousand ducats by the year
> Of fruitful land, all which shall be her jointure.

Gremio then makes a counter-offer, adding 'an argosy', but Tranio tops this with three argosies plus 'twice as much whate'er thou off'rest next' (2.1.359–76). This wild contention over jointures makes a ridiculous auction, doubly so because Tranio, a servant disguised as his master, lacks any authority to make his bids.

A danger in young Tranio's offers is noted by Baptista, for Tranio dispenses only 'his' father's (that is, Lucentio's father's) wealth. Baptista objects that Tranio's offers are unsafe, saying: 'let your father make her the assurance, / She is your own. Else, you must pardon me, / If you should die before him, where's her dower?' (2.1.383–5). This call for an assurance from the bridegroom's father matches the advice in a discussion of 'Dowment by the assent of the father' in Coke's *First Institute*:[95] 'That it behooveth the wife to have a Deed of the father, to proove his assent and consent to the endowment.'

The sale of Bianca may represent, or perhaps parody, typical hard bargaining over jointures. In accord with the image of an absurd auction, old Hortensio's settlement offer is kept in reserve by Baptista should Lucentio's father not agree.

In contrast, independently wealthy Petruchio seems particularly careful for Katherina, making old-fashioned unlimited dower available for her in widowhood. Petruchio's offer of dower might have struck a London audience of Shakespeare's time as either extraordinary or eccentric, for bargaining over jointures was very familiar to them. Perhaps due only to the rushed circumstances of his own marriage by special licence to Anne Hathaway, Shakespeare himself apparently did allow dower rights for her maintenance in widowhood.[96] Yet, some of Shakespeare's late-acquired property investments do appear to have been protected from dower by means of a trust not executed by the 1536 Statute,[97] another legal route apart from jointure to avoid allowing dower to the widow. Commonly, legal fees were expended to avoid just the arrangement that Petruchio apparently chose, one markedly generous to his wife.

The appearance of Petruchio's unusual or even extraordinary generosity in his marriage settlement would throw a peculiar light on the seeming maltreatment of Katherina in the play. This suggests that Petruchio intends to overcome shrewishness by applying unusual marital kindness: that even before the wedding he has begun a process that he names while refusing to change his wedding attire:

> To me she's married, not unto my clothes.
> Could I repair what she will wear in me
> As I can change these poor accoutrements,
> 'Twere well for Kate and better for myself.
> (*SHR* 3.2.117–20)

Such a suggestion is consistent with a reading that one of us has proposed on the different evidence of the use of quite specific psychological terminology in the play:[98]

In the name of tender concern [Petruchio] deprives [Katherina] of food, sleep, and sexual comforts. Since nothing is good enough for her she must have nothing. The results are twofold. Kate learns she has been spoiled, her froward rejection of goods has been in the context of a pampered life. Like Christopher Sly she must do without a bed and learn that comforts are not automatic. With this she also learns to show compassion; seeing herself in the mirror of Petruchio who is terribly froward with the poor Tailor she takes the side of the wretched man. Petruchio, on his side, learns how to love Katherina. Although he has enacted virtually an anthropological 'marriage by ritual abduction', pretending to steal his bride to assert his male forwardness, he does even that in the name of protecting her. When he restores her comforts he will never retract his kindly concern. His illusion becomes real, the mask grows to him.

This reading may contradict some twentieth-century views of the play which stress only Petruchio's cruel subordination of his wife.[99] But this reading does not in any way claim that patriarchal outlooks are not central to the legal meaning of early modern marriage. Nor are images of such outlooks absent in the play, yet we should recognise, as Shakespeare's audiences would have done, an additional legal dimension and its implications.

An afterword on method

It is hoped that our studies will be seen to have brought sharply into focus both well-known and formerly unexplored aspects of Shakespeare's theatre, texts, and themes. If we have achieved this, to our minds that alone will recommend our method of considering Shakespeare's legal and historical contexts.

We approach legal history as a part of cultural and social history, while at the same time recognising that early modern English law had its own particular disciplinary norms. Legal reasoning and procedure was not (and is not) identical to storytelling. Indeed, we believe, the operations of neither law nor storytelling can be seen as isomorphic with the unfoldings of 'ordinary' (whatever that is) life. Yet, neither fiction (no matter how esoteric its genre), nor law (no matter how abstruse its ratio), is ever altogether divorced from the social structures extant and the common lives lived at the time of its creation.

Thus, in particular, we view the laws and legal institutions of Shakespeare's age as both sources and consequences of the social, political, and intellectual dynamic of early modern England. This is in contrast to academic approaches that make trans-historical jurisprudential issues their main focus, or other technical historical approaches that make legal change alone their primary concern independently of the wider life of past times.

For such reasons we support a view that study of the relics of legal history may offer a holistic impression of the past. So J. H. Baker has recently said of the possibilities of legal history, 'few other fields apart from archaeology can offer as much opportunity to delve into unbroken ground and recover lost worlds'.[1] We aim to approach the study of law in history in the archaeological spirit, as much as we can manage, of unblinkered, and not pre-directed, empiricism.

Something similar may be said about our intentions in combining legal–historical with literary studies. Lately, while 'Law and Literature' has grown into a self-conscious established academic movement, the relations between such studies have inspired much debate. Positioning ourselves in relation to the Law and Literature movement is facilitated by Ian Ward's recent analyses and insights.[2] In terms of the distinction that Ward makes between law *in* literature, and law *as* literature,[3] our interests would seem to lean to the former. We certainly do not hold that a theory of narrativity is the whole key to understanding law in its contexts (nor do we believe that it is a key to understanding literature). However, Ward points out, these two modes of approaching law *in* or law *as* literature are really not wholly disjunct. In quite a different way from that of Ward, and of the many proponents of contending schools of Law and Literature well described by him, we too find an overlap. For we hold that law in history certainly has a human story to tell, and also that discussions of the representations of legal issues in literature can go far beyond the mere recognition that such representations exist, and may even offer insights into the impetus and the expressiveness of literary production.

Another distinction that needs to be made between the enterprises of the Law and Literature movement and our own is that the former have a main interest in gathering a contextualisation of law from the study of literature, while our enterprise aims to gather the contexts of literature from the workings of law in society.

Of course to understand the historical operations of law in society it is necessary to start from a correct understanding of what the law was, how it was instituted, and how it operated. To do otherwise causes some investigators to fall into such errors as assuming the practical effectiveness over English marriage practices of the never-enacted *Reformatio Legum Ecclesiasticarum* of 1553, or the Church canons of 1604, or to presume that the treatment of Elizabethan scolding wives was near akin to that of burned witches (English witches were no longer punished by burning after the witchcraft statute of 1542).[4] On the other hand, a precise understanding of the written law alone is insufficient for our purposes. To give a simple example, it is necessary to know which statutes were never effectively applied and represented legislators' aspirations rather than practice.[5]

Ian Ward also discusses the pedagogical possibilities of Law and Literature studies in legal education, and the alternative purposes of some whose main concern is to use legal–historical studies together with the witness of literature to critique our own current-day cultural and political condition. The bases of our partial divergence from such motives are rather subtle. It might seem that we share with those in the Law and Literature movement interested in 'critical legal studies' an emphasis on the nature of law as a historical and political construct. But we do not go so far as to join in what Ward calls '[t]he marked drift of critical legal studies towards the lure of postmodernism'. For us, the very great deal that is now unknown about legal history and its contexts is not, in theory, unknowable. We have no wish to replace investigation with tautological discussion of relativity, indeterminacy, or textuality. Moreover, we are suspicious of an emphasis on radical relativity that seems to be (monologically?) fixated on a critique of the traditions of 'liberal' legal discourse.

Our approach attempts rather to recover by any means available both broader and more chronologically and locally detailed historical contexts. For we have found that for our studies the most relevant cultural matters have included some infused into long traditions, and some responding to immediate or changing conditions.

We have become very wary of pre-ordaining theories that tend to turn the diverse and energetic human voices of Shakespeare's age into standardising discourses, or the subtle social networks of that time into simply repellent power-machines. Shakespeare's age, no less than his work, gives witness to diversity, inventiveness, subtlety, and an extended awareness (for many Elizabethans were capable of both avid present observation and imaginative historical-mindedness). We are certainly interested in non-pre-emptive theories about history or culture ('history' and 'culture' themselves are theoretical terms), but not when these would drown out such interesting voices. We are therefore attentive to theories only when they are susceptible to empirical refutation or corroboration; our concern has not been to engage with postmodern or historicist debates so much as to make an argument for including detailed historical investigation in the new discipline of Law and Literature.

We have had certain favoured uses for historical detail. We are not at all scornful of, but do not directly attempt to contribute to, the tradition of hunting for Shakespearian 'sources'. Neither do we aim to join some authors who have combed Shakespeare's texts to find any or all historical legal allusions. Although valuable insights may be built upon an awareness of allusions or references, we have not set out to play 'I spy'. Rather, we aim to approach law as a vital part of the cultural fabric, embodying considerably more than a set of technicalities, professional mysteries, or cloaked means to domination. (We aim to approach literature similarly, not presuming it possesses any benevolence, or malevolence, or indeed necessarily any moral intent, in advance of observation and analysis.)

We believe that consideration of law in the wide sense – which includes legal institutions, practice and procedures, law-texts (statutes, treatises, and commentaries), and texts concerned with law (literary, polemical, or political) – can contribute to an understanding of the structure of social order.[6] We refer here to the imperfectly understood structure that Peter Laslett held must be approached as a first step towards an understanding of individuals, groups, or the nature of society in general.[7] With Laslett as well, we think understanding the social order in early modern England is necessary for Shakespeare studies.

Providing the often missing legal dimension to historical investigations can be like opening a curtain in a darkened room. And that sort of light, we hope we have shown, may shine onto Shakespeare's plays.

Notes

INTRODUCTION

1. Burns v Burns [1984] Ch. 1 W.L.R. (Weekly Law Reports).
2. The late sixteenth-century estimate according to Stretton, 2002, p. 53, which cites Craig Muldrew, is 1,102,000 actions annually in the national and local courts. We may add that, typically, court actions involved multiple persons, although on the other hand (as pointed out by Christine Churches at the London Legal History Seminar on 15 November 2002) a single dispute might result in several actions and cross-actions. So, in a rough estimate, everyone was involved on average with about one cause of litigation every year!
3. Sokol and Sokol, 2000, pp. 125–8 and 201–4, explains certain intricate fictional actions used in conveyancing and how Shakespeare took note of them.
4. These were the words of the famous Justice of the Peace William Lambard, according to Read, 1962, pp. 68–9; see Knafla, 1983.
5. Baker, 1990b, p. 149.
6. See Kent, 1973.
7. See Firth and Rait, 1911, vol. 2, pp. 387–9, and chapter 6 below.
8. According to Neale, 1976, pp. 21–2.
9. See Barnes, 1977, p. 320.
10. However, violent poaching was among the wide range of offences dealt with by Star Chamber; see Manning, 1993, pp. 59–60, and *passim*.
11. The innovations of particular jurisdictions, for example various new misdemeanours in Star Chamber, or Chancery's actions of ejectment for copyhold tenants, were often eventually adopted by other courts, or made statutory.
12. For details and references see Sokol and Sokol, 2000, pp. 356–8.
13. Commercial debt, in particular, was still mainly enforced by recognisances, statutes, and especially bonds; however, actions on the case did open up the possibility of litigating on a wide range of other issues. For discussion and references see ibid., pp. 238–45.
14. Also, an action of *assumpsit*, being an action for trespass, required a jury trial and so avoided the possibility of the defendant 'waging his law' – a procedure that could favour the debtor over the creditor. See ibid.

15. Actions of *assumpsit* for debt were declared valid in Slade's Case in 1602.
16. See Sokol and Sokol, 2000, pp. 33–4, on the growth of the fictional Bills of Middlesex that had similar effects.
17. As detailed ibid., *passim*.
18. Coke, 1747 treats the over one hundred types of legal tribunals of Shakespeare's time; Baker, 1985, pp. 41–8, discusses this and gives a useful brief survey of the more important ones' procedures and personnel.
19. See Sokol and Sokol, 2000, pp. 207–12.
20. See chapter 8 below.
21. Sokol and Sokol, 1999b.
22. Later Elizabethan practices indicate particular co-operation and reciprocity between Chancery and other jurisdictions which was achieved by means of informal arrangements between judges, or by appointment of Chancery Commissioners drawing on other jurisdictions. See: Jones, W. J., 1967, pp. 481–4; Sokol and Sokol, 1999b, pp. 437–8; and other sources described in Sokol and Sokol, 2000, p. 115.
23. For example in Calvin's Case (1609) 7 Co. Rep. 1, on which see Sokol and Sokol, 1996, p. 370, and ibid., pp. 369–74, on its connections with *TMP*.
24. The rules of equity developed with increasing precision throughout Shakespeare's period; see Sokol and Sokol, 1999b, and Sokol and Sokol, 2000, pp. 113–15.
25. The strange history of an illusion, dating from 23 April 1964 or possibly as early as 1901, is detailed in Sokol and Sokol, 1999b, pp. 421–8.
26. See: Stretton, 1994, 1999.
27. Stretton, 2002, p. 51, but see Stone, 1979, pp. 661–2.
28. Stretton, 2002, p. 44.
29. This will have great bearing on our discussions of Petruchio's intentions when he marries Katherina in *SHR*.
30. Among the many treatments of this, see especially the classic book Laslett, 1983, first published as Laslett, 1965. Ward, Ian, 1999, p. 80, reiterates that 'the constitution of the English commonwealth was founded on the constitution of the family', and, p. 102, cites Sir Thomas Smith's contemporary generalisation of that idea. Yet Ward, pp. 101–14, holds that Shakespeare presented families, personal relationships, love, and marriage as 'fictions of the narrative imagination'.
31. A further, retrospective, discussion of our motivations and methods will conclude this book in its Afterword.

1 MAKING A VALID MARRIAGE: THE CONSENSUAL MODEL

1. Webster, 1974, pp. 35–6, 1.1.478–81.
2. We will reserve until chapter 5 a fuller discussion of that portrayal.
3. A marriage by spousals in Middleton's 1605–6 *A Mad World, My Masters* is concluded in just the two lines 4.5.103–4 (Middleton, 1995, p. 52).

4. Many alternative senses of 'spousals' are discussed in Swinburne, 1686, pp. 1–5, including a 'promise of future marriage', 'Love gifts, and Tokens', the wedding ring itself, the feast celebrating a marriage, and the 'portion' or goods given in consideration of marriage, with the final assertion that 'The Matter of Spousals is nothing else but Marriage.'
5. Clandestine marriages will be discussed in chapter 6.
6. This was first published as Swinburne, 1686.
7. An expression of intent could be seen as an instance of J. L. Austin's 'performative utterances'; discussions of Austin's speech act theory and Shakespearian promises or spousals include Kerrigan, 1999, pp. 13–15, and Nelson, 1998.
8. Did Webster provide only one witness to the Malfi marriage to gesture towards these?
9. Shakespeare testified he had forgotten long-ago events when he was called as a witness in the 1612 Bellot–Mountjoy suit over a marriage settlement; see Schoenbaum, 1986, pp. 260–4.
10. The real motive may have been mainly to validate the King's marriage with Katherine Howard.
11. 'Statutes of England', 1811, vol. 3, pp. 335–6.
12. The term 'pre-contracts' here is a misnomer with ancient origins (*OED* dates it to 1483), and is also used by Shakespeare in a crucial context, as we shall see.
13. 'Statutes of England', 1811, vol. 3, pp. 546–7. All Statutes will be cited from this edition.
14. See Brundage, 1987, pp. 229–55.
15. See Pedersen, 2000, pp. 2–8 and 64.
16. Ranald, 1963, p. 186, discusses the betrothal of the King's ward in *AWW*, suggesting that a *de praesenti* spousal required consummation to make a marriage indissoluble, which is mistaken. This error recurs in Ranald, 1987, pp. 37, 38, and 43. The true significance of sexual consummation in relation to *AWW* is fully discussed in Mukherji, 1996, which explains, p. 183, that with regard to the legal validity of a marriage 'consummation was as irrelevant "in law" as solemnization', yet illustrates the frequent value of consummation as legal or social evidence for true marital consent.
17. This was accepted in England by the Council of Westminster 1175.
18. For details see chapter 8.
19. See Houlbrooke, 1985, p. 344, and Swinburne, 1686, pp. 10, 86, 203–12.
20. See Swinburne, 1686, pp. 10, 154–92.
21. See Sheehan, 1996, p. 40.
22. See: Helmholz, 1974, p. 25; Ingram, 1987, p. 189; Ingram, 1981, p. 36.
23. These were the criteria for validity, on which see Helmholz, 1974, p. 72. However, see chapter 5 on solemnisation.
24. Sexual slander (as in a 1613 case brought by Shakespeare's married daughter Susanna, see Schoenbaum, 1986, pp. 289–90) was also tried in church courts; see Sharpe, 1980; Gowing, 1994; Gowing, 1996.
25. See Sokol and Sokol, 2000, pp. 50–5.

26. Ingram, 1987, p. 364. A recent study, Pedersen, 2000, has shown that the medieval church courts at York were often approached quite voluntarily, with trust, by litigants of all social and economic backgrounds, in disputes about marriage. For examples see pp. 118, 119–20, 206–8.

27. An especially moving instance described in Sokol, 1994a, pp. 39–40, appears in Hermione's wordless portion of the statue scene in *WT* culminating in Paulina's 'Nay, present your hand. / When she was young, you wooed her. Now, in age, / Is she become the suitor?', and Leontes' 'O, she's warm!' (*WT* 5.3.107–9).

28. As seen in *1H6* 5.1.46, *R3* 3.7.5, *ROM* 2.1.159, *1H4* 4.2.17, *WIV* 5.5.215, *AYL* 3.2.207, *TN* 5.1.154, *AWW* 2.3.179, *MM* 1.2.133, *LRF* 5.3.79, *CYM* 2.3.110, *WT* 4.4.388, and *TMP* 4.1.19. The few exceptions to this limited use are in mentions of peace treaties as 'contracts' in *1H6* 3.1.146 and *CYL* 1.1.38, and in Gonzalo's phrase 'contract, succession, / Bourn, bound of land, tilth, vineyard, none' (*TMP* 2.1.157–8), which is taken nearly exactly from Florio's translation of Montaigne's 'Of the Cannibals'.

29. Black, 1991, p. 33, seems mistaken in its analysis.

30. Liston, 1991, p. 157, claims Hermia 'has little trouble in persuading him', arguing their conventionality. But Wickham, 1980, p. 185, sees the forest as 'a testing ground of adolescent sexuality', comparing it with uses in *TNK* and in Milton's *Comus*.

31. Webster, 1975, pp. 69–70, 3.3.43–51.

32. An assertion that the spousals were made *per verba de praesenti* is the basis of the argument in McGlynn, 1999 that the final union of Hero and Claudio is presented as merely a business transaction gone badly wrong. This overlooks Claudio's penitence in *ADO* 5.3.1–23, which is, however, much more perfunctory than Leontes' or Posthumus' will be.

33. See Kent, 1973.

34. Swinburne, 1686, pp. 171–2.

35. Which would be an impediment of pre-contract: see chapter 8.

36. In parallel with his ingratitude to Titus, brutal Saturninus also ignores the need for Lavinia's consent to break her *de futuro* contract with him. As noted above, a spousal *per verba de futuro* could be dissolved by mutual agreement if not consummated, but one *per verba de praesenti* could not be.

37. Pollock and Maitland, 1898, vol. 2, pp. 368–9.

38. This is pointed out in Appendix B of Latham, 1975, pp. 133–5.

39. Priest, 1980 argues plausibly that Rosalind manifests a tendency to 'hypothetical' or 'subjunctive' gestures here and at other points of the play; her likely tendencies and the play's indubitable use of the modality of fantastical mooting are of course coherent.

40. Swinburne, 1686, p. 105. The Elizabethan autobiographer, the musician Thomas Whythorne, just avoided a handfasting with a girl he hardly knew by claiming as a reservation that he had exchanged the appellations 'husband' and 'wife' with her only in a spirit of jesting; a comparison with Orlando in *AYL* is developed in Berry, 1984, pp. 90–2.

41. Swinburne, 1686, pp. 121, 131.
42. Ibid., p. 227; see pp. 224–8.
43. A similar discussion has also been extensive on *AWW*. See: Ranald, 1963; Nuttall, 1975; Welsh, 1978; Bassnett-McGuire, 1984; Cohen, 1986; Adelman, 1989; Mukherji, 1996.
44. However, as Grivelet, 1987 ingeniously points out, thanks to its use of the marriage-shunning Lucio as messenger, *MM* is contrived so that Isabella is kept in ignorance of the spousals of her brother and Juliet.
45. See Jones, Emrys, 1971. On the nineteenth-century theory of a dual time scheme in *OTH* allowing Desdemona time for her supposed infidelity, and an alternative 'solution' to the time problem based on a hypothesised *de futuro* contract (for which there is, however, no textual warrant), see Wentersdorf, 1985. On the related question of the sexual consummation (or not) of Desdemona and Othello's marriage, see Lerner, 1979, p. 16, and the debate in Nelson and Haines, 1983 and Nathan, 1988. This topic is reviewed in relation to New Historicism, and identified as 'A Myth and the Mess It Made', in Bradshaw, 1992.
46. Wentersdorf, 1979 offers an analysis correcting common errors. For examples of errors see: Ranald, 1979, pp. 77–9, which seems to propose Shakespeare should have applied post-Tridentine canon law; Hamilton, 1992, pp. 121–3, which finds spousals less relevant to *MM* than the English Canons of 1604; Cacicedo, 1995, pp. 191–2 and 203, which states incorrectly that the Canons of 1604 invalidated marriage by spousals and that 'common law practice' demanded church marriage.
47. Schanzer, 1960. Although Hopkins, 1998, p. 82, claims that the private sexual act that enables this conversion radically threatens state control, it only verifies present consent in accord with the longstanding model of spousals. Marcus, 1988, pp. 178–82, presents views of the marriage of Angelo also not noting marriage laws.
48. Nagarajan, 1963.
49. Roscelli, 1962, pp. 216 and 217. Harding, 1950 argues that the two contracts would have had the same moral impact.
50. Suggested in Scott, 1982, and on a different basis in Hawkins, 1974.
51. On allowed and disallowed pre-contract conditions see Swinburne, 1686, pp. 109–53.
52. Ibid., pp. 237, 238.
53. See especially Hammond, 1986. Bernthal, 1992 takes a similar stance, but mistakenly claims, p. 262, that among the play's enigmas is that Angelo has not committed any chargeable crime (he is in fact guilty of the serious crime of 'champerty and maintenance', e.g. judicial corruption).
54. Mariana, in her moated grange, is miserable. Clare in George Wilkins's 1607 *The Miseries of Enforced Marriage* kills herself; see Wilkins, 1964 and Blayney, 1956.
55. The application of early modern English matrimonial law to *MM* is discounted by Hawkins, 1974, which prefers the common sense and sensibility of modern

readers to scholarly arguments over marriage pre-contracts in *MM*, 'an issue that is of no importance whatsoever' (p. 174). We certainly agree with the further dismissal by Hawkins of preposterous claims that 'Elizabethans lacked our modern capacities for mercy, pity, generosity and wonder' (p. 179), but note that this article supports an anti-historical position by citing history.

56. For discussion of changes in marriage law made by the Council of Trent see chapter 5.
57. Scott, 1982, p. 793.
58. *TIT, LLL, MND, SHR, ROM, H5, WIV, AYL, ADO, TN, AWW, LRF, WT,* and *TMP*.

2 ARRANGING MARRIAGES

1. The data and argument throughout O'Hara, 2000 are arranged to show that family involvement was predominant in sixteenth-century English marriage formation, even at the less wealthy social levels.
2. See Lerner, 1979, pp. 60–75, for a discussion arguing, mainly against Lawrence Stone, that the variety of arranged marriages was not a matter of historical phases, and that children's marriages were not simply commodified by families.
3. Crawford and Mendelson, 1998, p. 108–12.
4. See: Macfarlane, 1986, pp. 119–47, especially p. 124; Houlbrooke, 1984, pp. 72–3; Cook, 1991, p. 87; Macfarlane, 1970, pp. 95–8; and Crawford and Mendelson, 1998, pp. 110–14. On the other hand, Laslett, 1983, pp. 102–4, presents a possibly general model in which parents 'at least of yeoman stock' take a larger initial role in choosing marriage partners while Stone, 1977, p. 184, emphasises the 'authoritarian control by parents over the marriage of their children' which 'lasted longest in the richest and most aristocratic circles'. See also Ingram, 1987, pp. 137–42, on marriages of gentry and middling ranks, and Crawford and Mendelson, 1998, p. 115, for an example of an enforced plebeian marriage.
5. See Stone, 1977, pp. 46–54, and Houlbrooke, 1984, pp. 63–8. Ingram, 1987, p. 129, shows that seventeenth-century Wiltshire records give an average age for entering marriage of twenty-six to twenty-nine for men and twenty-four for women; Carlson, Eric Josef, 1994, p. 106, gives a national mean of twenty-seven for men and twenty-five for women. A number of other studies tabulated in Cook, 1991, pp. 265–7, indicate the average age for the first marriage of women was about twenty-six; a slightly younger age is indicated in Laslett, 1983, pp. 81–4.
6. Carlson, Eric Josef, 1994, p. 107.
7. Ibid., p. 109; also see Hurstfield, 1958, pp. 151–4, and Ingram, 1987, pp. 128–9.
8. See Ingram, 1987, p. 83, on the regulation of cottage building, and p. 131, on preventing marriages of the very poor (usually those who already had illegitimate children). Gillis, 1985 theorises on, pp. 84–6, and cites, pp. 86–9, even more vigorous prohibitions linked to the tearing down of cottages. See also Carlson, Eric Josef, 1994, p. 106.

9. See Carlson, Eric Josef, 1994, p. 21, and Helmholz, 1974, p. 90.
10. See Carlson, Eric Josef, 1994, p. 21.
11. Norsworthy, 1935, p. 37. In another instance of a forced marriage for political advantage, in 1553 Lady Jane Grey was married against her will to Guildford Dudley, son of the Duke of Northumberland.
12. Norsworthy, 1935, p. 62; Atkinson, 1986, p. 485.
13. See Helmholz, 1974, p. 91, and Swinburne, 1686, p. 225.
14. The frequency of early death of one or both parents must remain another factor. However, Outhwaite, 1995, p. 58, argues that it distorts the truth to insist that parental consent to marriage was not needed, because parents could stop a church marriage at the banns stage if their children were under twenty-one. This latter argument rests on Canon 100 of the Church Canons of 1603–4 which required banns to be read for all marriages and consent of parents to be given if prospective bride or groom was under twenty-one. But, as we shall see, Canon 100 did not make void those marriages which failed to meet its requirements.
15. Whately, 1619, p. 88.
16. Gouge, 1622, p. 428.
17. Ibid., pp. 446–7.
18. Ibid., p. 448.
19. Hoby, 1998, p. 66.
20. Ibid., pp. 229–37.
21. Bullard, 1934, pp. 106–7. Moreover, Parliament did not enact the 1603–4 Canons, and restricted any possibility of their reiteration; on this see chapter 5.
22. See Ingram, 1981, p. 48.
23. Gouge, 1622, pp. 448–9.
24. Ibid., pp. 452–3.
25. Carlson, Eric Josef, 1990, p. 450.
26. Ibid., p. 450.
27. For an excellent comparative survey of plays of this sort see Atkinson, 1986, which extends Blayney, 1956. Lindley, 1993, pp. 28–42, surveys and analyses the interaction of literature and society in order to investigate the first arranged marriage of Frances Howard, which led on to scandal, divorce, and murder. See also Williamson, 1986, pp. 59–74 and 101–5, which finds Shakespeare's problem plays paralleling many contemporary treatments of enforced marriage, and Campbell, Julie D., 1997, which compares Lady Mary Wroth's play *Love's Victory* with *MND* and finds only the former presents 'a strongly voiced protest' against arranged marriages (p. 115). According to Roberts, 1983, pp. 30–1, Lady Mary Wroth allegorised her own unhappy arranged marriage in the story of Lindamira in her enormous prose romance *Urania*; Prichard, 1996, p. 10, finds multiple such allegories in Wroth's writing.
28. See Cairncross, 1992, pp. l–li.
29. McGuire, 1989 examines the significance of Egeus' silence in terms of differences in the Quarto and Folio texts of *MND*, and of the recent stage history of

the play. This describes gestures that have been used to indicate reconciliation between father and daughter. Boose, 1982, p. 327, proposes that Egeus 'poses a threat that must be converted to a blessing to ensure the comic solution', but does not explain how this is to be portrayed on stage in the absence of any lines spoken.

30. Or love can arise after any marriage, an adage burlesqued in Touchstone on Audrey: 'Well, praised be the gods for thy foulness. Sluttishness may come hereafter' (*AYL* 3.3.35–6).
31. Horwich, 1992, p. 40, comments: 'the Pages, who have constructed a loving and companionate marriage for themselves, seem not at all interested in securing a similar blessing for Anne'.
32. Fenton's condemnation finds a close analogue in a passage of Henri Bullinger's influential *The Christen State of Matrimonye*, quoted in Pearson, 1987, p. 34.
33. By 4 & 5 Ph. & Mary c.8 (1558), or by the Statute of Wills 1540, discussed in chapter 9.
34. This is spoken by a witty servant, the usual accomplice in New Comedy, in *SHR* 1.2.136–7.
35. Gossett, 1991, p. 60. Boose, 1982, pp. 327–8, makes a similar point but subordinates this to a ritual pattern.
36. Gouge, 1622, p. 447.
37. Walzer, 1965, p. 185, notes that Jean Bodin revived 'the old Roman notion of *pater familias* – an idea in which love and concern were entirely replaced by legal sovereignty' and that 'the logic of this identification forced Bodin to give the father the same power of life and death that the king possessed'. Walzer adds that in 1606, the year that Knolles's translation of Bodin appeared, this conclusion was endorsed at the Anglican convocation. Ibid., p. 191, notes that the Puritan Perkins, 'who probably did not know Bodin's work', also held that just as a king '"the father hath authority to dispose of his child"', and cites parallels from Whately and Gouge.
38. Flandrin, 1979, pp. 130–8.
39. For an excellent discussion of this 'correspondence' see Collinson, 1988, pp. 60–3. In a reverse of the notion of the husband as king, the Virgin Queen imaged herself married to England, and rather more surprisingly King James told Parliament in 1603 that he was 'the Husband and the whole Isle is my lawful Wife; I am the Head, and it is my Body' (McIlwain, 1918, p. xxxv).
40. See Young, 1988, for comment on forced marriages in relation to *ROM*.
41. Laslett, 1983, pp. 81–90, and especially p. 87, with reference to Furnivall.
42. Hoby, 1998, p. 173.
43. Laslett, 1983, pp. 81–6, Cook, 1977, Pearson, 1983, Young, 1988, and Cook, 1991, pp. 28–31, discuss why Shakespeare chose to dramatise female child brides. The notion that the setting of *ROM* in Italy was significant is debated by some of these, and all think that Juliet's age at marriage was abnormal for England.
44. Yet as Gossett, 1991, pp. 63–5, persuasively argues, Princess Katherine 'has no choice, but this does not mean she is an unhappy victim'.
45. Ibid., p. 60.

46. In 1602 deliberate bigamy was used in a desperate unsucessful attempt to obtain divorce and remarriage, as described in Phillips, Roderick, 1988, pp. 107–8. The setting of *CYM* in pre-Christian Britain does not excuse the fact that Cymbeline's choice of her step-brother Cloten for Imogen is incestuous as well as bigamous; it has been suggested that the play's world is proto-Christian, and it does seem likely that indifference to the sins of bigamy and incest are transgressions of Cymbeline inspired by his ambitious and evil Queen's influence. For further details see chapter 8.

47. See Sokol, 1993.

3 WARDSHIP AND MARRIAGES ENFORCED BY LAW

1. On these see Sokol, 1994a, pp. 144–66, and especially p. 165.

2. These rights continued in Shakespeare's time. The prerogative Court of Wards and Liveries (discussed later in this chapter) was set up in 1540 to deal with the collection of royal revenues from wardship. It administered the estates of wards and of lunatics in royal custody, and had to grant a licence to a royal widow to allow her to remarry if her late husband's land had included tenure in knight service. The broader topic of remarriage of widows will be discussed in chapter 9.

3. See: Helmholz, 1974, pp. 172–81; Helmholz, 1987a, pp. 145–56; Pedersen, 2000, especially pp. 148–52.

4. Ibid., p. 88.

5. See chapter 1 on instance litigation.

6. Pedersen, 2000, pp. 148–51 and *passim*, details cases from the medieval church courts of the north of England.

7. See ibid., pp. 149 and 88, on this case.

8. On wardship as a feudal incident see Simpson, 1986, pp. 18–19, and Holdsworth, 1903, vol. 3, pp. 61–5. On medieval wardship see Walker, 1982, and Walker, 1988 (which also treats rape). On wardship contemporary with Shakespeare see especially Hurstfield, 1958, Croft, 1983, Bean, J. M. W., 1968, pp. 8–11, 14–20 and Dubrow, 1999, pp. 166–7.

9. Many discussions of the abuses of wardship seem to assume tacitly that military tenure alone is involved.

10. Baker, 1990b, pp. 275–6.

11. See Sokol and Sokol, 2000, pp. 364–5, 189–91, and 147.

12. Carlson, Eric Josef, 1994, pp. 28–9; Hurstfield, 1958, pp. 136–9.

13. Baker, 1990b, p. 278.

14. Also the king benefited more than other lords because he had a special right of wardship, known as 'prerogative wardship'. This arose if an infant was heir to several estates, and even just one of those estates was held of the king by military tenure. The king would then take wardship of all the heir's lands, irrespective of tenure and irrespective of the rights of any other lord. By the seventeenth century most of the great estates established by the Norman invaders had been fragmented, added to by inheritance and purchase, or alienated by inheritance

or sale. In consequence, it was usual for a landowner to hold lands subject to several different tenures which might well include socage and villein tenure as well as knight service. If that landowner died leaving a minor child, the king's prerogative wardship would then attach to all the land even if only one acre was held by military tenure.

15. Bell, 1953, p. 2, argues that 'the scientific development of livery and wardship as a regular source of royal income dates from the Tudor period'.

16. See ibid. on the Court of Wards and Liveries, and especially pp. 46–66 on its increased revenues in the Jacobean period. On the Elizabethan Court of Wards and Liveries (and the City of London's Court of Orphans), see Jones, W. J., 1967, pp. 383–9.

17. Hurstfield, 1958, pp. 138–41; on disparaging an heir by arranging a marriage with someone of inferior status see Bean, J. M. W., 1968, pp. 13, 14.

18. See Hurstfield, 1958, p. 142, and the semioticist excursion Murphy, 1997, which alleges Southampton's bastardy.

19. Hurstfield, 1958, pp. 58–71, describes the variety of people who petitioned for wardship. All grants had to go through the office of the Master of the Court of Wards.

20. Ibid., pp. 37, 65.

21. Ibid., pp. 33–46.

22. Sir Thomas Smith, *De Republica Anglorum*, first published in 1583 but partly written in the 1560s, quoted from its manuscripts in Notestein, 1971, pp. 120 and 121.

23. Durant, 1999, pp. 7, 10–11, 23. This speculates, p. 23, that the children of Bess's later marriage to the elderly Sir William Cavendish were protected from wardship by special property arrangements to ensure that Bess would be heir.

24. Printed in Emmison, 1978, pp. 11–12. Sir Richard, first Lord Ryche, was the grandfather of the Sir Robert who married the famous 'Stella' of Sidney's sonnets; her matrimonial story is further considered in chapter 8.

25. Hoby, 1998, p. xvii. Burghley was active in promoting Lady Margaret's third marriage to his nephew, Sir Thomas Posthumous Hoby.

26. Hurstfield, 1958, p. 119.

27. Notestein, 1971, p. 85, even claims that by the late Elizabethan and early Stuart decades for the landowning classes 'wardship had become a running sore in society and the body politic'.

28. Bell, 1953, pp. 48–9, notes that, despite criticism of Burghley's Court for its efforts to increase revenue, the amount of revenue actually raised by the Court for Queen Elizabeth was not high. It would become higher in the second decade of James's reign.

29. Munden, 1978 places this in a general context of growing mutual distrust between the King and Parliament, and Croft, 1983 explains that James had at first appeared willing to consider the abolition of wardship but then suddenly changed his mind.

30. Ibid., p. 40; Notestein, 1971, p. 88. This proposal was one of various schemes considered to raise royal revenues, such as the sale of freeholds to all royal

copyholders and the payment of a fee to end the expensive feudal duty of performing homage.

31. Ibid., p. 88, writes that Cecil's actions, probably taken with the approval of the King, were designed to raise money for the King while at the same time offering some limited relief from wardship. Croft, 1983, pp. 44–5, makes similar comments, and points out that after the failure of the Commons Committees' petitions to the King, Cecil's plan was revived in the Commons by Sir Robert Wroth, whom she believes to have been Cecil's client in the Commons.

32. At first the Lords wanted wardship linked with homage and other feudal incidents, and then the matter seemed to be left until later in the same year when the Commons proposed a petition to the King asking him for a composition for wardship and an end to the tenure that went with it. Such a plan did not have unanimous support in the Commons because it would have involved a major investigation into landholding throughout all England, the sort of proposal that landowners consistently resisted. A counter-proposal made by Sir Robert Wroth suggested that every man should pay a fee to the King and in return have the right to draw up a will leaving a composition for the wardship of his minor child. See Notestein, 1971, p. 93, and Croft, 1983, p. 41.

33. Although no copy or account of what James said can be found, Notestein, 1971, pp. 94–6, concludes that James must have indicated his displeasure with the Commons' interference with his revenues because the Lords sent word to the Commons that the last Commission for compounding wardship had brought the sum of four thousand pounds to the King whereas wardship had amounted to thirty-one thousand pounds. In other words it is likely that the King had early in his reign realised the value to him of wardship and had indicated to the Commons that they were unlikely to ever be able to offer him an adequate equivalent by way of composition.

34. Croft, 1983, p. 43. James's needs rapidly exceeded those of his predecessor as in the early years of his reign he set about making many gifts and granting generous pensions.

35. See Stone, 1977, p. 58.

36. Laslett, 1977, pp. 160–72, concludes that one statistic on parental deprivation that is more reliable than most is that it was much more common for a child to lose a father than a mother, and was rare to lose both.

37. Swinburne, 1590, leaves 98–9.

38. See Davies, J. Conway, 1954 on Nicholas Bacon's proposals for royal wards' education made to Burghley, Burghley's provision for his ward Edward de Vere, Earl of Oxford, and Sir Humphrey Gilbert's proposals for royal wards' education called *Queene Elizabethes Academy.*

39. Quoted in Hurstfield, 1958, p. 120, where educational reforms successively proposed by Hugh Latimer, Nicholas Bacon, and Gilbert are reported to have 'come to nothing'.

40. Oliver is a tightfisted guardian (*AYL* 1.1.81–2), but his malice against Orlando, self-admitted in 1.1.154–6, does not share the motive alleged by Sir Humphrey Gilbert for guardians' poor education of wards: 'of purpose to abase their minds

lest, being better qualified, they should distain to stoop to the marriage of such purchasers' daughters' (quoted ibid., p. 120). Although no doubt mirroring the poor treatment of some younger brothers by heirs, Orlando's plight was not necessarily typical. For example, it contrasts with the pattern exemplified in the good treatment and education given to his six younger brothers by the 9th Earl of Northumberland and his successor according to Nicholls, 1992. This article extends this point in general to younger brothers, and recounts some fascinating details of conflicts over wardship.

41. See Bateson, 1906, pp. cxxvii–cxxxv.
42. Clark, 1985 argues that this was not typically so in medieval rural England.
43. Jones, W. J., 1967, p. 383.
44. Ibid., pp. 384–9.
45. See ibid. and Bateson, 1906, pp. cxxvii–cxxxv.
46. Murphy, 1997 alleges some kind of relation between *VEN* and events in the wardship of Southampton and other actualities around the institution. In what seems a strained attempt to avoid conjecture about the actual attitudes of individual Elizabethan readers to wardship, this account provides semiotic diagrams to evince 'homologous systems [that] combine and interact and through that intersection they expose the conjunctive and disjunctive logic that shapes a given ideological matrix' (p. 338; see also pp. 326–7 on the approach). Despite the interest of the historical materials presented, this essay seems to us more evasive than constructive with regard to important questions regarding literature and history.
47. Elizabethan dramatists' wide range of attitudes to wardship are discussed in Clarkson and Warren, 1942, pp. 26–31.
48. Berry, 1984, p. 38; ibid., pp. 33–42, discusses the impact of such separations and possible reflections in Shakespeare's plays.
49. Levin, 1997, p. 30, finds it 'unclear whether any in Shakespeare's original audiences drew connections between the king's guardianship of Bertram and . . . the most serious abuse of wardship, enforced marriage', but notes, p. 31, that *AWW* 'may date from the beginning of James' reign, which coincides with a peak of agitation on wardship'.
50. Campbell, John Lord, 1859, p. 58n, supposes that since Helena was not of noble birth Bertram could have refused to marry her or pay any compensation, despite the powers of wardship.
51. Ranald, 1979, p. 80, asserts that 'the King outwits [Bertram] by granting Helena a title of nobility'. But there is no sign of this in the playtext.
52. Lowenthal, 1996, pp. 84–5, discussing *MND*.
53. Derogation in Imogen's marriage is asserted again by Cloten in *CYM* 2.3.110–21. He alleges hers is 'no contract' on the basis of aristocratic superiority to her husband. Jordan, 1994, pp. 54–5, n. 5, finds Cloten and his argument 'in the spirit of mercantilism', but Cloten's scorn is precisely for the possessors of that spirit, the 'meaner parties' than himself. Cloten's position on the validity of Imogen's marriage will be considered further in chapter 8.

54. Yet she later finds Cloten's body indistinguishable from Posthumus', although earlier we learn that Cloten smells bad after sword exercise.
55. Cymbeline indeed finally exults in Imogen's love: 'See, / Posthumus anchors upon Imogen, / And she, like harmless lightning, throws her eye / On him, her brothers, me, her master, hitting / Each object with a joy' (*CYM* 5.6.393–7), and calls Posthumus his 'son-in-law' (5.6.422).

4 FINANCING A MARRIAGE: PROVISION OF DOWRIES OR MARRIAGE PORTIONS

1. See Erickson, 1993, pp. 79–97, 114–22, and 129–39, on the form taken by marriage portions as evidenced in Chancery litigation and in probate of wills of married men.
2. In a partial confusion, Boose, 1982, p. 333, claims 'the terms of sixteenth-century dowries were required to be fully fixed before the wedding'. This was not true in law, for dowries were not required at all. The constraint probably referred to was that jointures had to be fixed before the marriage, or else the wife could demand her dower (usually more valuable) instead on widowhood; this will be discussed in chapter 9. Both Cook, 1990, pp. 156–7, and Black, 1991, p. 40, seem to equate the very different types of 'contract' that form marriages and set dowries. Cook, 1991 does not fully untangle this, correctly finding spousals essential for marriage, pp. 155, 157, but incorrectly adding consummation was necessary, pp. 165 and 227, and calling the negotiations over dowry concluded in *H5* 5.2.353 a 'marriage contract', p. 169, while supposing 'betrothal' is not 'matrimony itself', p. 192. Dreher, 1986, pp. 36–7, suggests that there were two sorts of marriage embodied in law, one replacing the other, confusing Elizabethan spousals with solemnisation (which distinction will be discussed in chapter 5). Recently Matchinske, 1998 seriously confuses litigation over dowries and other financial contracts with matrimonial contract litigation. The former was in fact more commonly seen in secular courts from the mid-sixteenth century because of increasing use of 'actions on the case' and particularly 'actions of *assumpsit*'. But in no way does this sixteenth-century development relate to Matchinske's claimed 'shift from ecclesial to secular *court* jurisdiction' relating to a reordering of 'the legal definition of marriage from sacrament to contract, from spiritual union to civil arrangement' (p. 93). Moreover, civil marriage was instituted legally only in 1651 (and did not last long).
3. The influence of the classical New Comedy, in which young lovers overcome the opposition of parents or guardians and marry according to their own wishes, was particularly strong. Such a model was considered sophisticated, and was used by Shakespeare in plays as varied as *MND* and *WIV*. However, Shakespeare also may have subverted or questioned the same model; in *SHR* and even *ROM* some children's autonomous marriage choices turn out disastrously for them.
4. The dual meanings of 'dower' (*OED* 1 and 2a) go back to Britton and to Chaucer. The problem with interpreting this spelling is that both Shakespearian orthography and the transmission of Shakespearian theatrical texts are

Notes to pages 58–65

areas of great complexity. Marjorie Hope Nicolson's famous misinterpretation of John Donne's 1611–12 spelling of 'shee', together with the many problems of interpreting manuscript and printing-house practices, may serve as warnings against finding great significance in variations of Elizabethan or Jacobean spelling. Nevertheless Reilley, 2001, pp. 392–9, does correctly note the technical differences and comments at length on the anomalies of 'dower' as used in *King Lear*.

5. See Glanvill, 1993, p. 69; Plucknett, 1956, pp. 546–8; Baker, 1990b, pp. 310–11, and also Ward, Jennifer, 1995, pp. 16–17.

6. Of course such mirroring in literature is never photographically exact, as pointed out in Steadman, 1996, p. 88. This essay offers a wide-ranging survey of dowries and dowry-hunting in Shakespeare's plays, but concludes that 'the economic aspects of marriage are normally secondary . . . to romantic and spiritual values'.

7. Pettet, 1945 illustrates venture capital borrowing in pursuit of marrying heiresses.

8. The Wooer continues 'and / I will estate your daughter in what I have promised' (*TNK* 2.1.10–11), showing willingness to arrange for her support in widowhood only on the basis of a non-enforceable promise. Much contention arose from promises of portions and other marriage provisions that were partially, tardily, or not at all delivered (see Foyster, 2001, pp. 319–23), but no doubt such promises were in many unrecorded instances kept faithfully and so did not result in conflict.

9. See, for instance, Norsworthy, 1935, p. 261, detailing Lady Hatton's provision in her will of marriage portions for poor maidservants. The Preamble to the 1601 Statute of Charitable Uses lists among acceptable 'charitable and godlie uses' gifts for 'marriages of poor maids'.

10. A 1706 case of an Essex father who actually carried out just such a threat is cited in Alleman, 1942, p. 53.

11. See Bonfield, 1986.

12. As we shall see in chapter 6, the abduction of an heiress was considered at law to be a wrong against the father; interestingly this and Lorenzo's taking of his ducats do not form part of Shylock's legal complaints (Shylock seems to expect justice only on the production of a commercial bond).

13. Berger, 1981 describes Portia's mercy, not her father's strictures, as a threat to masculinity.

14. In these classes marriages were also typically undertaken relatively late: see: Macfarlane, 1986, pp. 119–47 (especially p. 124); Houlbrooke, 1984, pp. 72–3; Cook, 1991, pp. 69–103 (especially p. 87); examples in Macfarlane, 1970, pp. 95–8; and partial reservations in Laslett, 1983, pp. 102–4.

15. For instance, Lady Julia in Tilney, 1568, B3r, states 'equalness causeth friendship', deploring marriages made with women 'ful of money wanting virtue and grace' and with women who 'having virtues, lacketh money'.

16. Such a suspicion of a rich woman is seen in the image of *TIM* 4.3.38–42, and perhaps even in Anne Page's marriage to Fenton in *WIV*.

17. This term, not in *LLL*, is used twice in *King Lear*, from whence it has its first *OED* citation.

18. Montaigne, 1942, vol. I, pp. 212–13, which even expresses approval of husbands who turn to other women to avoid excessive lust with their wives. However, the matter was complex; it is well if briefly reviewed in Bradshaw, 1992, pp. 225–6.

19. This is not unlike the euphemisms of Milton's Satan who cannot name God.

20. See Sokol, 1994a, pp. 117, 124–7, 129–32, 226. Stone, 1979, p. 663, claims that in early sixteenth-century England 'in practice, if not in theory . . . the nobility was a polygamous society'. Gillis, 1985, pp. 12–13, claims that 'in sixteenth-century Lancashire, many [of the aristocracy] lived in open adultery. They were shamed neither by their concubines nor by their bastards.' Soon after, and aside from the possible influence of English Puritanism, there was a change in extra-marital mores throughout Europe; Flandrin, 1979, pp. 180–4, sees the Catholic Church as instrumental in the final decline in the early seventeenth century of the former widespread toleration of concubinage. Stone, 1979, pp. 662–3, claims that 'between 1610 and 1660 evidence for the maintenance of regular, semi-official mistresses becomes rare' in England. However, Stone goes on, pp. 665–8, to highlight open promiscuity in the court of James I; on the contrary, Cook, 1991, pp. 186–9, comments on its rarity.

21. But O'Hara, 2000, pp. 217–18, does instance some few marriages that were, or were purported to be, 'anti-materialistic'.

22. Laslett, 1983, pp. 90–9. This does not deny that elderly parents sometimes found care in their children's households, but states that this was not common. See chapter 9 and Foyster, 2001, especially pp. 321–2, on objections to the co-residence of widows with married children.

23. Described in Elliott, 1981.

24. Hotine, 1990 discusses both Englishwomen who emigrated to Catholic Europe to become Poor Clares at about the time of *MM*, and brief hopes for Catholic emancipation in 1604. Gurr, 1997, pp. 93–7, suggests how Shakespeare may have had direct knowledge of some Poor Clares still living in London, and speculates that the play may reflect an 'Isabella Rule' of the Clares.

25. Kliman, 1982, pp. 138–9. McFeely, 1995, pp. 204 and 214n26, comments that if the Poor Clares were not absolutely 'the only possible refuge for dowerless Isabella', as Kliman had suggested, they were still unlike 'most orders [that] required dowries'. McFeely, p. 211n3, further points out that dowries for daughters were sometimes explicitly provided in the middle ages by the wealthy 'for their marriage or entering a religious house'.

26. It is apparent in the tone of the married outcomes in their cases that the reluctance of a Beatrice, or the dubiety of a Rosalind, are set up to be overturned, as are Luciana's doubts expressed in *ERR* 2.1.27.

27. Her silence on this question does not preclude, but rather demands, an answer to the question of how she reacts to Vincentio's 'Give me your hand, and say you will be mine' (*MM* 5.1.491). On this see McGuire, 1985 and Spotswood, 1994. See also Sokol, 1991, which finds structural reasons to suppose that Isabella will

gesturally say 'yes'; in addition this study finds patterns of three throughout the play, and it is arguable that Isabella as the third dowryless woman will marry as do the others.

28. Of the sort that Rose, Mary Beth, 1988, pp. 186–235, argues came to dominate Jacobean tragicomedy.

29. The insult here concerns both sexuality and status; it is overtopped by Lucio's calumny of Vincentio: 'Yes, your beggar of fifty; and his use was to put a ducat in her clack-dish' (*MM* 3.1.389–90).

30. This illustrates one of the ways in which Hal as Prince and Hal as a private man brings together these two aspects of himself to his advantage. But, of course, to do so he must be a victor.

31. See Sokol and Sokol, 2000, p. 108.

5 THE SOLEMNISATION OF MARRIAGE

1. 1.1.488 and 1.1.491–3, Webster, 1974, pp. 35–7.

2. Smith, 1986, p. 49, summarising work of Michael Sheehan and others.

3. Carlson, Eric Josef, 1994, p. 24.

4. There was a form of marriage by ritual in Roman law, but it was of very limited application. See ibid., pp. 24–5, and Clarke, 1936, pp. 458–71.

5. See Brundage, 1987, pp. 561–5.

6. There were, for instance, 32 Hen. VIII c.38, discussed in chapter 1, and a Commonwealth Statute of 24 August 1653, which invalidated all but marriages made by civil magistrates. This latter, Firth and Rait, 1911, vol. 2, pp. 715–17, required 'consent of their Parents or Guardians, if either of the said parties shall be under the age of One and twenty years', and specified that 'no other [kind of] marriage . . . shall be accompted a Marriage according to the Laws of England'. This exclusive validity of civil marriage was repealed 26 June 1657, Firth and Rait, 1911, vol. 2, p. 1139, and the rest of the Act effectively lapsed, as is discussed in Outhwaite, 1995, pp. 11–13.

7. Ibid., p. 4.

8. MacCulloch, 1996, p. 41.

9. See Carlson, Eric Josef, 1994, pp. 37–8.

10. This legislation included The Submission of the Clergy 1532 (confirmed by statute in 1534), The Act in Restraint of Appeals 24 Hen. VIII c.12 (1533), The Act for the Submission of the Clergy and Restraint of Appeals 25 Hen. VIII c.19 (1534), The Act Restraining the Payment of Annates and Concerning the Election of Bishops 25 Hen. VIII c.20 (1534), The Act of Dispensations 25 Henry VIII c.21 (1534), and The Act of Supremacy 26 Hen. VIII c.1 (1534).

11. Printed and described in a useful compendium, Bray, 1994, p. 86.

12. MacCulloch, 1996, p. 121.

13. Carlson, Eric Josef, 1994, p. 71.

14. Ibid., p. 43, and MacCulloch, 1996, pp. 187–8, and especially p. 212.

15. Carlson, Eric Josef, 1994, p. 42. Matrimony, confirmation, extreme unction, and religious orders were removed from the list of sacraments leaving

only baptism, eucharist, and confessions. Carlson, Eric Josef, 1992 discusses the history of clerical marriage in Tudor England, arguing that Henry opposed it strenuously, but Elizabeth's opposition was mainly to avoid scandals.

16. See Carlson, Eric Josef, 1994, p. 45.
17. Gloucester, 1910, pp. 252–8.
18. Ibid, p. 252; see Carlson, Eric Josef, 1994, p. 45.
19. Gloucester, 1910, p. 254.
20. MacCulloch, 1996, pp. 410–11.
21. Carlson, Eric Josef, 1994, p. 74. See the detailed introduction of Bray, 2000.
22. Bray, 2000, pp. cxxv–cxxvii and 247–79. Ibid., pp. 21 and 93–107, also translates the 1535 Henrician marriage canons, also not enacted.
23. This Act compelled also, for the first time ever, weekly attendance at church, and this requirement was repeated in the 1559 Act of Uniformity.
24. Gloucester, 1910, p. 392. Cranmer's 1552 rubric was amended in the 1662 Prayer Book which stipulated any unused elements were to be consumed in church by the priest there and then, not away from the church. See MacCulloch, 1996, pp. 506–7.
25. See Gloucester, 1910, pp. 386, 510. See Booty, 1976, p. 374, for details of the required critical self-examination.
26. See generally MacCulloch, 1996, p. 511.
27. See Gloucester, 1910, pp. 254 and 412.
28. See Haigh, 1987, pp. 6–7; for an earlier view see Dickens, 1967, especially pp. 228–9, 444.
29. Starkey, 1985, pp. 15–17, 29, 103–23, 167.
30. Haigh, 1987, p. 8.
31. MacCulloch, 1996, pp. 620–1 and 625–8; Collinson, 1967, pp. 31–5.
32. Collinson, 1967, p. 35. On Elizabeth's religious orientation see Collinson, 1994, pp. 87–118, especially pp. 109–11.
33. Bowers, 2000, which also explains the politics of her actions. This proof was anticipated in Booty, 1976, pp. 338, 340, and Collinson, 1967, p. 32.
34. MacCulloch, 1996, p. 620.
35. Ibid., p. 620 and see pp. 620–2; on Elizabeth's moves to halt further reform see Crankshaw, 1998.
36. See Booty, 1976, p. 346, and Collinson, 1967, pp. 165, 364–7.
37. Bray, 2000, p. xciv.
38. Proctor, 1955, pp. 136–7.
39. See Hamilton, 1992, pp. 115–18, on this outcome.
40. Collinson, 1967, pp. 458–60.
41. See ibid., pp. 456–62.
42. See Bullard, 1934, pp. 106–7.
43. Ibid., p. xvii.
44. For instance Hamilton, 1992, pp. 121–3, and Powers, 1988, p. 29, which seemingly on this basis asks, p. 30, '[a]re Proteus and Julia married under Anglican canon law?'

45. See Carlson, Eric Josef, 1994, p. 78, and Kent, 1973.
46. This older view is questioned in Carlson, Eric Josef, 1992.
47. Carlson, Eric Josef, 1994, p. 87.
48. Ibid., p. 6, reports Luther refusing to become involved in disputed legal cases of marriage because he believed such matters were the business of secular courts. When he received a letter from a pastor seeking advice on a marriage case Luther retorted 'I'll give him something to remember me by for implicating me in such matters that belong to the government.'
49. Ibid. describes Germany and Switzerland, where 'adopting the Reformation usually created a legal vacuum' when the old ecclesiastical tribunals were abandoned because the laity did not necessarily want to hand power over to Protestant clergy and because the reformers did not necessarily have a uniform policy. Perhaps the English experience was not so unlike that of their European neighbours.
50. Collinson, 1994, pp. 222 and 223.
51. MacCulloch, 1996, pp. 420–1. For more on 'companionate marriage' and Shakespeare see chapter 7.
52. See: Booty, 1976, p. 408; Collinson, 1967, p. 36; and Cressy, 1997, pp. 337 and 342–7. As mentioned above, objections to the ring appeared in the 1603 Millenary Petition as well.
53. See Booty, 1976, p. 409.
54. See Rose, Mark, 1989, especially pp. 293–4, on this in relation to Shakespeare's *JC*. This argues that imaged opposition to ceremony feeds the 'strategic ambivalence' (p. 304) of *JC* concerning questions of the authority of the crown c. 1599.
55. Collinson, 1967, pp. 244–5.
56. After the Act to Restrain the Abuses of Players, 3 Jac. I c.21, the naming of God, Christ, or the Holy Ghost was outlawed on stage. Of course the Prayer Book marriage ceremony was not blasphemous, but it did name God and Christ. Some of Shakespeare's plays post 1606 name God, but none name Christ. See Clare, 1999, pp. 124–8, on the Act's patchy observance.
57. Powers, 1988, p. 29.
58. The imagery of Shakespeare's sonnet 52 associates 'feasts so solemn and so rare' with 'seldom pleasure', and the solemnity of the Capulets' ball is specifically identified as a long-unprecedented event in *ROM* 1.5.32–40.
59. See chapter 1 on this much-discussed matter.
60. It is thus in 1549, 1552, and 1559: see Gloucester, 1910, pp. 252 and 410, and Booty, 1976, p. 290.
61. More than a decade later a second handfasting takes place between Leontes and Hermione's statue, creating, in a sense, a second more valid marriage. See Sokol, 1994a.
62. Booty, 1976, p. 290. Subsequent quotations from the Prayer Book marriage ceremony and its rubrics will be from this edition of the 1559 text, pp. 290–9.
63. See Jones, Emrys, 1971 on this convention.
64. See: Shaheen, 1987, 1989, 1993, 1999.

65. Booty, 1976, p. 290.
66. These instances are noted in Shaheen, 1993, pp. 154 and 167, and the note on 'joined together' arises in relation to *RDY* in Shaheen, 1989, p. 69. The 1559 Prayer Book passages are printed in Booty, 1976, pp. 290 and 293.
67. Elizabeth Wheeler, accused of brawling and not attending church, appeared before the Stratford-on-Avon bawdy court on 1 October 1595 where she said 'Goodes wooneds, a plague a God on you all, a fart of ons ars for you' (Brinkworth, 1972, p. 128). Ibid., p. 63, describes her blasphemous words 'God's wounds' as 'an old Catholic oath still in currency – the Queen used it'.
68. First in 1552, Gloucester, 1910, p. 392; repeated in 1559, Booty, 1976, p. 267.
69. See the 1549 rubric in Gloucester, 1910, p. 254, and the comment in Booty, 1976, p. 408.
70. Kirsch, 1981, pp. 43–4, cites the ceremony in detail and claims it is highly relevant to the truncated marriage in *ADO*, but overlooks a total deviation of the staged ceremony from the prescribed form.
71. This silent role is subjected to a strenuous and debatable interpretation in Boose, 1982, pp. 326–7.
72. So Shaheen, 1993, p. 209, has on these passages: 'the specific texts that lie behind his words in this and the previous two passages are not easily recognizable'. This is repeated in Shaheen, 1999, p. 270. Kirsch, 1981, pp. 139–40, says Lavatch in these passages parodies 'the Bible' but misses the structural basis and the thrust of the parody of the Prayer Book. Simonds, 1989, pp. 47–9, makes similar observations.
73. Falstaff's uses of logic and mock-godly habits of speech are connected with actual perceptions of Puritans, not with a mocking by Falstaff of Puritans, in Poole, 1995. Tiffany, 1998 takes this position further, arguing that Puritans may have liked the representation of anti-authoritarianism in the Henriad, and not believed the portrayal of Falstaff to be an embodiment of their values. This sophisticated article concludes that there is no single valid interpretation of these multivalent plays.
74. Hunter, 1959, p. 22n. This note identifies the same phrase used in *ADO* 2.1.298–300.
75. MacCulloch, 1996, pp. 58–9 and 420–1, traces Cranmer's coming to accept a companionate theory of Christian marriage.
76. Ibid., p. 421.
77. *Homilie of Matrimonie*, 1968, p. 239.
78. It parodies the notion of man and wife being 'one flesh' as well, discussed in relation to law below in chapter 7.
79. Booty, 1976, p. 339; on the long-running vestments controversy see Collinson, 1967, pp. 68–9, 71–83, 94–6, 123, and Collinson, 1994, pp. 198, 240–1.
80. Booty, 1976, p. 48.
81. Shaheen, 1993, p. 210, comments: 'Not a biblical reference'.
82. Lavatch's implied critique of marriage in general is made explicit in the discussion of *ADO* in Berger, 1982. The even more scurrilous Thersites of *TRO* is

claimed to make a 'bitter prayer, a perversion of the Prayer Book' in Shaheen, 1997, pp. 503–5.

83. See Sokol, 1995 on the ubiquitous rings of *MV* and their 'trajectories'.

84. The single valency of rings as love tokens is undermined by their Shakespearian use in moments as diverse as the perverse wooing in *R3* 1.2.189–212 and the romantic anguish in *ROM* 3.2.142.

85. This dual disapproval does not help prove Shakespeare was, or was not, a Roman Catholic. His views seem inclusive rather of both sides of an argument. Observing only one side can be misleading. For instance, Beauregard, 1999 argues that *AWW* is built around principles of Catholic theology. But this misses Lavatch's Prayer Book parody, with its equivocal bias, which we have noted. It also, p. 221, excuses Lavatch's simile 'as the nun's lip to the friar's mouth' (*AWW* 2.2.25), claiming this is satiric of abuses but not evidence of a 'Reformed sensibility at work'; yet such images are characteristic of Reformation repugnance.

86. This position accords with a view, outlined in Collinson, 1994, p. 228, of the probable importance for those aiming to understand Shakespeare of centre-of-the-road 'parish Anglicanism', although Collinson concludes there is insufficient evidence to allow with any assurance the religious placement of Shakespeare himself.

6 CLANDESTINE MARRIAGE, ELOPEMENT, ABDUCTION, AND RAPE: IRREGULAR MARRIAGE FORMATION

1. See Sheehan, 1996, p. 47, and Outhwaite, 1995, pp. 19–49. Finch, 1990 discusses the problem of clandestine marriage in the middle ages, and distinguishes it from the issue of parental control.

2. Furnivall, 1887, p. 140, notes marriages using the Prayer Book and rings, but lacking banns, or held in a 'howse' or in fields by moonlight.

3. Outhwaite, 1995, p. 7.

4. See Bald, 1986, p. 136.

5. Helmholz, 1990, pp. 71–3; Donaghue, 1983, pp. 153–5, says that earlier there was a similar practice in northern France, but not in England.

6. Gillis, 1985, p. 84.

7. Ingram, 1987, pp. 192–3.

8. Ibid., pp. 206–9.

9. Houlbrooke, 1985, p. 351.

10. Historians' continuing debates over interpretation of similar church court data, outlined in Pedersen, 2000, pp. 177–80, are questioned ibid., pp. 180–206, in terms of the likelihood that statistical comparability and demographic representativeness are likely to be deficient in the varied and patchy surviving records.

11. Helmholz, 1974, p. 31.

12. See Outhwaite, 1995, pp. 19–49.

13. Ibid., p. 8.

14. See: ibid., pp. 21–35; Houlbrooke, 1984, pp. 85–7; and Brown, 1981, p. 119. Emmison, 1973, pp. 155–9, gives examples of cases of irregular marriages brought before church courts in Essex.
15. Ibid., p. 155.
16. Durant, 1999, p. 1.
17. See: Norsworthy, 1935, pp. 8–15; Bowen, 1957, pp. 101–9, 342–3, 354–5; and Outhwaite, 1995, p. 23.
18. On Swinburne see Baker, 1993, and on Swinburne's second, unpublished, treatise on marriage see Doyle, 1998 and also Mukherji, 1996.
19. Swinburne, 1686, p. 108.
20. Ibid., pp. 233–4.
21. Ibid., pp. 234–5.
22. Pollock and Maitland, 1898, vol. 2, pp. 383–5.
23. See Smith, 1986, p. 65.
24. Ibid., pp. 59–60.
25. Ibid., p. 62.
26. Stone, 1992, p. 18.
27. See Aveling, 1963.
28. There are, however, statements that all clandestinely married women lost dower rights in some (perhaps propagandistic) eighteenth-century pamphlets and law dictionaries; see Outhwaite, 1995, pp. 35–6.
29. Norsworthy, 1935, pp. 8–15, 22–4; Bowen, 1957, pp. 101–9, 342–3, 354–5; Outhwaite, 1995, p. 23.
30. Outhwaite, 1995, p. 62, identifies this as 'snobbery' in the Elizabethan period and in the eighteenth century.
31. Aubrey, 1983, p. 76, reports that 'Coke, laying his hand on [his new wife's] belly (when he came to bed) and finding a child stir, "What", said he, "flesh in the pot?" "Yes", quoth she, "or else I would not have married a cook."'
32. Hotson, 1937, pp. 125–40, 209–11, which notes that Russell was the overseer of Shakespeare's own will. This marriage was first mentioned as relevant to *MM* in Empson, 1952, p. 286, and since has been less over-simplified than usual in Scouten, 1975, p. 70.
33. When these arrangements broke down the heir and Russell resorted to Chancery from 1626.
34. 1623 Chancery Pleadings PRO c/8/23/19, order PRO c/33/146 51v–52r; see Sokol and Sokol, 2002 for detail on all the relevant cases.
35. The manuscript is badly damaged, but we can read 'since that time he hath married'.
36. This incident is considered in more detail in Sokol and Sokol, 2002.
37. The records of the southern Court of High Commission for the period are lost, but this is the conclusion drawn from the records of the northern branch summarised in Carlson, Eric Josef, 1990.
38. See chapter 8 on problems of jurisdiction and bastardy.
39. As noted just above 'fast married' unambiguously means indissolubly so in *OTH* 1.2.11, but perhaps not so simply just that in *MM*. According to *OED*,

'fast' as an adjective always meant firm and secure, but as an adverb in the sense 4.a it could refer to very close proximity. Therefore Claudio's qualification might express ambiguously either an assurance of a legal certainty, or (at a stretch) the legal uncertainty of an approximation.

40. See Kent, 1973, and for background Gowing, 1996 and Ingram, 1996. The Commonwealth 'Act for suppressing the detestable sins of Incest, Adultery and Fornication' of 10 May 1650, printed in Firth and Rait, 1911, vol. 2, pp. 387–9, made a second conviction for fornication a non-clergyable felony (see chapters 7 and 9), punishable by death. The Act did not, however, penalise wider families, for it excluded 'corruption of Blood, loss of Dower forfeiture of Goods, disinherison of Heir or Heirs'. Contrary to the harsher law used against Claudio in *MM*, the 1650 Act made a first conviction for fornication punishable by three months in prison without possibility of bail.

41. A marriage such as Fenton and Anne's could have been allowed, even after the fact, by a dispensation such as Thomas Egerton, and his employee Thomas Conninsby, obtained (see Bald, 1986, pp. 131–2).

42. See Gillis, 1985, pp. 55–86, on the importance of big weddings.

43. Still it might have been noticed by Shakespeare's audiences that the mistaken identity of Sebastian is the sort of error that the required reading of banns before solemnisation was intended to avoid; no tragic consequences arise here from marital haste and error but could and did do in 'reality'.

44. According to Walton, 1966, p. 35, even the outraged father-in-law of John Donne, Sir George More, eventually paid Ann More's portion of 800 pounds, although after much worse than a sputter. The long-term consequences of his dismissal from office were dire for Donne.

45. Furnivall, 1887, pp. l–li, claims an actual case matches this!

46. On *gradatio* and its manifestations in *MM* see Sokol, 1991.

47. Quaife, 1979, pp. 187–8, explains why many *ex officio* cases were not presented by local churchwardens in cases of sexual immorality; similar reasons could apply, with perhaps better reasons, in cases of clandestinity where no parties were injured.

48. Brinkworth, 1972, pp. 108–9; ibid., pp. 14–15, states that a sentence of embarrassing full penance was usually dreaded but that the typical fine for part or whole commutation of penance there was 12 pence.

49. See Quaife, 1979, pp. 195–6.

50. *Pace* Beauregard, 1999, p. 236, Shakespeare does not offer an unusual 'favourable portrayal of Franciscan friars', either generally or here. Friar Lawrence's figure is an ambiguous one in which political machinations taint the good advice that he offers the impassioned lovers. He may also be verging on necromancy in arranging a fake resurrection; in this he shares an image of a conjurer with the other friars in *ADO* and *MM*, whom Beauregard also thinks are portrayed only positively. Also Lawrence's knowledge of fatal-seeming drugs links in Juliet's mind with suspicions that he may poison her; similarly in *CYM* cunning sleeping potions are confused with poisons.

51. See Outhwaite, 1995, pp. 22–31.

52. Furnivall, 1887 details many cases of cynical seductions under the pretext of marriage by handfasting, and Quaife, 1979, p. 63, confirms generally that deceptive promises to marry were used in seductions.
53. Helmholz, 1974, p. 79.
54. But in Sebastian's marriage, as we have noted, mistaken identity could have caused harm.
55. For an overview of the law of rape see Temkin, 1987, pp. 43–8.
56. Holdsworth, 1903, vol. 8, p. 427.
57. See Baker, 1990b, pp. 517–20, on the development of actions in trespass for loss of services of servants, wives, and daughters.
58. Carter, 1985, p. 35; p. 31 lists the records examined.
59. If an appeal of felony resulted in conviction the property of the offender went to the crown. See ibid., pp. 39–40.
60. Bracton, 1968, vol. 2 pp. 345, 415; see Carter, 1985, pp. 94–5.
61. See Thomas, 1959. Carter, 1985, pp. 128–31, argues that the incidence of rape, as a physical attack, is not constant in different periods of history or geographical areas, and high or low levels of rape must depend on complex political factors, such as an outbreak of war.
62. Brundage, 1993, VIII:63–6.
63. Ibid., VIII:66–74.
64. Ibid., I:372.
65. Ibid., VIII:64–5, 74.
66. Glanvill, 1993, p. 176.
67. But Bracton did stress the serious moral failure of this offence which should be punished accordingly. He approvingly tells the tale of the beautiful Jewish wife of a court jester in France, raped by her husband's lord, who ran to the King for protection. The wrongdoing nobleman offered to marry his victim but the King rejected his offer and insisted on punishing him because of the seriousness of his offence. Bracton, 1968, vol. 2, pp. 418–19.
68. See Post, 1978, pp. 151–3.
69. 'Britton', 1865, vol. 1, p. 55.
70. Women were allowed to bring an appeal of felony for only two reasons, rape, or the murder of their husband.
71. Baker, 1990b, p. 603, says that in practice the punishment was death. Post, 1978, p. 152, reports that only one case of mutilation has been discovered in the plea rolls and it is not mentioned by later legal commentators. Carter, 1985, p. 41, argues that the local communities who comprised the jury only rarely imposed corporal punishment for rape and more often a monetary fine. As a general rule, by the fifteenth century physical punishments, apart from execution, were confined to whipping, branding, the stocks and the pillory; mutilation as a punishment was reserved for offences committed in the court itself, such as threatening a jury or throwing a brick at the judge. Later Star Chamber did impose mutilation.
72. Post, 1980 describes the Act as following a complaint made by Sir Thomas West about the abduction in 1382 in the New Forest of his daughter Eleanor

by Nicolas Clifton. Soon after this legislation became law Sir Thomas unsuccessfully petitioned Parliament to make its application retrospective so that his daughter and Nicolas Clifton would be punished.

73. Coke, 1797, vol. 2, p. 60.

74. In the words of the first Act, 3 Hen. VII c.2 (1487), commented on by Thomas, 1959, p. 211.

75. Ives, 1978 argues the Act is a response to the abduction of Margery Ruyton in 1487. Cameron, 1978 documents the case of Jane Sacheverell which may have been a contributory factor behind the Act.

76. See Ives, 1978, p. 25, on the relation of this Act to 3 Hen. VII.

77. Firth and Rait, 1911, vol. 2, pp. 715–18. On the earlier statutes in action, as influences on Restoration comedy, see Alleman, 1942, pp. 52–3.

78. Post, 1978, p. 160; see also Stephen, 1883, vol. 2, p. 201, and Bashar, 1983, p. 30.

79. See Bellamy, 1973, p. 58, and Walker, 1987, p. 237.

80. After an elopement a new husband of a ward would be compelled to purchase a pardon from the crown. The cost of such a pardon was worked out according to a scheme which took into account the status of the offender; the price of a pardon for rape was the same as for murder.

81. See Bald, 1986, pp. 132–3: in 1600 the Court of High Commission dissolved the clandestine marriage of Walter Aston and Anne Barnes; excommunication was 'denounced against all present at the clandestine marriage, according to the *Canon*, and thereby they are disabled to give witnesse'; Anne spent almost a year in the Fleet prison.

82. See Ingram, 1987, p. 266, and Cockburn, 1977 on the incidence of criminal indictments for rape in Essex, Hertfordshire, and Sussex assize records, p. 58.

83. Rape in *LUC* is treated in terms of a military siege and of treason in Ranald, 1987, pp. 153–72, and in terms of social discontent and the law of treason in Nass, 1996. Paying no heed to the 'constant man' test, Catty, 1999, pp. 66–8, wonders if Shakespeare found it 'hard to stomach a definition of rape as "yielding under duress"'.

84. Turner, 1967, pp. 93–111, treats initiation rituals as a liminal period. Although many important specifics are described, some general descriptions are most relevant here. These include 'Liminality may perhaps be regarded as the Nay to all positive structural assertions, but as in some sense the source of them all, and more than that as a realm of pure possibility whence novel configurations of ideas and relations may arise' (p. 97). The use of monstrous masks or images in liminal initiation festivals is ascribed to an educative process in which the constituents of a culture are 'made into objects of reflection' (p. 105). The 'liberty' of monstrous mixing or mismatching that allows such insight has 'fairly narrow [time] limits', after which the 'neophytes return to secular society' and perhaps knowing better 'how things work' are again 'subject to custom and law' (p. 106).

85. The festivities following the 15 August Feast of the Assumption in modern rural France hilariously portray inversions of popular rituals. In Gascony we saw a village parade by members of a local rugby club dressed up as 'majoreaux' – in

pompoms, cheer-leader skirts, and silver-sprayed wellington boots – high-stepping and tripping over their batons. This occurred the day after a serious parade of majorettes. So also the once-a-year tradition in which officers of the British Army act as servitors to enlisted men (on Christmas eve), although fun, also makes in effect a clear assertion that the deference will go the other way around for the rest of the year.

86. As in some Scottish border ballads in earnest, or in a tribal ritual in simulation, Katherina is abducted from her own wedding feast by Petruchio; this is commented on in Sokol, 1985. Here her friends' and family's willingness to be rid of Katherina apparently overrides her traditional bride's right to a public feast; Gillis, 1985, pp. 55–86, analyses the great traditional importance of wedding feasts, 'the big wedding', of the sort that Katherina is denied.

87. As it is also in the story of multiply-male-beset Florimel running through Books 3 and 4 of *The Faerie Queene*. The desperate plight of an unprotected woman in a society with no safe haven for her continues its cogency until Fanny Burney's 1814 novel *The Wanderer*, and beyond.

88. Julia in the same scene faints as her only means of registering her dismay at Proteus' inconstancy to her.

89. This is one of the anxious aspects of the play considered in Sokol, 1995.

90. For a survey of recent discussions of rape in *TIT* see Bate, 1995, especially pp. 36–7.

91. Lavinia is mutilated and raped partly in revenge for Titus killing a brother, and partly to spite Lavinia's marital fidelity. These horrors may be reminiscent of blood feud mutilations allowed by obsolete English laws noted in Selden Society, 1987, p. 93.

92. Young, 1988, p. 466.

7 THE EFFECTS OF MARRIAGE ON LEGAL STATUS

1. See Staves, 1990, pp. 1–3, for a brief summary.
2. Ingram, 1987, p. 125.
3. Gouge, 1622, p. 17.
4. See: Laslett, 1983, pp. 153–81, Houlbrooke, 1984, p. 23, and Collinson, 1988, pp. 61–2. Community surveillance of sexual matters is claimed to have been extensive and deeply intrusive in Shakespeare's England; see Quaife, 1979, especially pp. 50–2, and Laslett, 1983, p. 180. Ingram, 1987, pp. 238–81, presents an image of greater tolerance. Attempted enlargements of legal regulation of personal conduct are discussed in Kent, 1973, and in Ingram, 1996. The relevance of these matters to *MM* is discussed in Roscelli, 1962, Hotine, 1990, Bennett, 1993, Hayne, 1993, Cacicedo, 1995, Widmayer, 1995, Carlson, Cindy, 1996, and Powers, 1996.
5. For an example of each see respectively Gouge, 1622, Whately, 1619, and Fitzherbert, 1652. For useful lists and surveys of conduct books see Powell, 1917, pp. 101–46, and Camden, 1952, pp. 109–49. A detailed consideration of conduct books is generally outside our scope, but nevertheless they are of interest

because they reflect contemporary expectations of duties and obligations owed by husband and wife to each other. Yet conduct books may have expressed contemporary aspirations, exhortations, anxieties, actualities, or any combination of these; see McLuskie, 1989, pp. 40–1, and Amussen, 1994, p. 72. Also see Foyster, 1999a, pp. 3–4, for an argument that patriarchal ideas gained a new force in the seventeenth century in the setting out of 'appropriate' gender roles.

6. *Homilie of Matrimonie*, 1968, p. 239, which then adds the motives of procreation and avoidance of fornication. The order of these three reasons is commented upon in chapter 5.
7. These views are legion. Wrightson, 1982, pp. 102–4, criticises some of them.
8. See Johnson, 1971, on the covenantal idea of marriage. The relations between God and His Church are often described in Christian thought as a marriage.
9. On these teachings see Camden, 1952, pp. 109–49, Ingram, 1987, p. 143, and especially Collinson, 1988, pp. 60–93.
10. Maine, 1930, p. 182. Henry Maine's thesis is best illustrated by the example of the transformation of the agricultural labourer in medieval England from the allodial villein into the wage labourer, free to contract his work in return for money.
11. Blackstone, 1766, 1:442 (Bk 1, ch. xv).
12. 'Lawes Resolutions', 1632, p. 6.
13. See Houlbrooke, 1984, p. 96.
14. Booty, 1976, pp. 298–9, prints the 1559 version that was current in Shakespeare's time. On the marriage ceremony generally, see chapter 5.
15. Houlbrooke, 1984, p. 96.
16. Doggett, 1992, p. 38, explains how the original statement of this in Coke's First Institute had many descendants.
17. 'Lawes Resolutions', 1632, pp. 120–2. This treatise has been mentioned above as mistakenly equating religion's 'one flesh' with law's 'one person'. Doggett, 1992, p. 6, considers it to have been written in the first few years of the seventeenth century, while Prest, 1991 more fully analyses its origins, purposes, uses, and significance. On a similar point see the not wholly accurate Swinburne, 1686, pp. 234–5, which has been analysed in chapter 6.
18. 'Lawes Resolutions', 1632, p. 124.
19. Ibid., p. 4.
20. See Kreps, 2002 for a discussion of such inconsistency in relation to Dekker's *The Honest Whore*.
21. Stretton, 2002, p. 48. See chapter 9 on the church courts and inheritance.
22. Ibid., pp. 48–9. Stretton, 1994 shows that the central equity court of Requests sometimes upheld such customary rights, even where local or manorial courts 'forgot' them. See chapter 9 on inheritance patterns.
23. On the use of the equity court of Chancery by women see Cioni, 1982, and Cioni, 1985. See also: Stretton, 1994, Stretton, 1998, and Stretton, 1999 on women's use of the less-expensive equity court of Requests. However, Spring,

1993, pp. 14–17, and Stretton, 2002, pp. 49–51, argue that some of the legal devices upheld by equity, such as uses or trusts, which were initially beneficial to married women (by allowing a wife's rights to separate property) later became disadvantageous to them.

24. See Baker, 1990b, pp. 551–7, and Finn, 1996, pp. 708–10. The wife's rights to maintenance extended if she was deserted by her husband.

25. Women could defer a sentence of death by proving their pregnancy to a jury of matrons. It has been suggested that deferred capital sentences on pregnant women were not carried out after the child's birth. See Laurence, 1994, pp. 268–71, on the punishment of women for crime.

26. See chapter 6 on appeals of felony for rape. Although prosecutions by appeal were common in the sixteenth century, some historians argue that they had all but died out by 1660 while others hold that appeals continued to be brought throughout the seventeenth and eighteenth century. See Baker, 1986, p. 262, Whittick, 1984, p. 57, and Ernst, 1984, p. 168.

27. Russell, 1980, pp. 137, 140.

28. See Baker, 1978, p. 116. Battle was restricted to appeals of homicide where no other evidence existed apart from the appellor's accusation. A 'presumption of malice' was automatically applied to every appeal of felony. Every appellor was presumed to have malicious intent and therefore defendants were allowed legal counsel after 1488 in appeals of death (where the accusation was for a capital crime).

29. See Whittick, 1984, pp. 58–9.

30. The appeal process was also more flexible than indictment. For instance, it was not necessary to distinguish between the principal and accessory to a homicide.

31. See Sokol and Sokol, 2000, pp. 212–18.

32. Gowing, 1994, p. 44, n. 5.

33. Stretton, 1994, p. 173.

34. Ibid., p. 184.

35. Stretton, 1999, pp. 196–7, citing Juan Luis Vives. See also Todd, 1999, pp. 69–70. Stretton, 2002, pp. 52–3, shows that only 8 per cent of early modern plaintiffs in the Court of Star Chamber were women, but cites Gowing's contrasting statistics on London church courts, as are seen above. This mentions that the range was less dramatic in the central courts of London, whose varied jurisdictions saw women as between 10 per cent and 15 per cent of the plaintiffs (in a wide range of actions not at all exclusively matrimonial in focus). Women were either plaintiffs or defendants in up to one-third of all actions in the main central courts. More detail is given in Stretton, 1999, pp. 194–6.

36. The Act 25 Edw. III st. 5 c.2 (1352) defined petty treason as the killing of a husband by his wife, a master by his servant, or of his superior by a monk. Although statutory and judicial changes were made in subsequent centuries the basic definition remained as set out in the fourteenth-century statute. Petty treason was reduced to ordinary murder in 1828 (9 Geo. IV c.31).

37. A conviction of petty treason resulted in escheat of lands and goods to the defendant's lord and for men drawing on a hurdle and then hanging, while for women burning to death. See Bellamy, 1970, pp. 225–31, and on the punishment of women by burning for petty treason see Campbell, Ruth, 1985 and 'Lawes Resolutions', 1632, p. 208.
38. See Holdsworth, 1903, vol. 3, p. 527.
39. See Staves, 1990, p. 135; Cornwall v Earl of Montague (1701) 1 Eq. Ca. Abr. 66.
40. Ibid., p. 134.
41. Erickson, 1993, p. 103.
42. See Laurence, 1994, pp. 125–43, on women who were in trade or in waged work in the seventeenth and early eighteenth centuries.
43. Ibid., p. 125.
44. This situation was to cause scandal and was used to support demands for reform in the eighteenth century.
45. See Sokol and Sokol, 2000, pp. 125–8.
46. Plucknett, 1956, pp. 567–8.
47. As a widower Sir Thomas would have had a possible interest in her lands because of his right to 'curtesy', described in chapter 9. But curtesy rights for widowers depended on the birth of a live child during the marriage, and the Hobys had no children.
48. Hoby, 1998, pp. 222–6. See also Houlbrooke, 1984, p. 100, who gives details of a father's letter to his daughter urging her not to agree to her husband's proposed conveyance of her lands because in the future some of her children might be dependent on her for their support.
49. Hoby, 1998, p. 224.
50. See Sokol and Sokol, 2000, pp. 110–12, on this.
51. Erickson, 1993, p. 102.
52. See Sokol and Sokol, 1999a.
53. Erickson, 1993, pp. 102–13, gives details from manuals such as William West's 1594 *The First Part of Symboleography* and Thomas Phayer's 1543 *New Boke of Presidents*. She argues that Chancery would uphold such agreements, but that these were not always made to benefit married women, and may have had other purposes.
54. Ibid., p. 107.
55. 'Lawes Resolutions', 1632, p. 123.
56. Shakespeare does allude to the witch Medea in *CYL* 5.3.57–9, *MV* 1.1.170–2 and 5.1.13–14, and 'quotes' her from Ovid in *TMP* 5.1.33–50. But her revenge on her absconding husband Jason in the form of killing his new wife (and from Euripides' version onwards also by means of infanticide) does not get much prominence.
57. See Sokol and Sokol, 2000, pp. 369–80.
58. Treason and petty treason in *CYL* are analysed in Bernthal, 1991 and Levine, Nina, 1994. Cunningham, 1994 proposes that the Henrician treason statutes concerning the succession, and particular details of the attainder for treason of Katherine Howard (attainted for her promiscuity before her marriage to

Henry VIII), inform the trial of female fidelity in *CYM*. Dolan, 1992b considers petty treason in relation to *TMP*. Dolan, 1994, *passim*, considers this together with broader representations of domestic violence and wives' acts of petty treason, and Dolan, 1992a considers murderous wives.

59. This point is noted in Bean, John C., 1980, pp. 70–1.
60. For instance, Lady Julia in Tilney, 1568, D5r, states (on behalf of the male author) 'howe much more the husbande be evill, and out of order, so much more it is the woman's prayse, if she love him'.
61. For a very interesting discussion of Elizabethan views on whether the subjects of tyrants must always exercise 'patience', considering Shakespeare's plays and differing religious views on sovereignty and 'human rights', see Titlestad, 1988.
62. See Ward, Ian, 1995, pp. 59–89, and Ward, Ian, 1996.
63. See chapter 9 for a review of varied positions, and some new evidence that bears on them.
64. See Williamson, 1986, pp. 39 and 51, and Berger, 1981, concerning Portia.
65. Bean, John C., 1974.
66. Dash, 1981, p. 93.
67. Dreher, 1986, p. 38.
68. Boone, 1987, pp. 54–6 and 49. Such a sectarian view is seen as highly dubious by Professor Robert Miola (private communication). In accord with this, Sommerville, 1995, p. 129, cites the Catholic St Peter Canisius as listing in 1592–6 all three of the ends of marriage, including the companionate one, but continues that John Milton's preference for the companionate basis of marriage, echoing Bucer's, was 'completely heterodox'.
69. Hagstrum, 1992, pp. 374–404; p. 403.
70. For applications to particular Shakespeare plays see, for example, Fisch, 1974, Bean, John C., 1974, Dash, 1981, Hennings, 1986, McLuskie, 1989, Hagstrum, 1992, Kegl, 1994, and Belsey, 1999.
71. So (as we have seen in chapter 2) King James told his first English Parliament that he was 'the Husband and the whole Isle is my lawful Wife; I am the Head, and it is my Body', McIlwain, 1918, p. xxxv, and here *MM* may exhibit another among many other more obvious reflections of the new monarchy.
72. This instance will be discussed further in chapter 8 in relation to notions of divorce for adultery.
73. See Amussen, 1994, p. 73 and p. 86n17, for a survey of the literature.
74. See ibid., p. 73, and Sommerville, 1995, pp. 92–7.
75. Doggett, 1992, pp. 6–8, investigates claims made for a 1660 statute enacted to put a common law right to beat into statutory form, but draws a blank at uncovering either the statute or any repealing legislation.
76. Ibid., p. 8. According to Jeaffreson, 1872, vol. 1, pp. 317–18, the 'old Welsh law empowered him to give her "three blows with a broomstick on any part of her person except the head"'.
77. Later in the seventeenth century the central royal courts ceased to instruct the justices and themselves took sureties for good behaviour from assailants. See Lambard, 1592, pp. 80–1, Dalton, 1635, pp. 157–8, and Doggett, 1992, p. 5.

78. Fitzherbert, 1652, p. 595.
79. Ibid. See Doggett, 1992, p. 5, for a careful account of the development of these processes.
80. Lambard, 1592, p. 130.
81. Ibid., pp. 80–1. To the same ends, to instruct Justices of the Peace, Dalton, 1635, pp. 157–8, explains the technicalities of justices either ordering themselves or obtaining a writ of *supplicavit* 'to find sureties for the Peace', and then, p. 163, states a wife or husband may demand sureties against the other.
82. Amussen, 1994, p. 72.
83. Wrightson, 1982, p. 98.
84. Ibid., pp. 98–100. On wife-beating see also: Phillips, Roderick, 1988, p. 54 (on Calvin), p. 89 (on the *Reformatio Legum Ecclesiasticarum*), and especially pp. 323–44; Dolan, 1994, pp. 32–4 and 102–3; Amussen, 1994; Foyster, 1996; Foyster, 1999a, pp. 181–95; and Stretton, 2002, p. 43.
85. Carlson, Eric Josef, 1994, p. 153; Houlbrooke, 1984, pp. 117–18.
86. Foyster, 1996, pp. 215–16. On disapproval see also Foyster, 1999a, pp. 185–93.
87. See Foyster, 1999a, pp. 109–15. Purkiss, 1992, p. 81, states that 'Ridings were used when a wife beat her husband, or was thought insubordinate in some other clear way. It was the husband or a surrogate, not the wife, who received the punishment, so that again the social problem of female unruliness is figured as a defect in man.'
88. Foyster, 1996, p. 216.
89. 'Lawes Resolutions', 1632, p. 128. This also mentions Fitzherbert's remedy available for wives fearful of assault, the writ of *supplicavit*.
90. This Oxford 'Act' or preached thesis of a new Doctor of Divinity (*OED* 8.) of Gouger is treated scathingly in Jeaffreson, 1872, vol. 1, p. 332; this is part of a polemical account ibid., pp. 317–42.
91. H[eale], 1609, which is dedicated to the honourable and virtuous Lady M. H., possibly the three-times-married Lady Margaret Hoby.
92. Ibid., p. 12. Heale uses the traditional analogy of Virgil's 'common–wealth of Bees' for the happy household of husband, wife, children, and servants.
93. Ibid., p. 27.
94. Ibid., pp. 28–30. See Jeaffreson, 1872, vol. 1, pp. 333–4.
95. *Homilie of Matrimonie*, 1968, p. 245. William Whateley rhetorically asks his readers if it is right for a husband to 'correct' his wife with 'blowes' and reminds husbands that their wives are not slaves, see Whately, 1619, pp. 106–7. See also: Camden, 1952, pp. 114–16; Davies, Kathleen M., 1981, p. 68; Houlbrooke, 1984, pp. 22, 117–18; and Ingram, 1987, p. 144, and p. 180 on community disapproval of wife-beating.
96. Lord Seymour's Case 1613 Godb. 215, 72 English Reports 966; see Doggett, 1992, p. 8.
97. Doggett, 1992, pp. 12–13.
98. See Ingram, 1987, pp. 13 and 180.
99. Ibid., pp. 180–1, 183; see examples in Pedersen, 2000, pp. 134–5.

100. In 1674 in Lord Leigh's Case (2 Keb. 433, 84 English Reports 807) Lord Chief Justice Hale denied that a husband had an unlimited right to beat his wife, but only a right to admonish and to confine her to the house 'in case of her extravagance'.

101. Because divorce was not available and separation orders were hard to obtain (see chapter 8), husbands and wives sometimes entered into private agreements to live apart. Such an agreement was typically obtained by a woman who had brought property into a marriage, and it usually provided her with annual maintenance funded by her own property. Typically such a wife (through trustees) indemnified the husband from liability for her future debts. But such agreements were not recognised by either church courts or common law courts. So if the wife breached such an agreement and pledged her husband's name for credit, the common law courts would not help him against her, while there was no help for the wife if her husband obtained an order from a church court for her to resume cohabitation. By the eighteenth century separation agreements commonly provided that a husband would not subsequently seek to enforce cohabitation, yet even then cases of confinement of wives, often accompanied by physical abuse, arose when the estranged wife was due to inherit property, or if a larger share of her property was wanted. See Doggett, 1992, pp. 18–22, for examples of cases where separation agreements were notoriously breached by husbands in order to extract property.

102. There were tangled problems of definition and of sentencing with regard to the early modern crime of homicide, but details of these are topics outside our concerns. See Sokol and Sokol, 2000, pp. 228–37, and references there.

103. See Houlbrooke, 1998, pp. 24–5.

104. For an analysis of these plays see Lieblein, 1983.

105. Fortier, 1996, p. 587, equates Leontes' threats to 'burn Hermione at the stake' with wife-beating. No such threat is made, however. Only Paulina is threatened with burning for witchcraft/heresy; Hermione is tried for treason, but not assaulted.

106. His preceding interchange with Desdemona, 4.1.235–40, is impossible to emend, wholly unclear, yet wholly poetically correct.

107. The loss of companionable potential in *OTH* is emphasised in Hagstrum, 1992, p. 403.

108. The range of these dramatic purposes for servant abuse includes the comic in *ERR* and *SHR*, the politically potent in *LRF* (the stocking of Kent, threats against the Fool), and the symbolically weighty in *TMP* (punishment of Caliban and his confederates, threats against Ariel). On the legality of beating servants and apprentices see Cornish and Clark, 1989, p. 287. Sokol, 1994b discusses the threats against Ariel in *TMP*. On *ERR* and servants see Hunt, 1997.

109. In repentance Ford promises his wife a total trust which Page finds excessive (*WIV* 4.4.5–11).

110. See Barton, 1994, pp. 3–30, for an investigation of this remarkable position.

111. Montaigne, 1942, vol. 3, pp. 62–128.
112. The Archbishop of York's images and their thrust unconsciously echo the opening words of the preceding play, spoken by the exhausted King Henry IV: 'So shaken as we are, so wan with care, / Find we a time for frighted peace to pant . . . / No more the thirsty entrance of this soil / Shall daub her lips with her own children's blood' (*1H4* 1–6). The Archbishop fails to reckon with the vigour of the royal younger generation.
113. The stage direction is from Shakespeare, 1968, folio 216, tln 1096.
114. On the contrary, the play does actually show Kate assaulting a range of others, male and female. Arguably this may lend a deliberately misleading farcical element to a play that subverts taming farces.
115. However, the stumbling horse and the weak bridle are described in 3.2.57–8 as of Petruchio's choosing.
116. She even wades through mud in an attempt to protect Grumio, as described in 4.1.69–70.
117. Sokol, 1985 argues that when Kate is deprived of accustomed comforts she learns to correct her 'froward' rejection of the goods of the world, and also learns to show compassion for the victim (e.g. the tailor) of a 'frowardness' in Petruchio much like her own. The play's conceptual or psychological language of forwardness and frowardness (taken from Spenser) first differentiates and then unites the married pair; at the start of the marriage a servant remarks of Petruchio 'he is more shrew than she' (*SHR* 4.1.76). Unlike the Lord of the Induction, who acts upon Sly but changes in himself not a whit, Petruchio is an artificer who transforms himself; his 'forward' disposition is modified permanently by his concern for Kate, at first paradoxically enacted by depriving her of inferior goods.
118. See Nevo, 1980, Bean, John C., 1980, Perret, 1983, Daniell, 1984, and Mikesell, 1989.
119. Martin, 1991, p. 14. Martin holds that the humanist ideals of the age and in the play lose out to patriarchy in social practice.

8   MARRIAGE BREAKDOWN: SEPARATION, DIVORCE, ILLEGITIMACY

1. However, a man was not free to marry again after he had been divorced *a vinculo* due to the dirimentary impediment of impotence – for any subsequent marriage would be equally invalid.
2. See: Pollock and Maitland, 1898, vol. 2, pp. 392–6; Helmholz, 1974, pp. 74–107; Houlbrooke, 1979, pp. 67–75; Ingram, 1987, p. 146; Baker, 1990b, p. 562; Carlson, Eric Josef, 1994, p. 22.
3. See Brooke, 1981, pp. 18–26, on the informal matrimonial practices of earlier medieval clergy and nobility, and on popular practices see Smith, 1986, pp. 52–69.
4. Helmholz, 1974, pp. 75–6. On the complex history of European and English divorce and separation see especially Phillips, Roderick, 1988. See also Stone, 1990 and Laurence, 1994, pp. 47–54.

5. Baker, 1990b, pp. 560–2; Helmholz, 1974, pp. 76–100; and Ingram, 1987, p. 145.
6. Swinburne, 1686, pp. 223–4.
7. See Helmholz, 1974, p. 90.
8. On the history of the often-shifting rules creating impediments to marriage on account of affinity, and on problems of the definition and history of 'incest', see McCabe, 1993, pp. 3–63.
9. Hoby, 1998, p. 32.
10. Pollock and Maitland, 1898, vol. 2, p. 393.
11. Sheehan, 1996, p. 84; see also Ingram, 1987, p. 146. Sheehan, p. 85, claims the subject has not been studied fully, but agrees that the Church's stress on marriage by consent alone, requiring no formalities, did create a dilemma in late medieval and early modern England. It was all too easy for couples to be ignorant of, or even choose to forget, an impediment.
12. Helmholz, 1974, pp. 79–80.
13. See Phillips, Roderick, 1988, pp. 71–7.
14. Helmholz, 1974, pp. 94–8.
15. See the note to 4.1.26–7 in Webster, 1975, p. 85, which derives from Webster, 1927, vol. 2, p. 346.
16. See Lindley, 1993, pp. 77–122.
17. Pedersen, 2000, pp. 88, 115–18, 119, 136, 137, 145–8, 189–90, discusses church court litigation over two particular medieval divorce actions based on male sexual incapacity (modern discussions of other cases are listed ibid., p. 117n.). In one of Pedersen's two cases, detailed pp. 145–8, the high-born husband was probably severely malformed, and he resisted physical investigation. In the other case, detailed ibid., pp. 116–18, malformation was physically confirmed. Lindley, 1993, pp. 99–100, shows that Essex successfully resisted attempts to examine his potency, although, pp. 107–13, his wife Frances Howard was inspected for virginity.
18. Helmholz, 1974, pp. 87–90. Although Helmholz's cases of women carrying out physical examinations are medieval, lawyers discussing such matters (and alternative possibilities for divorce) are lampooned in the last scene of Ben Jonson's 1609 *Epicoene*, in Jonson, 1925, vol. 5, pp. 254–71.
19. Helmbolz, 1974, p. 100; Baker, 1990b, p. 562.
20. See Helmholz, 1977.
21. Helmholz, 1974, p. 101; see also Poos, 1995, and Pedersen, 2000, pp. 137 and 210. It seems the normal rules about the need for evidence which applied in annulment were not insisted on for divorce *a mensa et thoro*, leaving the court free to counsel the parties to reach an accommodation with each other.
22. Durant, 1999, pp. 122, 136–8. This Commission ordered a financial settlement and ordered Shrewsbury to take Bess back into his house, but he did not do so.
23. Bowen, 1957, p. 354.
24. See: Thurston, 1904; Scarisbrick, 1974, pp. 218–316, 367–75, 452–6, 479–84, 554–9; and Phillips, Roderick, 1988, pp. 71–7, especially p. 74.

25. This revival was in line with Protestant thought, as described in Sommerville, 1995, pp. 197–8.
26. Also see chapter 5 on the abortive *Reformatio* of 1553. The bitter early modern contentions over the reform of divorce are discussed in Powell, 1917, pp. 61–100.
27. See Stone, 1990, pp. 301–13, and for further examples Stone, 1993. On the asymmetry between men and women in English divorce see Thomas, 1959, pp. 200–3.
28. Stone, 1979, pp. 661–2, which suggests that this surprising statistic may have been due to these peers' wives' dissatisfaction coupled with improving legal conditions allowing a wife's separate estate in equity. Stone may be accepted as reliable about the aristocracy, if not other social levels. We might note that Penelope Rich's marital separation and cohabitation was not a scandal until she married Lord Mountjoy.
29. A commentary on *AWW* which sees these legal aspects clearly is found in Mukherji, 1996.
30. Pedersen, 2000, p. 211. But this did not mean that sexual consummation was necessary to validate marriage generally.
31. See Bassnett-McGuire, 1984 on the political dimensions of the Elizabethan 'divorce issue' reflected in *AWW*.
32. There is a huge critical literature on the reinstated marriage at the ending of *AWW*. For diametrical views see Friedman, 1995 versus Hill, 1975, or Babula, 1977, or Beauregard, 1999.
33. Although not all Shakespeare critics seem to know this; see, for instance, Simonds, 1989, p. 58.
34. Cranmer never gave any reasons for this, but he could have argued the impediment of affinity due to Henry's prior affair with Anne's sister, or else the existence of a pre-contract for another marriage previously entered into by Anne.
35. *CYM* is at one time or another a history play, a Renaissance melodrama, a wild classical Romance, a tragedy, a comedy, and a Roman play.
36. Barton, 1994, pp. 3–30.
37. We may compare hers with the sad fate of Arbella Stuart, whose marriage plans were thwarted by Queen Elizabeth I, and who died mad in the Tower following an abortive runaway marriage under James I.
38. Carlson, Eric Josef, 1994, pp. 81–2. See also Head, 1982.
39. See Brooke, 1981, pp. 22–6. The informal marrying and remarrying of those times is reflected in the institutions of concubinage, as noted above, and may accord with King Cymbeline calling Posthumus Imogen's 'minion' (*CYM* 2.3.39).
40. Ibid., pp. 31–2.
41. Swinburne, 1686, p. 237. Contrarily, if sexual relations had taken place between parties to a marriage contract *per verba de futuro*, this would immediately make the relationship into a valid marriage. In accord with this Claudio adds in response to the suggestion that it was he that has had sexual relations with Hero, that if true this would 'extenuate the forehand sin' (4.1.50). See chapter 1.

42. See the cases discussed in Pedersen, 2000, pp. 140–5.
43. The impediment could have been one of pre-contract with Cleopatra, except that any promise made to Cleopatra during Fulvia's lifetime would have been made void by the impediment of 'crime'.
44. On historical, definitional, and other complexities concerning incest see: Marienstras, 1981, pp. 186–92; Thomas, 1983, p. 39; Neely, 1985, pp. 166–209; Forker, 1990, pp. 141–68; and McCabe, 1993, pp. 3–63.
45. Brooke, 1981, p. 26.
46. Ibid., pp. 32–3.
47. Sokol, 1991 gives reason to doubt such interpretations of *MM*. Isabella's silence is discussed, for instance, in McGuire, 1985 and Spotswood, 1994.
48. The Folio has Albany join Regan with Edmund 'in thy arrest' (Shakespeare, 1968, tln 3028), but the Oxford *LRF* 5.3.76 and other editions adopt 'attaint' from 'in thy attaint' in *LRQ* s.24.81.
49. This is astutely analysed in Kreps, 1999, which connects the treatment in *AIT* of the royal divorce with Buckingham's fall as depicted in it, and other of 'the play's telegraphic reminders of Henry's talent for adjusting legal "facts" to his convenience' (p. 181).
50. On the canon law (as opposed to civil law) background of the *recusatio* in Katherine's challenge to Wolsey, see Helmholz, 1987b.
51. See: Keeton, 1930, pp. 206–16; Phillips, O. Hood, 1967, p. 186; Phillips, O. Hood, 1972, pp. 86–7.
52. See Neill, 1993, p. 277, on the ordination of the Bishop of Winchester in *1H6*.
53. See Pollock and Maitland, 1898, vol. 2, pp. 396–9.
54. Helmholz, 1977, p. 446.
55. The most serious sanction awarded by church courts was excommunication, which brought with it civil and religious disabilities. See ibid., p. 445.
56. See Helmholz, 1977.
57. Osborne, 1960, pp. 67–9.
58. See: Pollock and Maitland, 1898, vol. 2, pp. 382, 396–9; Farrer, 1917; Adams, 1946; Helmholz, 1969; Helmholz, 1977; Baker, 1990b, pp. 557–9.
59. A limited exception to the rigid position of the common law arose in the complex circumstances of a *bastard eigné*. Here the requirement was that an elder son was born before his parents' marriage, then later a second son was born to the same parents but after the date of their marriage. If the elder son took possession of his inheritance and no objection was raised at the time, then after the elder's death his son was able to inherit.
60. The bishops strenuously objected to having their authority circumvented and suggested that 'the barons change the common law to accord with the canon law'. In the Provisions of Merton (1236) 'all the Earls and Barons replied with one voice that they did not wish to change the laws of England which were customary and had been approved'. See Adams, 1946, p. 369, and Baker, 1990b, p. 558.
61. See Helmholz, 1969, p. 370.
62. See Keeton, 1930, pp. 1–7.

63. Helmholz, 1969, p. 370, also Keeton, 1930, p. 7.
64. See Adams, 1946, pp. 378–81.
65. Baker, 1990b, p. 558.
66. On bastardy in English Renaissance drama see Neill, 1993 and Findlay, 1994. On bastardy as portrayed by Shakespeare see Draper, 1938 and Williamson, 1986, pp. 81–5, 91–9. Widmayer, 1995 makes a case that bastard-bearing was sometimes very severely punished in Shakespeare's age, and applies this to *MM*.
67. 'Bastard', meaning sweet wine, is certainly not disparaged in *1H4* 2.5.26 and 72.
68. See Webster, 1975, p. 103, *The Devil's Law-Case* 4.2.327–30: 'When do we name Don John of Austria, / The emperor's son, but with reverence? / And I have known in diverse families, / The bastards the greater spirits.' Don John was the illegitimate son of the Emperor Charles V, and the hero of the great battle of Lepanto (1571). Also see especially Elton, 1966, pp. 131–5, on the possibly positive implications of Edmund's bastardy.
69. Yet, when dying, Edmund expresses very odd ideas of love: 'Yet Edmund was beloved. / The one the other poisoned for my sake, / And after slew herself' (*LRF* 5.3.215–17). Murder, suicide, bigamy, and incest seem the unwanted son's proofs of love, and this may be connected with Gloucester's scant acknowledgement.
70. Brennan, 1990 suggests that biblical resonances make blasphemous (as well as subversive) the bastard son Edmund's attempt to usurp legitimate Edgar. On scriptural condemnations of bastardy also see Neill, 1993, pp. 276–8.
71. See Sokol, 1998.
72. On the bastardy trial in *JN* see: Keeton, 1930, pp. 1–9; Clarkson and Warren, 1942, pp. 212–15; Phillips, O. Hood, 1967, p. 186; Phillips, O. Hood, 1972, pp. 85–6; Hamilton, 1992, pp. 34–42.
73. See Flandrin, 1979, pp. 180–4.
74. See Stone, 1979, p. 663, which claims, perhaps with exaggeration, that in early sixteenth-century England 'in practice, if not in theory . . . the nobility was a polygamous society'. Gillis, 1985, pp. 12–13, states that 'The aristocracy also continued to give pride of place to kin and lineage . . . in sixteenth-century Lancashire, many lived in open adultery. They were shamed neither by their concubines nor by their bastards.' See also Cook, 1991, pp. 186–9.
75. See: Shorter, 1976, pp. 82, 332–6; Laslett, 1977, pp. 102–55; Levine, David and Wrightson, 1980; Laslett, 1983, pp. 153–74; Neill, 1993, p. 273.
76. See: Wrightson, 1980; Houlbrooke, 1984, p. 81; Ingram, 1985, p. 159; Laslett, 1983, p. 162.
77. Flandrin, 1979, p. 182.
78. Schoenbaum, 1986, pp. 275–6.
79. Metzger, 1991, p. 160, spelling modernised. Ibid., p. 162, describes the displeasure of Carl Ludwig at having 'his marital affairs mentioned in print; when he met the author of one such report, the elector forced him publicly to eat the pages containing the indiscretion'.

80. The possibility of concubinage is bluntly expressed in the play's source, Greene's *Pandosto*, but only insinuated in *WT*.
81. On these fears and the sexual dynamic of the pastoral scene see Sokol, 1994a, pp. 116–41.

9 'TIL DEATH US DO PART

1. See Houlbrooke, 1998, pp. 1–27, on the perceived 'Face of Death' in an age of high mortality and death.
2. Stone, 1977, pp. 54–60, paints a picture of low-key, unaffectionate, undemanding, and unstable family relations, but this has been much questioned. See: Macfarlane, 1979; Laslett, 1983, pp. 119–20; Ingram, 1987, pp. 143–4; Wrightson, 1982, pp. 106–18; and Cook, 1991, pp. 12–13, which has a bibliographical footnote. Spring, 1984, pp. 184–7, argues that the legal–historical basis of Stone's 'impressionistic' theory of unaffectionate early modern family life 'is largely misperceived'. Theories of non-affection for children in Stone, 1977 are linked to ideas allegedly taken from Ariès, 1973 that 'childhood' was a late concept. But Ariès, p. 123, states that medieval children were not 'neglected, forsaken or despised. The idea of childhood is not to be confused with affection for children.' Dubrow, 1999, pp. 142–93, gives careful consideration to the impect on Shakespeare's writing and milieu of frequent early parental death.
3. On these rules see Simpson, 1986, pp. 56–63, and Baker, 1990b, pp. 304–7.
4. Such a tenant, however, could be liable for 'waste', as is discussed in Sokol and Sokol, 2000, pp. 408–10.
5. See Stone, 1977, p. 56. Pelling, 1999, p. 39, claims that early modern widowers who did not remarry were so scarce that they can hardly be traced statistically: 'widowers were such mainly for the fleeting period just before a second marriage'.
6. Another possible problem about remarriage derives from the doctrine in Ephesians 5:23 equating the husband as the head of the wife with Christ as the head of the Church. Remarriage might confuse this equivalence, but note John Donne's astonishing metaphor in 'Show me deare Christ, thy spouse, so bright and clear' (Donne, 1960, p. 301), in which the most promiscuous spouse for Christ is seen as the best.
7. Claiming benefit of clergy nominally required the reading of a 'neck verse' from a Latin text. Various statutes imposed branding on the hand to ensure that it could not be used twice for the same offence. A number of felonies were not clergyable. See Sokol and Sokol, 2000, pp. 41–3 and 231.
8. See Coke, 1797, vol. 2, pp. 272–4. By the Act 1 Edw. VI c.12 (1547) such 'bigamy' was not a bar, and peers of the realm did not have to read and were excused branding.
9. By 18 Eliz. I c.7 (1575) those receiving benefit of clergy were not handed over to ecclesiastical authorities at all, but could be discharged at once or could be imprisoned for one year.

10. In particular certain murders were excluded in the series of statutes 12 Hen. VII c.7 (1496), 4 Hen. VIII c.2 (1512), 23 Hen. VIII c.1, ch. 3–4 (1531), 1 Edw. VI c.12, ch. 10 (1547).

11. The other contexts of 'widower' in Shakespeare are in the mocking or bitter remarks seen in *RDY* 3.3.227 (repeated in 4.1.97) and *TMP* 2.1.84.

12. See Laslett, 1977, pp. 160–72, and Stone, 1977, p. 58.

13. Schofield, 1986 shows that death in childbed or as a result of pregnancy was not the leading cause of absent mothers in Shakespeare's England. The careful statistical work in this study is summarised, p. 260, in: 'the risk of dying in childbed was not greater than the risk [a woman] ran every year of dying from infectious disease and a whole variety of other causes'.

14. See Shakespeare, 2001, p. 92, on a possible influence on *King Lear*.

15. See Foyster, 2001, especially pp. 321–2, which cites William Gouge, but explains some advantages of co-residence as well.

16. Laslett, 1983, pp. 90–9, explains that this rarity was for demographic reasons.

17. Stretton, 1999, pp. 201–3, gives examples of widows who immediately took advantage of this new opportunity for litigiousness following a husband's death.

18. Kusunoki, 1995 discusses attitudinal contexts at large, and shows that emergent cultural forces favoured remarriage of widows. Ibid., p. 176, notes, however, Barbara Todd's discovery of an apparent decline in remarriage rates for English widows in the seventeenth century, which may have had demographic causes.

19. Brodsky, 1986, pp. 128–34.

20. Ibid., p. 141.

21. For an overview on early modern Englishwomen and their work see Mendelson, 2002.

22. For example, when the wealthy Lady Margaret Hoby's first husband died her parents accepted she was under the protection of the Earl and Countess of Huntingdon who quickly arranged a new marriage. This pattern was repeated when she was widowed for the second time.

23. See Loengard, 1993.

24. Panek, 2000, pp. 324 and 341n.

25. Brodsky, 1986, pp. 125–6.

26. Foyster, 1999b, p. 109.

27. See Brodsky, 1986 and Elliott, 1981. These hold that the motives were often economic.

28. Foyster, 1999b, p. 117.

29. Ibid. argues *passim* that the reason widows were often portrayed as lustful on the Jacobean stage and in other literature was an expression of male anxiety about female autonomy.

30. See Sheehan, 1996, p. 18, and Brundage, 1992.

31. See Stretton, 1999, pp. 205–8, on litigious widows' frequent ploy of playing on this 'defenceless' stereotype.

32. Kusunoki, 1995. This essay is based on close considerations of social and legal history, contemporary views of sexuality and of women's agency, and the play

itself. It covers similar ground to Jardine, 1991, but reaches wholly different conclusions.

33. These rules divided a husband's chattels on his death into three parts. One-third belonged to his widow, one-third, known as the *legitim*, belonged to his children, and one-third was available to the testator to leave as he wished. If a man had only a wife, or only children, then half of his personal property was available to the wife or the children, and half was available for him to leave as he wished. If a man had neither wife nor children then all his personal property was his to dispose of as he wished. See Helmholz, 1987c on the decline of *legitim*. Charitable or pious gifts were often made from this remaining third. Contrary to some recently expressed beliefs, a degree of autonomy in leaving property existed before the 1540 Statute of Wills which applied only to real property.

34. See Helmholz, 1993.

35. See Sheehan, 1996, p. 34.

36. The administration of the estates of intestates was in the hands of admin-istrators appointed by the church court; they were usually the next of kin. These administrators could sue or be sued in the same way as executors, but scandalous tales were told of the failure of ecclesiastical courts to control their activities.

37. See the differences on women making wills between Houlbrooke, 1998, p. 87, and Erickson, 1993, pp. 204–21.

38. Baker, 1990b, p. 303.

39. Ibid.

40. Land from dissolved monasteries in Kent was 'disgavelled' when passed on to new owners by 31 Hen. VIII c.3 (as well as all land in Wales by 34 & 35 Hen. VIII c.26), indicating the desire of new landowners to prevent partition among sons. See Baker, 1978, p. 209; see also Bonfield, 1983, p. 22.

41. See Sokol and Sokol, 2000, pp. 151–2, on the rules applied for the descent of real property, known as the *parentelic scheme*. These rules favoured male descent except that if there were no sons then collateral male relatives were not preferred to daughters, so a daughter took property in preference to an uncle.

42. This rule came into use following the *statutum decretum* of Henry I. However, inheritance of the crown was excluded from the coparceny rule, and an eldest sister took to the exclusion of others. See Baker, 1990b, pp. 306–7, Clarkson and Warren, 1942, pp. 218–19, and Sokol and Sokol, 2000, pp. 56, 150–4, and 312–13.

43. See Archer, 1984 on inheritance patterns in late medieval landed families.

44. See Erickson, 1993, p. 221. This is emphatically backed up in an analysis of women and property in the Cumbrian town Whitehaven, albeit in the later early modern period 1660–1750, in Churches, 1998, pp. 165 and 180.

45. Spring, 1993, pp. 41–2.

46. See examples in Emmison, 1976, pp. 95–102.

47. Whately, 1619, pp. 185–8.

48. See Stretton, 1994 on the equity court of Requests and copyhold inheritances, and Stretton, 1999 on a wider range of courts used and legal actions taken by women, including cases involving bonds, debts, and duties as executors of estates.

49. The proportion of sole executors who were wives was 80 per cent, according to Brodsky, 1986, p. 145.

50. Ibid., pp. 144–6.

51. The King redistributed a traitor's forfeited lands as reward or sold them. Before Henry VIII's 1534 Treason Act a conviction for treason would result in the forfeiture of lands held in fee-simple, but (except briefly during the last part of the reign of Richard II, from 1397) it had been necessary to obtain Parliamentary Acts of attainder to forfeit entailed lands, or lands held in use; see Bellamy, 1979, p. 34.

52. Baker, 1990b, p. 572.

53. See Plucknett, 1956, p. 567. The English witchcraft statutes of 1542 and 1604 specifically excluded disinheritance, as did the 1650 interregnum Act against incest, adultery, and fornication. Until 1870 some felonies did still result in disinheritance of the felon's family.

54. Abjuring the realm (swearing to leave the country for ever in lieu of standing trial) is described as an 'English invention' in Baker, 1990a, p. 9. The abjurer's land and chattels were forfeit to the King, and even if a pardon was later granted the goods would not be returned.

55. See Baker, 1990b, pp. 585–6.

56. See Sokol and Sokol, 2000, pp. 376–8.

57. Clarkson and Warren, 1942, pp. 204–6.

58. The widows of his barons were assured their dower in the coronation charter of Henry I (1100). Magna Carta confirmed rights to dower but with ambiguities and confusions that produced a period of 'transition'; see Loengard, 1993 and Walker, 1993.

59. The notion that property rights were simply not conferred in a private marriage by spousals alone is expressed, for instance, in Black, 1991, p. 33.

60. Pollock and Maitland, 1898, vol. 2, p. 375; Plucknett, 1956, p. 566; Loengard, 1985; Biancalana, 1988, pp. 257 and 288–92; Carlson, Eric Josef, 1994, p. 29; Outhwaite, 1995, pp. 5, 36 and 40.

61. Archer, 1984, p. 17. Smith, 1986, pp. 62–3, holds that really the problem was largely the practical one of obtaining sufficient independent evidence from witnesses that the marriage had taken place, other than just the widow's word, to allow the court to award dower in disputed cases.

62. This is translated from Bracton in Ward, Jennifer, 1995, p. 44.

63. Smith, 1986, pp. 63–4, commenting on Pollock and Maitland, 1898, vol. 2, p. 374.

64. Fitzherbert, 1652, pp. 367–8, first published 1534.

65. Coke, 1628, sections 36–55 (book 1, leaves 30–41).

66. Some local inheritance customs would allow the widow more, so for instance in gavelkind the widow was allowed a life interest in half the husband's property.

67. Plucknett, 1956, pp. 566–7.
68. Milsom, 1976, p. 167; Baker, 1990b, p. 308.
69. Milsom, 1976, p. 167; Baker, 1990b, p. 308.
70. Milsom, 1976, p. 167.
71. See Sokol and Sokol, 2000, pp. 125–8 and 222–3.
72. Clarkson and Warren, 1942, p. 135.
73. Spring, 1993, pp. 47–9. Stone, 1979, pp. 642–5, also shows that the Statute was to the husband's advantage. Yet Bonfield, 1983, p. 6, points out that there were some advantages to a widow to receive a jointure instead of dower.
74. Stone, 1979, p. 645. A sharp sixteenth-century dowry inflation at all social levels is discussed in O'Hara, 2000, especially pp. 191–3 and 207–12.
75. Erickson, 1993, p. 119, but see Reynolds, 1996, p. 331. A desired proportion of 10:1 between wealth and beauty is implied in Portia's wish to be, for her husband's sake, 'A thousand times more fair, ten thousand times more rich' (*MV* 3.2.154) – is there an allusion here to an emerging standard for jointures?
76. Erickson, 1993, p. 120.
77. Spring, 1993, p. 50.
78. Erickson, 1993, pp. 121–2.
79. Ibid., pp. 129–30.
80. Freebench inheritance of copyhold estates included only lands held at the time of death, not those held during life as in dower; see Plucknett, 1956, pp. 566–9.
81. They were less so for brides of yeomen and others, where less property meant the estate could not be subdivided and yet realistically provide for widows and heirs.
82. *WIV* 1.1.46–55. This seven hundred pounds appears to be hers absolutely, but of course becomes Fenton's upon her marriage. Emmison, 1978, p. 9, describes a provision in the 1567 will of Sir Richard Ryche for the marriage portions for his grand-daughters.
83. On possible complexities of Slender's jointure see Reynolds, 1996.
84. A few striking examples ranged roughly along the scale from condemnation to praise follow; the standard bibliographies of Shakespeare criticism and of feminist criticism provide many more. Maguire, 1995 sees 'uncivilized' male violence imaged in the play, and Katherina (or 'women animals and the environment') as a victim of this and not ennobled or positively transformed. Heffernan, 1985 sees an abusive bourgeois pattern of marriage nearly satirised by Petruchio's outrageousness, but that is too serious a matter for a comedy. Martin, 1991 finds the play less than the 'vexatious social comedy' of revisionist critics, because while it acknowledges the pressure of reforming or emancipating sexual ideals it (like the society) does not enact them. Kahn, 1975 finds that the submission of Kate to taming fulfils a stack of fantasies, the top one masculinist, the middle one feminist, and the deepest again serving men's needs. Bean, John C., 1980 sees the genuine humanising of Kate uncomfortably enclosed within a 'dehumanized' farcical plot. Mikesell, 1989 finds that the play 'deconstructs' both New Comedy and farcical 'threats' to allow Kate and Petruchio to strive for a 'viable, intimate marriage structured by hierarchy'. Daniell, 1984 sees a

good marriage arising from a mutual learning to use artistically contrived situations; their growth betters the fact that Katherina is no longer a shrew and Petruchio no longer a bully. Nevo, 1980, pp. 37–52, sees the shrew's marriage as a spiritually generous love-match with the super-asset of an unusual, great *joie de vivre*.

85. See, for instance, Heffernan, 1985, which deals with *SHR* and money, and Steadman, 1996, which treats the theme of dowries and inheritance and focuses on *SHR*, pp. 84–6. These note but do not analyse the offer made by Petruchio.

86. Jardine, 1983, p. 60.

87. Pettet, 1945 identifies Elizabethan dowry-seekers' borrowing to furnish their quest.

88. The man, his servant, and his horse are described in some of the finest comic prose ever written in *SHR* 3.2.43–69. This passage may also contain a masterly parody of the celebrated (and self-consciously proud of itself) word-portrait of a horse in *VEN* 293–300 (that is, if the play was written after the poem). In deliberate contrast to his appearance at the wedding, Petruchio has arranged for his household to be prepared with great care to receive Kate, putting among other things his 'servingmen in their new fustian, the white stockings, and every officer his wedding garment on' (*SHR* 4.1.40–3; see also 4.1.80–2, 4.1.101–2, 4.1.118–22 which underscore this), but this is done wholly out of the public view. Perret, 1983 thinks the household arrangements made by Petruchio are part of a training programme run to show Katherina how to be a housewife; Sokol, 1985 argues for a more paradoxical meaning for Petruchio's atypical fastidiousness, implying self-education.

89. Cook, 1991, p. 140, n. 80 critiques the readings in Kahn, 1975, Jardine, 1983, and Ranald, 1987. This note also correctly finds that a notion of reversion of dowries is 'wrongly' asserted in Jardine, 1983, p. 80. Such a reading is also crucial in the argument of Black, 1991, p. 40.

90. Ranald, 1979 calls the 'widowhood' named in *SHR* 2.1.123–5 a 'jointure', but seems to conflate the term with 'dower' in a note, pp. 69–70. Boose, 1982, p. 344, n. 13, follows Ranald. Boose, 1988, p. 245, again suggests a jointure is implicit in Petruchio's marriage settlement in *SHR*, and this leads to Kate's ritual prostration and offering of her hand for stepping on in 5.2.

91. Cook, 1981, p. 86.

92. Ibid., pp. 88 and 89.

93. Cook, 1991, p. 140.

94. Nor can Gremio guarantee an eventual inheritance, for after the 1540 Statute of Wills (32 Hen. VIII c.1) a will could be changed at any time before death.

95. Coke, 1628, section 40 (book 1, leaves 35–6).

96. Schoenbaum, 1985, p. 52, revises Schoenbaum's earlier belief that Anne received a customary *legitim* in chattels, but still sees her dower rights maintained.

97. Schoenbaum, 1986, p. 274.

98. Sokol, 1985, pp. 314–15. This is argued on the basis of the play's unique analysis of 'forward' versus 'froward' tendencies, this language and concept taken from *The Faerie Queene*.

99. It does not contradict, but accords with, some feminist readings, such as Dusinberre, 1975, pp. 105–10, that find in the play's outcome mutuality between Petruchio and Katherina.

AN AFTERWORD ON METHOD

1. Baker, 2000, p. 84.
2. See Ward, Ian, 1995, pp. 3–56, and Ward, Ian, 1999, pp. 1–19.
3. Ward, Ian, 1995, pp. 4–22.
4. The 1604 Act of Parliament against witchcraft, 1 Jac. I, c.12, replaced 5 Eliz., c.16, and stood until repealed in 1736. Although this act was more severe than the earlier statutes of 1542 and 1563, its severity still fell far short of many early modern continental laws.
5. See Collinson, 1994, pp. 222–3 and chapter 5 above on the marriage provisions of the Elizabethan Act of Uniformity. Another example would be the operations of jury mitigation, discussed in Sokol and Sokol, 2000, pp. 173–6.
6. Our sort of studies can contribute to the three approaches to the study of social structures identified by Keith Wrightson in Wrightson, 1986. Firstly, legal commentaries, treatises, and political admonitions can contribute greatly to investigations of contemporary perceptions of the social order, including hierarchies and ranking, and challenges to these. Secondly, Wrightson's 'social–distributional approach' which investigates quantitative historical evidence also needs to draw on legal–historical material. For example, the vexed question of how litigious early modern society really was can only be answered by detailed analysis of a variety of local and national court records. Finally, legal history may contribute to the investigation of social relations, which is Wrightson's third kind of approach to understanding the social order. For example, an understanding of the application of the legal doctrine of coverture, and of the laws concerning dower and jointure, can contribute to an appreciation of gender relations in early modern England.
7. See Laslett, 1965, pp. 22–52, and the comments in Wrightson, 1986, p. 178.

Bibliography

Adams, J. (1946). 'Nullius Filius', *University of Toronto Law Journal* 6: 361–84.

Adelman, Janet (1989). 'Bed Tricks: on Marriage as the End of Comedy in *All's Well That Ends Well* and *Measure for Measure*', in *Shakespeare's Personality*. Ed. Norman N. Holland, Sidney Homan, and Bernard J. Paris. 151–74. Berkeley: University of California Press.

Alleman, Gellert Spencer (1942). *Matrimonial Law and the Materials of Restoration Comedy*. Philadelphia: University of Pensylvania.

Amussen, Susan Dwyer (1994). 'Violence and Domestic Violence in Early Modern England', *Journal of Women's History* 6,1: 69–89.

Archer, Rowena E. (1984). 'Rich Old Ladies: the Problem of Late Medieval Dowagers', in *Property and Politics: Essays in Later Medieval English History*. Ed. Tony Pollard. 13–31. Gloucester: Alan Sutton.

Ariès, Philippe (1973). *Centuries of Childhood: A Social History of Family Life*. In French, 1960. Reprint of translation by Robert Baldick, first published by Jonathan Cape, London, 1962. Harmondsworth: Penguin.

Atkinson, David (1986). 'Marriage Under Compulsion in English Renaissance Drama', *English Studies* 67: 483–504.

Aubrey, John (1983). *Brief Lives*. Ed. Richard Barber. London: Book Club Associates.

Aveling, Hugh (1963). 'The Marriage of Catholic Recusants, 1559–1642', *Journal of Ecclesiastical History* 14: 68–83.

Babula, William (1977). 'The Character and the Conclusion: Bertram and the Ending of *All's Well That Ends Well*', *South Atlantic Review* 42: 94–100.

Baker, J. H. (ed.) (1978). *The Reports of Sir John Spellman*. Vol. 94. London: Selden Society.

(1985). 'Law and Legal Institutions', in *William Shakespeare: His World, His Work, His Influence*. Ed. John F. Andrews. 3 vols. Vol 1. 41–54. New York: Scribner's.

(1986). 'Criminal Courts and Procedure, 1550–1800', in *The Legal Profession and the Common Law*. 259–301. London: Hambledon.

(1990a). 'The English Law of Sanctuary', *Ecclesiastical Law Journal* 2: 8–13.

(1990b). *An Introduction to English Legal History*. Third edition. London: Butterworths.

(1993). 'Famous English Canon Lawyers: Henry Swinburne', *Ecclesiastical Law Journal* 3: 5–9.

(2000). 'Why the History of English Law Has Not Been Finished', *Cambridge Law Review* 59: 62–84.

Bald, R. C. (1986). *John Donne: A Life*. Corrected edition, originally 1970. Oxford: Clarendon Press.

Barnes, Thomas G. (1977). 'Star Chamber and the Sophistication of the Criminal Law', *Criminal Law Review*: 316–26.

Barton, Anne (1994). *Essays, Mainly Shakespearean*. Cambridge University Press.

Bashar, Nazife (1983). 'Rape in England between 1550 and 1700', in *The Sexual Dynamics of History*. Ed. London Feminist History Group. 28–42. London: Pluto Press.

Bassnett-McGuire, Susan (1984). 'An Ill Marriage in an Ill Government: Patterns of Unresolved Conflict in *All's Well That Ends Well*', *Shakespeare-Jahrbuch* (*Weimar*) 120: 97–102.

Bate, Jonathan (ed.) (1995). William Shakespeare, *Titus Andronicus*. Third Arden edition. London: Routledge.

Bateson, Mary (ed.) (1906). *Borough Customs II*. Vol. 21. London: The Selden Society.

Bean, J. M. W. (1968). *The Decline of English Feudalism*. Manchester University Press.

Bean, John C. (1974). 'Passion versus Friendship in the Tudor Matrimonial Handbooks and Some Shakespearean Implications', *Wascana Review* 9: 231–40.

(1980). 'Comic Structure and the Humanizing of Kate in *The Taming of the Shrew*', in *The Woman's Part: Feminist Criticism of Shakespeare*. Ed. Carolyn R. S. Lenz, Gayle Greene, and Carol Thomas Neely. 65–78. Urbana: University of Illinois Press.

Beauregard, David N. (1999). '"Inspired merit": Shakespeare's Theology of Grace in *All's Well That Ends Well*', *Renascence* 51: 219–39.

Bell, H. E. (1953). *An Introduction to the History and Records of the Court of Wards and Liveries*. Cambridge University Press.

Bellamy, John (1970). *The Law of Treason in England in the Later Middle Ages*. Cambridge University Press.

(1973). *Crime and Public Order in England in the Later Middle Ages*. London: Routledge & Kegan Paul.

(1979). *The Tudor Law of Treason*. London: Routledge & Kegan Paul.

Belsey, Catherine (1999). *Shakespeare and the Loss of Eden: The Construction of Family Values in Early Modern Culture*. Houndsmill: Macmillan.

Bennett, Robert B. (1993). 'The Law Enforces Itself: Richard Hooker and the Law against Fornication in *Measure for Measure*', *Shakespeare and Renaissance Association of West Virginia: Selected Papers* 16: 43–51.

Berger, Harry, Jr (1981). 'Marriage and Mercifixation in *The Merchant of Venice*: The Casket Scene Revisited', *Shakespeare Quarterly* 22: 155–62.

(1982). 'Against the Sink-a-Pace: Sexual and Family Politics in *Much Ado about Nothing*', *Shakespeare Quarterly* 33: 302–13.

Bernthal, Craig A. (1991). 'Treason in the Family: the Trial of Thumpe v Horner', *Shakespeare Quarterly* 42: 44–54.

(1992). 'Staging Justice: James I and the Trial Scenes of *Measure for Measure*', *SEL: Studies in English Literature, 1500–1900* 32: 247–69.

Berry, Edward (1984). *Shakespeare's Comic Rites*. Cambridge University Press.

Biancalana, Joseph (1988). 'Widows at Common Law: the Development of Common Law Dower', *Irish Jurist* 23: 255–329.

Black, James (1991). 'The Latter End of Prospero's Commonwealth', *Shakespeare Survey* 43: 29–41.

Blackstone, William (1766). *Commentaries on the Laws of England*. 4 vols. Oxford: Clarendon Press.

Blayney, Glenn H. (1956). 'Wardship in English Drama (1600–1650)', *Studies in Philology* 53: 470–84.

Bonfield, Lloyd (1983). *Marriage Settlements, 1601–1740: The Adoption of the Strict Settlement*. Cambridge University Press.

(1986). 'Normative Rules and Property Transmission: Reflections on the Link between Marriage and Inheritance in Early Modern England', in *The World We Have Gained*. Ed. Lloyd Bonfield, Richard M. Smith, and Keith Wrightson. 155–76. Oxford: Basil Blackwell.

Boone, Joseph Allen (1987). *Tradition Counter Tradition: Love and the Form of Fiction*. University of Chicago Press.

Boose, Lynda E. (1982). 'The Father and the Bride in Shakespeare', *PMLA* 97: 325–47.

(1988). 'The Comic Contract and Portia's Golden Ring', *Shakespeare Studies* 20: 241–54.

Booty, John E. (ed.) (1976). *The Book of Common Prayer 1559*. Washington: Folger Library.

Bowen, Catherine Drinker (1957). *The Lion and the Throne: The Life and Times of Sir Edward Coke 1552–1634*. London: Hamish Hamilton.

Bowers, Roger (2000). 'The Chapel Royal, the First Edwardian Prayer Book, and Elizabeth's Settlement of Religion, 1559', *The Historical Journal* 43: 317–44.

Bracton (1968). *On the Laws and Customs of England*. Trans. Samuel E. Thorne. Ed. George E. Woodbine. Cambridge, MA: Harvard University Press.

Bradshaw, Graham (1992). 'Obeying the Time in *Othello*: a Myth and the Mess It Made', *English Studies* 73: 211–28.

Bray, Gerald (ed.) (1994). *Documents of the English Reformation*. Cambridge: James Clark.

(2000). *Tudor Church Reform: The Henrician Canons of 1535 and the Reformatio Legum Ecclesiasticarum*. London: Church of England Record Society.

Brennan, Michael G. (1990). '"Now gods, stand up for bastards" (*King Lear*, I.ii.22) and the Epistle to the Hebrews 12:5–8', *Notes and Queries* 37: 186–8.

Brinkworth, E. R. C. (1972). *Shakespeare and the Bawdy Court of Stratford*. London: Phillmore.

Britton (1865). Ed. Francis Morgan Nichols. 2 vols. Oxford: Clarendon Press.

Brodsky, Vivien (1986). 'Widows in Late Elizabethan London: Remarriage, Economic Opportunity and Family Orientation', in *The World We Have Gained*. Ed. Lloyd Bonfield, Richard M. Smith, and Keith Wrightson. 122–54. Oxford: Basil Blackwell.

Brooke, Christopher N. L. (1981). 'Marriage and Society in the Central Middle Ages', in *Marriage and Society: Studies in the Social History of Marriage*. Ed. R. B. Outhwaite. 17–34. London: Europa.

Brown, Roger Lee (1981). 'The Rise and Fall of the Fleet Marriages', in *Marriage and Society: Studies in the Social History of Marriage*. Ed. R. B. Outhwaite. 117–36. London: Europa.

Brundage, James A. (1987). *Law, Sex, and Christian Society in Medieval Europe*. University of Chicago Press.

(1992). 'Widows as Disadvantaged Persons in Medieval Canon Law', in *Upon my Husband's Death: Widows in the Literature and Histories of Medieval Europe*. Ed. Louise Mirrer. 193–206. Ann Arbor: University of Michigan Press.

(1993). *Sex, Law and Marriage in the Middle Ages*. Aldershot: Variorum.

Bullard, J. V. (ed.) (1934). *Constitutions and Canons Ecclesiastical 1604: Latin and English*. London: Faith Press.

Cacicedo, Alberto (1995). '"She is fast my wife": Sex, Marriage, and Ducal Authority in *Measure for Measure*', *Shakespeare Studies* 23: 187–209.

Cairncross, Andrew S. (ed.) (1992). William Shakespeare, *King Henry VI, Part 1*. London: Routledge.

Camden, Caroll (1952). *The Elizabethan Woman: A Panorama of English Womanhood, 1540 to 1640*. London: Cleaver-Hume Press.

Cameron, A. (1978). 'Complaint and Reform in Henry VII's Reign: the Origins of the Statute of 3 Henry VII, c.2?', *Bulletin of the Institute of Historical Research*: 83–9.

Campbell, John Lord (1859). *Shakespeare's Legal Acquirements Considered*. London: John Murray.

Campbell, Julie D. (1997). '*Love's Victory* and *La Mirtilla* in the Canon of Renaissance Tragicomedy: an Examination of the Influence of Salon and Social Debates', *Women's Writing* 4: 103–24.

Campbell, Ruth (1985). 'Sentence of Death by Burning for Women', *The Journal of Legal History* 5: 44–59.

Carlson, Cindy (1996). 'Trials of Marriage in *Measure for Measure*', *Shakespeare Yearbook* 6: 355–81.

Carlson, Eric Josef (1990). 'Marriage Reform and the Elizabethan High Commission', *The Sixteenth Century Journal* 21: 437–51.

(1992). 'Clerical Marriage and the English Reformation', *The Journal of British Studies* 31: 1–31.

(1994). *Marriage and the English Reformation*. Oxford: Blackwell.

Carter, John Marshall (1985). *Rape in Medieval England*. Lanham, MD: University Press of America.

Catty, Jocelyn (1999). *Writing Rape, Writing Women in Early Modern England*. Manchester University Press.

Churches, Christine (1998). 'Women and Property in Early Modern England: a Case Study', *Social History* 23: 165–250.

Cioni, Maria L. (1982). 'The Elizabethan Chancery and Women', in *Tudor Rule and Revolution: Essays for G. R. Elton*. Ed. John W. McKenna and Delloyd J. Guth. 159–82. Cambridge University Press.

(1985). *Women and Law in Elizabethan England with Particular Reference to the Court of Chancery*. New York: Garland Publishing.

Clare, Janet (1999). *'Art made tongue-tied by authority': Elizabethan and Jacobean Dramatic Censorship*. Manchester University Press.

Clark, Elaine (1985). 'The Custody of Children in English Manor Courts', *Law and History Review* 3: 333–48.

Clarke, W. K. L. (1936). *Liturgy and Worship*. London: Society for Promoting Christian Knowledge.

Clarkson, Paul S., and Clyde T. Warren (1942). *The Law of Property in Shakespeare and the Elizabethan Drama*. Baltimore: Johns Hopkins Press.

Cockburn, J. S. (1977). 'The Nature and Incidence of Crime in England 1559–1625: a Preliminary Survey', in *Crime in England*. Ed. J. S. Cockburn. 49–71. London: Methuen.

Cohen, Eileen Z. (1986). '"Virtue is bold": the Bed-trick and Characterization in *All's Well That Ends Well* and *Measure for Measure*', *Philological Quarterly* 65: 71–86.

Coke, Edward (1628). *A Commentarie upon Littleton (The First Part of the Institutes of the Lawes of England)*. London.

(1747). *The Fourth Part of the Institutes of the Laws of England*. London.

(1797). *Second, Third, and Fourth Parts of the Institutes of the Laws of England*. 3 vols. London: E. and R. Brooke.

Collinson, Patrick (1967). *The Elizabethan Puritan Movement*. London: Jonathan Cape.

(1988). *The Birthpangs of Protestant England: Religious and Cultural Change in the Sixteenth and Seventeenth Centuries*. Houndsmill: Macmillan.

(1994). *Elizabethan Essays*. London: Hambledon Press.

Cook, Ann Jennalie (1977). 'The Mode of Marriage in Shakespearean England', *Southern Humanities Review* 11: 126–32.

(1981). 'Wooing and Wedding: Shakespeare's Dramatic Distortion of the Customs of His Time', in *Shakespeare's Art from a Comparative Perspective*. Ed. Wendell M. Aycock. 83–101. Lubbock: Texas Tech Press.

(1990). 'The Transformation of Stage Courtship', in *The Elizabethan Theatre XI. Papers Given at the Eleventh International Conference on Elizabethan Theatre Held at the University of Waterloo, Waterloo, Ontario, in July 1985*. Ed. A. L. Magnusson and C. E. McGee. 155–75. Port Credit, Ontario: Meany.

(1991). *Making a Match: Courtship in Shakespeare and his Society*. Princeton University Press.

Cornish, W. R., and G. de N. Clark (1989). *Law and Society in England, 1750–1950*. London: Sweet and Maxwell.

Crankshaw, D. J. (1998). 'Preparations for the Canterbury Provincial Convocation of 1562–63: a Question of Attribution', in *Belief and Practice in Reformation England: A Tribute to Patrick Collinson from his Students*. Ed. S. Wabuda and C. Litzenberger. 60–94. Aldershot: Ashgate.

Crawford, Patricia, and Sara H. Mendelson (1998). *Women in Early Modern England*. Oxford: Clarendon Press.

Cressy, David (1997). *Birth, Marriage and Death: Ritual, Religion and the Life-Cycle in Tudor and Stuart England*. Oxford University Press.

Croft, Pauline (1983). 'Wardship in the Parliament of 1604', *Parliamentary History* 2: 39–48.

Cunningham, Karen (1994). 'Female Fidelities on Trial', *Renaissance Drama* 25: 1–31.

Dalton, Michael (1635). *The Countrey Justice, Containing the Practice of the Justices of the Peace out of their Sessions, Gathered for the Better Helpe of such Justices of the Peace as have not been much conversant in the Studie of the Lawes of this Realme*. London.

Daniell, David (1984). 'The Good Marriage of Katherine and Petruchio', *Shakespeare Survey* 37: 23–31.

Dash, Irene G. (1981). *Wooing, Wedding, and Power: Women in Shakespeare's Plays*. New York: Columbia University Press.

Davies, J. Conway (1954). 'Elizabethan Plans and Proposals for Education', *Durham Research Review* 2: 1–5.

Davies, Kathleen M. (1981). 'Continuity and Change in Literary Advice on Marriage', in *Marriage and Society: Studies in the Social History of Marriage*. Ed. R. B. Outhwaite. 58–80. London: Europa.

Dickens, A. G. (1967). *The English Reformation*. London: Fontana Collins.

Doggett, Maeve E. (1992). *Marriage, Wife-Beating and Law in Victorian England*. London: Weidenfeld and Nicolson.

Dolan, Frances E. (1992a). 'Home Rebels and House-Traitors: Murderous Wives in Early Modern England', *Yale Journal of Law and the Humanities* 4: 1–31.

(1992b). 'The Subordinate('s) Plot: Petty Treason and the Forms of Domestic Rebellion', *Shakespeare Quarterly* 43: 317–40.

(1994). *Dangerous Familiars: Representations of Domestic Crime in England 1500–1700*. Ithaca, NY: Cornell University Press.

Donaghue, Charles (1983). 'The Canon Law on the Formation of Marriage and Social Practice in the Later Middle Ages', *Journal of Family History* 8: 144–58.

Donne, John (1960). *Poems*. Ed. Sir Herbert Grierson. Oxford University Press.

Doyle, Sheila (1998). 'An Uncompleted Work by Henry Swinburne on Matrimony', *The Journal of Legal History* 19: 162–72.

Draper, J. W. (1938). 'Bastardy in Shakespeare's Plays', *Shakespeare Jahrbuch* 74: 123–36.

Dreher, Diane Elizabeth (1986). *Domination and Defiance: Fathers and Daughters in Shakespeare*. Lexington: University Press of Kentucky.

Dubrow, Heather (1999). *Shakespeare and Domestic Loss*. Cambridge University Press.

Durant, David N. (1999). *Bess of Hardwick: Portrait of an Elizabethan Dynast.* London: Peter Owen.

Dusinberre, Juliet (1975). *Shakespeare and the Nature of Women.* London: Macmillan.

Elliott, Vivien Brodsky (1981). 'Single Women in the London Marriage Market: Age, Status and Mobility, 1598–1619', in *Marriage and Society: Studies in the Social History of Marriage.* Ed. R. B. Outhwaite. 81–100. London: Europa.

Elton, William R. (1966). *King Lear and the Gods.* San Marino, CA: The Huntington Library.

Emmison, F. G. (1973). *Elizabethan Life: Morals and the Church Courts.* Chelmsford: Essex County Council.

(1976). *Elizabethan Life: Home, Work and Land.* Chelmsford: Essex County Council.

(1978). *Elizabethan Life: Wills of Essex Gentry and Merchants.* Chelmsford: Essex County Council.

Empson, William (1952). *The Structure of Complex Words.* London: Chatto & Windus.

Erickson, Amy Louise (1993). *Women and Property in Early Modern England.* London: Routledge.

Ernst, D. R. (1984). 'The Moribund Appeal of Death', *American Journal of Legal History* 28: 164–88.

Farrer, F. E. (1917). 'The Bastard Eigne', *Law Quarterly Review* 33: 135–53.

Finch, Andrew J. (1990). 'Parental Authority and the Problem of Clandestine Marriage in the Later Middle Ages', *Law and History Review* 8: 189–204.

Findlay, Alison (1994). *Illegitimate Power: Bastardy in English Renaissance Drama.* Manchester University Press.

Finn, Margot (1996). 'Women, Consumption and Coverture in England, c. 1760–1860', *The Historical Journal* 39: 703–22.

Firth, C. H., and R. S. Rait (eds.) (1911). *Acts and Ordinances of the Interregnum 1642–1660.* 3 vols. London: His Majesty's Stationery Office.

Fisch, Harold (1974). 'Shakespeare and the Puritan Dynamic', *Shakespeare Survey* 27: 81–92.

Fitzherbert, Anthony (1652). *New Natura Brevium.* London.

Flandrin, Jean-Louis (1979). *Families in Former Times.* Trans. Richard Southern. London: Cambridge University Press.

Forker, Charles R. (1990). *Fancy's Images: Contexts, Settings, and Perspectives in Shakespeare and his Contemporaries.* Carbondale: Southern Illinois University Press.

Fortier, Mark (1996). 'Married with Children: *The Winter's Tale* and Social History; or, Infanticide in Earlier Seventeenth-Century England', *Modern Language Quarterly* 57: 579–603.

Foyster, Elizabeth (1996). 'Male Honour, Social Control and Wife Beating in Late Stuart England', *Transactions of the Royal Historical Society* 6: 215–24.

(1999a). *Manhood in Early Modern England: Honour, Sex and Marriage.* Harlow: Longman.

(1999b). 'Marrying the Experienced Widow in Early Modern England: the Male Perspective', in *Widowhood in Medieval and Early Modern Europe*. Ed. Sandra Cavallo and Lyndan Warner. 108–24. Harlow: Longman.

(2001). 'Parenting Was for Life, Not Just for Childhood: the Role of Parents in the Married Lives of their Children in Early Modern England', *History* 283: 313–27.

Friedman, Michael D. (1995). '"Service is no heritage": Bertram and the Ideology of Procreation', *Studies in Philology* 92: 80–101.

Furnivall, Frederick J. (ed.) (1887). *Child-Marriages, Divorces, and Ratifications, &c in the Diocese of Chester, A. D. 1561–6*. EETS o.s. 108. London: Kegan, Paul Trench, Trubner.

Gillis, John R. (1985). *For Better, For Worse: British Marriages 1600 to the Present*. Oxford University Press.

Glanvill (1993). *The Treatise on the Laws and Customs of the Realm of England Commonly Called Glanvill*. Ed. G. D. G. Hall. Oxford: Clarendon Press.

Gloucester, Edgar C. S. (ed.) (1910). *The First and Second Prayer Books of King Edward the Sixth*. London: J. M. Dent.

Gossett, Suzanne (1991). '"I'll look to like": Arranged Marriages in Shakespeare's Plays', in *Sexuality and Politics in Renaissance Drama*. Ed. Carole Levin and Karen Robertson. 57–74. Lampeter: Mellen.

Gouge, William (1622). *Of Domesticall Duties*. London.

Gowing, Laura (1994). 'Language, Power and the Law: Women's Slander Litigation in Early Modern London', in *Women, Crime and the Courts in Early Modern England*. Ed. Jenny Kermode and Garthine Walker. 26–47. London: UCL Press.

(1996). *Domestic Dangers: Women, Words, and Sex in Early Modern London*. Oxford: Clarendon Press.

Grivelet, Michel (1987). '"Word of Fear"', in *KM 80: A Birthday Album for Kenneth Muir*. 58–9. Liverpool University Press for Private Circulation.

Gurr, Andrew (1997). '*Measure for Measure*'s Hoods and Masks: the Duke, Isabella, and Liberty', *English Literary Renaissance* 27: 89–105.

Hagstrum, Jean H. (1992). *Esteem Enlivened by Desire*. London: University of Chicago Press.

Haigh, Christopher (ed.) (1987). *The English Reformation Revised*. Cambridge University Press.

Hamilton, Donna B. (1992). *Shakespeare and the Politics of Protestant England*. Louisville: University of Kentucky Press.

Hammond, Paul (1986). 'The Argument of *Measure for Measure*', *English Literary Renaissance* 16: 496–519.

Harding, Davis P. (1950). 'Elizabethan Betrothal and *Measure for Measure*', *Journal of English and Germanic Philology* 49: 139–58.

Hawkins, Harriett (1974). 'What Kind of Pre-Contract Had Angelo? A Note on Some Non-problems in Elizabethan Drama', *College English* 36: 173–9.

Hayne, Victoria (1993). 'Performing Social Practice: the Example of *Measure for Measure*', *Shakespeare Quarterly* 44: 1–29.

Head, David (1982). '"Beyng Ledde and Seduced by the Devyll": the Attainder of Lord Thomas Howard and the Tudor Law of Treason', *The Sixteenth Century Journal* 13: 3–16.

H[eale], W[illiam[(1609). *An Apologie for Women or An Opposition to Mr. Dr. G. his assertion. Who held in the Act of Oxforde. Anno. 1608. That it was lawfull for husbands to beate their wives.* Oxford.

Heffernan, Carol F. (1985). '*The Taming of the Shrew*: the Bourgeoisie in Love', *Essays in Literature* 12: 3–14.

Helmholz, R. H. (1969). 'Bastardy Litigation in Medieval England', *American Journal of Legal History* 12: 360–83.

(1974). *Marriage Litigation in Medieval England.* Cambridge University Press.

(1977). 'Support Orders, Church Courts, and the Role of *Filius Nullius*: a Reassessment of the Common Law', *University of Virginia Law Review* 63: 431–48.

(1987a). *Canon Law and the Law of England.* London: Hambledon.

(1987b). 'Canonists and Standards of Impartiality for Papal Judges Delegate', in *Canon Law and the Law of England.* 21–40. London: Hambledon.

(1987c). '*Legitim* in English Legal History', in *Canon Law and the Law of England.* 247–62. London: Hambledon.

(1990). *Roman Canon Law in Reformation England.* Cambridge University Press.

(1993). 'Married Women's Wills in Later Medieval England', in *Wife and Widow in Medieval England.* Ed. Sue Sheridan Walker. 165–82. Ann Arbor: University of Michigan Press.

Hennings, Thomas P. (1986). 'The Anglican Doctrine of the Affectionate Marriage in *The Comedy of Errors*', *Modern Language Quarterly* 47: 91–107.

Hill, W. Speed (1975). 'Marriage as Destiny: an Essay on *All's Well That Ends Well*', *English Literary Renaissance* 5: 344–59.

Hoby, Lady Margaret (1998). *The Private Life of an Elizabethan Lady: The Diary of Lady Margaret Hoby 1599–1605.* Ed. Joanna Moody. Stroud: Sutton Publishing.

Holdsworth, Sir William (1903–). *A History of English Law.* 14 vols. London: Methuen.

An Homilie of the State of Matrimonie (1968), in *Certaine Sermons or Homilies.* Ed. Mary Ellen Rickey and Thomas B. Stroup. Fac. 1623 edn. 239–48. Gainsville: Scholars' Facsimiles and Reprints.

Hopkins, Lisa (1998). *The Shakespearean Marriage: Merry Wives and Heavy Husbands.* Basingstoke: Macmillan.

Horwich, Richard (1992). '*The Merry Wives of Windsor* and the Conventions of Companionate Marriage', *Shakespeare Yearbook* 3: 31–43.

Hotine, Margaret (1990). '*Measure for Measure*: Further Contemporary Notes', *Notes and Queries* 37: 186–8.

Hotson, Leslie (1937). *I, William Shakespeare.* London: Jonathan Cape.

Houlbrooke, Ralph A. (1979). *Church Courts and the People during the English Reformation.* Oxford University Press.

(1984). *The English Family 1450–1700.* Harlow, Essex: Longman.

(1985). 'The Making of Marriage in Mid-Tudor England: Evidence from the Records of Matrimonial Contract Litigation', *Journal of Family History* 10: 339–52.

(1998). *Death, Religion and the Family in England 1480–1750*. Oxford: Clarendon Press.

Hunt, Maurice (1997). 'Slavery, English Servitude and *The Comedy of Errors*', *English Literary Renaissance* 27: 29–56.

Hunter, G. K. (ed.) (1959). *Shakespeare, All's Well that Ends Well*. London: Methuen.

Hurstfield, Joel (1958). *The Queen's Wards: Wardship and Marriage under Elizabeth I*. London: Longmans Green.

Ingram, Martin (1981). 'Spousals Litigation in the English Ecclesiastical Courts, c.1350–c.1640', in *Marriage and Society: Studies in the Social History of Marriage*. Ed. R. B. Outhwaite. 35–57. London: Europa.

(1985). 'The Reform of Popular Culture?: Sex and Marriage in Early Modern England', in *Popular Culture in Seventeenth-Century England*. Ed. Barry Reay. 129–65. Beckenham: Croom Helm.

(1987). *Church Courts, Sex and Marriage in England, 1570–1640*. Cambridge University Press.

(1996). 'Reformation of Manners in Early Modern England', in *The Experience of Authority in Early Modern England*. Ed. P. Griffiths, A. Fox, and S. Hindle. 47–88. Basingstoke: Macmillan.

Ives, E. W. (1978). '"Agaynst taking awaye of Women": the Inception and Operation of the Abduction Act of 1487', in *Wealth and Power in Tudor England*. Ed. E. W. Ives, R. J. Knecht, and J. J. Scarisbrick. 21–44. London: Athlone Press.

Jardine, Lisa (1983). *Still Harping on Daughters: Women and Drama in the Age of Shakespeare*. Hemel Hempstead: Harvester.

(1991). '"No offence i' th' world": *Hamlet* and Unlawful Marriage', in *Uses of History: Marxism, Postmodernism, and the Renaissance*. Ed. Francis Barker, Peter Hulme, and Margaret Iversen. 123–39. Manchester University Press.

Jeaffreson, John Cordy (1872). *Brides and Bridals*. 2 vols. London.

Johnson, James T. (1971). 'The Covenant Idea and the Puritan View of Marriage', *The Journal of the History of Ideas* 32: 117.

Jones, Emrys (1971). *Scenic Form in Shakespeare*. Oxford: Clarendon Press.

Jones, W. J. (1967). *The Elizabethan Court of Chancery*. Oxford: Clarendon Press.

Jonson, Ben (1925–52). *Works*. Ed. C. H. Herford, P. and E. Simpson. 11 vols. Oxford University Press.

Jordan, Constance (1994). 'Contract and Conscience in *Cymbeline*', *Renaissance Drama* 25: 33–58.

Kahn, Coppélia (1975). '*The Taming of the Shrew*: Shakespeare's Mirror of Marriage', *Modern Language Studies* 5: 88–102.

Keeton, George W. (1930). *Shakespeare and his Legal Problems*. London: A. & C. Black.

Kegl, Rosmary (1994). *The Rhetoric of Concealment*. Ithaca, NY: Cornell University Press.

Kent, Joan (1973). 'Attitudes of Members of the House of Commons to Regulation of Personal Conduct', *University of London Bulletin of the Institute of Historical Research* 46: 41–71.

Kerrigan, William (1999). *Shakespeare's Promises*. Baltimore: Johns Hopkins University Press.

Kirsch, Arthur (1981). *Shakespeare and the Experience of Love*. Cambridge University Press.

Kliman, Bernice W. (1982). 'Isabella in *Measure for Measure*', *Shakespeare Studies* 15: 137–48.

Knafla, Louis A. (1983). '"Sin of all Sorts Swarmeth": Criminal Litigation in an English County in the Early Seventeenth Century', in *Law, Litigants and the Legal Profession*. Ed. E. W. Ives and A. H. Manchester. 50–67. London: Royal Historical Society.

Kreps, Barbara (1999). 'When All Is True: Law, History, and Problems of Knowledge in *Henry VIII*', *Shakespeare Survey* 52: 166–82.

(2002). 'The Paradox of Women: the Legal Position of Early Modern Wives and Thomas Dekker's *The Honest Whore*', *ELH* 69: 83–102.

Kusunoki, Akiko (1995). '"Oh most pernicious woman": Gertrude in the Light of Ideas on Remarriage in Early Seventeenth-Century England', in *Hamlet and Japan*. Ed. Yoshiko Ueno. 169–84. New York: AMS Press.

Lambard, William (1592). *Eirenarcha: or the Offices of the Justices of the Peace revised, corrected and enlarged*. London.

Laslett, Peter (1965). *The World We Have Lost*. London: Methuen.

(1977). *Family Life and Illicit Love in Earlier Generations: Essays in Historical Sociology*. Cambridge University Press.

(1983). *The World We Have Lost: Further Explored*. Revised, first edition 1965. London: Methuen.

Latham, Agnes (ed.) (1975). *Shakespeare, As You Like It*. Second Arden edition. London: Methuen.

Laurence, Anne (1994). *Women in England 1500–1760*. London: Weidenfeld and Nicolson.

The Lawes Resolutions of Womens Rights: or, the Lawes Provision for Women (1632). London.

Lerner, Lawrence (1979). *Love and Marriage: Literature in its Social Context*. London: Edward Arnold.

Levin, Richard (1997). 'The Opening of *All's Well that Ends Well*', *Connotations: A Journal for Critical Debate* 7: 18–32.

Levine, David, and Keith Wrightson (1980). 'The Social Context of Illegitimacy in Early Modern England', in *Bastardy and its Comparative History*. Ed. Peter Laslett, Karla Oosterveen, and Richard M. Smith. 158–75. London: Edward Arnold.

Levine, Nina (1994). 'Lawful Symmetry: the Politics of Treason in *2 Henry VI*', *Renaissance Drama* 25: 197–218.

Lieblein, Leanore (1983). 'The Context of Murder in English Domestic Plays, 1590–1610', *SEL: Studies in English Literature, 1500–1900* 23: 181–96.

Lindley, David (1993). *The Trials of Frances Howard*. London: Routledge.

Liston, William T. (1991). 'Paradoxical Chastity in *A Midsummer Night's Dream*', *University of Dayton Review* 21: 153–60.

Loengard, Janet Senderowitz (1985). '"Of the Gift Of her Husband": English Dower and its Consequences in the Year 1200', in *Women of the Medieval World*. Ed. Julius Kirshner and Suzanne F. Wemple. 215–55. Oxford: Basil Blackwell.

  (1993). '*Rationabilis Dos*: Magna Carta and the Widow's "Fair Share" in the Earlier Thirteenth Century', in *Wife and Widow in Medieval England*. Ed. Sue Sheridan Walker. 59–80. Ann Arbor: University of Michigan Press.

Lowenthal, David (1996). 'The Portrait of Athens in *A Midsummer Night's Dream*', in *Shakespeare's Political Pageant: Essays in Literature and Politics*. Ed. Joseph Alulis and Vickie Sullivan. 77–88. Lanham, MD: Rowman and Littlefield.

MacCulloch, Diarmaid (1996). *Thomas Cranmer: A Life*. New Haven, CT: Yale University Press.

Macfarlane, Alan (1970). *The Family Life of Ralph Josselin: A Seventeenth-Century Clergyman*. Cambridge University Press.

  (1979). 'Review of *The Family, Sex and Marriage in England 1500–1800* by Lawrence Stone', *History and Theory* 18: 103–26.

  (1986). *Marriage and Love in England: Modes of Reproduction 1300–1840*. Oxford: Blackwell.

Maguire, Laurie E. (1995). 'Cultural Control in *The Taming of the Shrew*', *Renaissance Drama* 26: 83–104.

Maine, Henry Sumner (1930). *Ancient Law: Its Connection with the Early History of Society and its Relation to Modern Ideas*. London: John Murray.

Manning, Roger B. (1993). *Poachers and Hunters: A Cultural and Social History of Unlawful Hunting in England 1485–1640*. Oxford University Press.

Marcus, Leah S. (1988). *Puzzling Shakespeare: Local Reading and its Discontents*. London: University of California Press.

Marienstras, Richard (1981). *New Perspectives on the Shakespearean World*. Cambridge University Press.

Martin, Randall (1991). 'Kates for the Table and Kates of the Mind: a Social Metaphor in *The Taming of the Shrew*', *English Studies in Canada* 17: 1–20.

Matchinske, Megan (1998). *Writing, Gender, and State in Early Modern England*. Cambridge University Press.

McCabe, Richard A. (1993). *Incest, Drama and Nature's Law 1500–1700*. Cambridge University Press.

McFeely, Maureen Connolly (1995). '"This day my sister should the cloister enter": the Convent as Refuge in *Measure for Measure*', in *Subjects on the World Stage: Essays on British Literature of the Middle Ages and the Renaissance*. Ed. David G. Allen and Robert A. White. 200–16. Newark: University of Delaware Press.

McGlynn, Mary (1999). 'Buyer Beware: the Business of Marriage Contracts in Shakespeare's *Much Ado about Nothing*', in *Proceedings of the Seventh Northern Plains Conference on Early British Literature*. Ed. Jay Ruud. 90–100. Aberdeen, SD: Northern State University Press.

McGuire, Philip C. (1985). 'Silence and Genre: the Example of *Measure for Measure*', *Iowa State Journal of Research* 59: 241–51.

    (1989). 'Egeus and the Implications of Silence', in *Shakespeare and the Sense of Performance: Essays in the Tradition of Performance Criticism in Honor of Bernard Beckerman*. Ed. Ruth Thompson and Marvin Thompson. 103–15. Newark: University of Delaware Press.

McIlwain, Charles H. (ed.) (1918). *The Political Works of James I*. Cambridge, MA: Harvard University Press.

McLuskie, Kathleen (1989). *Renaissance Dramatists*. London: Harvester Wheatsheaf.

Mendelson, Sara H. (2002). 'Women and Work', in *Early Modern Women's Writing*. Ed. Anita Pacheco. 58–76. Oxford: Blackwell.

Metzger, Michael M. (1991). 'Of Princes and Poets: Lohenstein's Verse Epistles on the Divorce of the Elector Palatine Carl Ludwig', in *Literary Culture in the Holy Roman Empire, 1550–1720*. Ed. James A. Parente Jr, Richard Erich Schade, and George C. Schoolfield. 159–75. Chapel Hill: University of North Carolina Press.

Middleton, Thomas (1995). *A Mad World My Masters, and Other Plays*. Ed. Michael Taylor. Oxford University Press.

Mikesell, Margaret Lael (1989). '"Love wrought these miracles": Marriage and Genre in *The Taming of the Shrew*', *Renaissance Drama* 20: 141–67.

Milsom, S. F. C. (1976). *The Legal Framework of English Feudalism*. Cambridge University Press.

Montaigne, Michel, Lord of (1942). *Essays*. Trans. John Florio. 3 vols. London: J. M. Dent & Sons.

Mukherji, Subha (1996). '"Lawful deed": Consummation, Custom and Law in *All's Well that Ends Well*', *Shakespeare Survey* 49: 181–200.

Munden, R. C. (1978). 'James I and "the growth of mutual distrust": King, Commons, and Reform, 1603–4', in *Faction and Parliament: Essays on Early Stuart History*. Ed. Kevin Sharpe. 43–72. Oxford: Clarendon Press.

Murphy, Patrick M. (1997). 'Wriothesley's Resistance: Wardship Practices and Ovidian Narratives in Shakespeare's *Venus and Adonis*', in *'Venus and Adonis': Critical Essays*. Ed. Philip C. Kolin. 323–40. New York: Garland.

Nagarajan, S. (1963). '*Measure for Measure* and Elizabethan Betrothals', *Shakespeare Quarterly* 14: 115–19.

Nass, Barry (1996). 'The Law and Politics of Treason in Shakespeare's *Lucrece*', in *Shakespeare Yearbook 7*. Ed. Holger Klein, Peter Davidhazi, and B. J. Sokol. 291–311. Lewistown, NY: Edwin Mellen Press.

Nathan, Norman (1988). 'Othello's Marriage Is Consummated', *Cahiers Elisabethains: Etudes sur la Pre-Renaissance et la Renaissance Anglaises* 34: 79–82.

Neale, J. E. (1976). *The Elizabethan House of Commons*. London: Fontana.

Neely, Carol Thomas (1985). *Broken Nuptials in Shakespeare's Plays*. New Haven, CT: Yale University Press.

Neill, Michael (1993). '"In Everything Illegitimate": Imagining the Bastard in Renaissance Drama', *Yearbook of English Studies* 23: 270–92.

Nelson, T. G. A. (1998). 'Doing Things with Words: Another Look at Marriage Rites and Spousals in Renaissance Drama and Fiction', *Studies in Philology* 95: 351–73.

Nelson, T. G. A., and Charles Haines (1983). 'Othello's Unconsummated Marriage', *Essays in Criticism* 33: 1–18.

Nevo, Ruth (1980). *Comic Transformations in Shakespeare*. London: Methuen.

Nicholls, Mark (1992). '"As Happy a Fortune as I Desire": the Pursuit of Financial Security by the Younger Brothers of Henry Percy, 9th Earl of Northumberland', *Historical Review* 65: 296–314.

Norsworthy, Laura (1935). *The Lady of Bleeding Heart Yard: Lady Elizabeth Hatton 1578–1646*. London: John Murray.

Notestein, Wallace (1971). *The House of Commons 1604–1610*. London: Yale University Press.

Nuttall, A. D. (1975). '*Measure for Measure*: the Bed-Trick', *Shakespeare Survey* 28: 51–6.

O'Hara, Diana (2000). *Courtship and Constraint: Rethinking the Making of Marriage in Tudor England*. Manchester University Press.

Osborne, Bertram (1960). *Justices of the Peace 1361–1848*. Shaftesbury, Dorset: Sedgehill Press.

Outhwaite, R. B. (1995). *Clandestine Marriage in England, 1500–1850*. London: Hambledon.

Panek, Jennifer (2000). '"My Naked Weapon": Male Anxiety and the Violent Courtship of the Jacobean Stage Widow', *Comparative Drama* 34: 321–44.

Pearson, D'Orsay W. (1983). 'Renaissance Adolescent Marriage: Another Look at Hymen', *Cithara* 1: 17–27.

—— (1987). 'Male Sovereignty, Harmony and Irony in *A Midsummer Night's Dream*', *The Upstart Crow* 7: 24–35.

Pedersen, Frederik (2000). *Marriage Disputes in Medieval England*. London: Hambledon and London.

Pelling, Margaret (1999). 'Finding Widowers: Men Without Women in English Towns Before 1700', in *Widowhood in Medieval and Early Modern Europe*. Ed. Sandra Cavallo and Lydan Warner. 37–54. Harlow: Longman.

Perret, Marion (1983). 'Petruchio: the Model Wife', *SEL: Studies in English Literature, 1500–1900* 23: 223–35.

Pettet, E. C. (1945). '*The Merchant of Venice* and the Problem of Usury', *Essays and Studies* 31: 19–33.

Phillips, O. Hood (1967). 'The Law Relating to Shakespeare 1564–1964', *Law Quarterly Review* 80: 172–202.

—— (1972). *Shakespeare and the Lawyers*. London: Methuen.

Phillips, Roderick (1988). *Putting Asunder: A History of Divorce in Western Society*. Cambridge University Press.

Plucknett, T. F. T. (1956). *A Concise History of the Common Law*. Fifth edition. London: Butterworth.

Pollock, Sir Frederick, and F. W. Maitland (1898). *The History of English Law Before the Reign of Edward I*. Second edition, reissued 1968. 2 vols. Cambridge University Press.

Poole, Kristen (1995). 'Saints Alive! Falstaff, Martin Marprelate, and the Staging of Puritanism', *Shakespeare Quarterly* 46: 47–75.

Poos, L. R. (1995). 'The Heavy-Handed Marriage Counsellor: Regulating Marriage in Some Later-Medieval Ecclesiastical-Court Jurisdictions', *American Journal of Legal History* 39: 291–309.

Post, J. B. (1978). 'Ravishment of Women and the Statutes of Westminster', in *Legal Records and the Historian*. Ed. J. H. Baker. 150–64. London: Royal Historical Society.

(1980). 'Sir Thomas West and the Statute of Rapes, 1382', *Bulletin of the Institute of Historical Research* 53: 24–30.

Powell, Chilton Latham (1917). *English Domestic Relations 1487–1653*. New York: Columbia University Press.

Powers, Alan (1988). '"Meaner Parties": Spousal Conventions and Oral Culture in *Measure for Measure* and *All's Well That Ends Well*', *The Upstart Crow* 8: 28–41.

(1996). '*Measure for Measure* and Law Reform in 1604', *The Upstart Crow* 15: 35–47.

Prest, Wilfred R. (1991). 'Law and Women's Rights in Early Modern England', *The Seventeenth Century* 6: 169–87.

Prichard, R. E. (ed.) (1996). *Lady Mary Wroth, Poems, A Modernized Edition*. Keele University Press.

Priest, Dale G. (1980). 'Rosalind's Child's Father', *Notes and Queries* 27 (225): 166.

Proctor, F. (1955). *A New History of the Book of Common Prayer with a Rationale of its Offices*. Revised by Walter Howard Frere. London: Macmillan.

Purkiss, Diane (1992). 'Material Girls: the Seventeenth-Century Woman Debate', in *Women, Texts and Histories 1575–1760*. Ed. Clare Brant and Diane Purkiss. 69–101. London: Routledge.

Quaife, G. R. (1979). *Wanton Wenches and Wayward Wives: Peasants and Illicit Sex in Early Seventeenth-Century England*. London: Croom Helm.

Ranald, Margaret Loftus (1963). 'The Betrothals of *All's Well that Ends Well*', *Huntington Library Quarterly* 26: 179–192.

(1979). 'As Marriage Binds and Blood Breaks: English Marriage and Shakespeare', *Shakespeare Quarterly* 30: 68–81.

(1987). *Shakespeare and His Social Context: Essays in Osmotic Knowledge and Literary Interpretation*. New York: AMS Press.

Read, Conyers (1962). *William Lambarde and Local Government*. Ithaca, NY: Folger Shakespeare Library and Cornell University Press.

Reilley, Terry (2001). 'King Lear: the Kentish Forest and the Problem of Thirds', *Oklahoma City Law Review* 26: 379–401.

Reynolds, Simon (1996). 'The Lawful Name of Marrying: Contracts and Stratagems in *The Merry Wives of Windsor*', in *Shakespeare Yearbook 7*. Ed. Holger Klein, Peter Davidhazi, and B. J. Sokol. 313–31. Lewistown, NY: Edwin Mellen Press.

Roberts, Josephine A. (ed.) (1983). *The Poems of Lady Mary Wroth*. Baton Rouge: Louisiana State University Press.

Roscelli, William John (1962). 'Isabella, Sin and Civil Law', *University of Kansas City Review* 28: 215–27.

Rose, Mark (1989). 'Conjuring Caesar: Ceremony, History, and Authority in 1599', *English Literary Renaissance* 19: 291–304.

Rose, Mary Beth (1988). *The Expense of Spirit: Love and Sexuality in English Drama*. Ithaca, NY: Cornell University Press.

Russell, M. J. (1980). '2 Trial by Battle and the Appeals of Felony', *The Journal of Legal History* 1: 135–64.

Scarisbrick, J. J. (1974). *Henry VIII*. Harmondsworth: Penguin.

Schanzer, Ernest (1960). 'Marriage Contracts in *Measure for Measure*', *Shakespeare Survey* 13: 81–9.

Schoenbaum, S. (1985). 'William Bott, the Widow's Portion, and Shakespearean Biography', in *Shakespeare and Others*. Ed. S. Schoenbaum. 47–53. London: Scolar Press.

(1986). *William Shakespeare: A Compact Documentary Life*. Reprint of Oxford University Press edition, 1977. New York: New American Library.

Schofield, Roger (1986). 'Did the Mothers Really Die? Three Centuries of Maternal Mortality in "The World we have Lost"', in *The World We Have Gained*. Ed. Lloyd Bonfield, Richard M. Smith, and Keith Wrightson. 231–60. Oxford: Basil Blackwell.

Scott, Margaret (1982). '"Our City's Institutions": Some Further Reflections on the Marriage Contracts in *Measure for Measure*', *ELH* 49: 790–804.

Scouten, Arthur (1975). 'An Historical Approach to *Measure for Measure*', *Philological Quarterly* 54: 68–84.

Selden Society (1987). *A Centenary Guide to the Publications of the Selden Society*. London: The Selden Society.

Shaheen, Naseeb (1987). *Biblical References in Shakespeare's Tragedies*. Newark: University of Delaware Press.

(1989). *Biblical References in Shakespeare's History Plays*. Newark: University of Delaware Press.

(1993). *Biblical References in Shakespeare's Comedies*. Newark: University of Delaware Press.

(1997). 'A Note on *Troilus and Cressida*, II.iii.1–37', *Notes and Queries* 44: 503–5.

(1999). *Biblical References in Shakespeare's Plays*. Newark: University of Delaware Press.

Shakespeare, William (1968). *The First Folio*. Facsimile of 1623 prepared by Charlton Hinman. New York: W. W. Norton.

(1989). *The Complete Works*. Ed. Stanley Wells and Gary Taylor. Electronic edition. Oxford University Press.

(2001). *King Lear* (*Third Arden Edition*). Ed. R. A. Foakes. London: Thomson Learning.

Sharpe, J. A. (1980). *Defamation and Sexual Slander in Early Modern England: The Church Courts at York*. Borthwick Papers No. 58. York: University of York Borthwick Institute of Historical Research.

Sheehan, Michael M. (1996). *Marriage, Family, and Law in Medieval Europe: Collected Studies*. University of Toronto Press.

Shorter, Edward (1976). *The Making of the Modern Family*. London: Collins.

Simonds, Peggy Munoz (1989). 'Sacred and Sexual Motifs in *All's Well That Ends Well*', *Renaissance Quarterly* 42: 33–59.

Simpson, A. W. B. (1986). *A History of the Land Law*. Second edition. Oxford: Clarendon Press.

Smith, Richard M. (1986). 'Marriage Processes in the English Past: Some Continuities', in *The World We Have Gained*. Ed. Lloyd Bonfield, Richard M. Smith, and Keith Wrightson. 43–99. Oxford: Basil Blackwell.

Sokol, B. J. (1985). 'A Spenserian Idea in *The Taming of the Shrew*', *English Studies* 66: 310–16.

(1991). 'Figures of Repetition in Sidney's *Astrophil and Stella* and in the Scenic Form of *Measure for Measure*', *Rhetorica* 9: 131–46.

(1993). '*The Tempest*, "All torment trouble, wonder and amazement": a Kleinian reading', in *The Undiscover'd Country*. Ed. B. J. Sokol. 179–216. London: Free Association Books.

(1994a). *Art and Illusion in 'The Winter's Tale'*. Manchester University Press.

(1994b). 'Numerology in the Time Scheme of *The Tempest*', *Notes and Queries* 41: 53–5.

(1995). 'Constitutive Signifiers or Fetishes in *The Merchant of Venice*?', *International Journal of Psycho-Analysis*. 76: 373–87.

(1998). 'Prejudice and Law in *The Merchant of Venice*', in *Shakespeare Survey 51*. Ed. Stanley Wells. 159–73. Cambridge University Press.

Sokol, B. J., and Mary Sokol (1996). '*The Tempest* and Legal Justification of Plantation in Virginia', *Shakespeare Yearbook* 7: 353–80.

(1999a). 'Legal Terms Implying Extended Meanings in *As You Like It* III.ii.331–2 and *Troilus and Cressida* III.ii.89–91', *Notes and Queries* 46: 236–8.

(1999b). 'Shakespeare and the English Equity Jurisdiction: *The Merchant of Venice* and the Two Texts of *King Lear*', *Review of English Studies* 50: 417–39.

(2000). *Shakespeare's Legal Language*. London: Athlone.

(2002). 'Where are We in Legal–Historical Studies of Shakespeare?: The Case of Marriage and Property', in *Shakespearean International Yearbook 2*. Ed. John M. Mucciolo and W. R. Elton. 249–71. Burlington: Ashgate.

Sommerville, Margaret R. (1995). *Sex and Subjection: Attitudes to Women in Early Modern Society*. London: Arnold.

Spotswood, Jerald W. (1994). 'Isabella's 'Speechless Dialect': Subversive Silence in *Measure for Measure*', *Explorations in Renaissance Culture* 20: 107–25.

Spring, Eileen (1984). 'The Family, Strict Settlement and Historians', in *Law, Economy and Society, 1750–1914: Essays in the History of English Law*. Ed. G. R. Rubin and David Sugarman. 168–91. Abingdon: Professional Books.

(1993). *Law, Land and Family: Aristocratic Inheritance in England 1300–1800*. Chapel Hill and London: University of North Carolina Press.

Starkey, David (1985). *The Reign of Henry VIII*. London: George Philip.

The Statutes at Large of England (1811). 20 vols. London.

Staves, Susan (1990). *Married Women's Separate Property in England, 1660–1833*. Cambridge, MA: Harvard University Press.

Steadman, John M. (1996). '"Respects of Fortune": Dowries and Inheritances in Shakespeare, Spenser, and Marvell – an Overview', in *Shakespeare's Universe: Renaissance Ideas and Conventions: Essays in Honour of W. R. Elton*. Ed. John M. Mucciolo. 71–94. Aldershot: Scolar Press.

Stephen, Sir James Fitzjames (1883). *A History of the Criminal Law of England*. Vol. 3. London: Macmillan.

Stone, Lawrence (1977). *The Family, Sex and Marriage in England 1500–1800*. London: Weidenfeld and Nicolson.

(1979). *The Crisis of the Aristocracy, 1558–1641*. Revised, originally 1965. Oxford: Clarendon Press.

(1990). *Road to Divorce: England 1530–1987*. Oxford University Press.

(1992). *Uncertain Unions: Marriage in England 1660–1753*. Oxford University Press.

(1993). *Broken Lives: Separation and Divorce in England 1660–1857*. Oxford University Press.

Stretton, Tim (1994). 'Women, Custom and Equity in the Court of Requests', in *Women, Crime and the Courts in Early Modern England*. Ed. Jenny Kermode and Garthine Walker. 170–89. London: UCL Press.

(1998). *Women Waging Law in Elizabethan England*. Cambridge University Press.

(1999). 'Widows at Law in Tudor and Stuart England', in *Widowhood in Medieval and Early Modern Europe*. Ed. Sandra Cavallo and Lydan Warner. 193–208. Harlow: Longman.

(2002). 'Women, Property and Law', in *Early Modern Women's Writing*. Ed. Anita Pacheco. 40–57. Oxford: Blackwell.

Swinburne, Henry (1590). *A Briefe Treatise of Testaments and Last Willes*. London.

(1686). *A Treatise of Spousals or Matrimonial Contracts*. London.

Temkin, Jennifer (1987). *Rape and the Legal Process*. London: Sweet and Maxwell.

Thomas, Keith (1959). 'The Double Standard', *The Journal of the History of Ideas* 20: 195–216.

(1983). *Man and the Natural World: Changing Attitudes in England 1500–1800*. London: Allen Lane.

Thurston, Herbert (1904). 'The Canon Law of the Divorce', *English Historical Review* 19: 632–45.

Tiffany, Grace (1998). 'Puritanism in Comic History: Exposing Royalty in the Henry Plays', *Shakespeare Studies* 26: 256–87.

Tilney, Edmunde (1568). *A Briefe and Pleasaunt Discourse of the Duties of Marriage*. London.

Titlestad, P. J. H. (1988). 'Religion, Politics and Literature: the Elizabethan Background New Modelled', *Shakespeare in Southern Africa* 2: 42–50.

Todd, Barbara J. (1999). 'The Virtous Widow in Protestant England', in *Widowhood in Medieval and Early Modern Europe*. Ed. Sandra Cavallo and Lydan Warner. 66–83. London: Pearson.

Turner, Victor (1967). *The Forest of Symbols: Aspects of Ndembu Ritual*. Ithaca, NY: Cornell University Press.

Walker, Sue Sheridan (1982). 'Free Consent and Marriage of Feudal Wards in Medieval England', *Journal of Medieval History* 8: 123–34.

　　(1987). 'Punishing Convicted Ravishers: Statutory Strictures and Actual Practice in Thirteenth- and Fourteenth-Century England', *Journal of Medieval History* 13: 237–50.

　　(1988). 'Wrongdoing and Compensation: the Pleas of Wardship in Thirteenth- and Fourteenth-Century England', *The Journal of Legal History* 9: 267–307.

　　(1993). 'Litigation as Personal Quest: Suing for Dower in the Royal Courts, circa 1272–1350', in *Wife and Widow in Medieval England*. Ed. Sue Sheridan Walker. 81–108. Ann Arbor: University of Michigan Press.

Walton, Izaak (1966). *The Lives of Doctor John Donne, Sir Henry Wotton, etc.* Introduction by George Saintsbury. London: Oxford University Press.

Walzer, Michael (1965). *The Revolution of the Saints*. London: Weidenfeld and Nicolson.

Ward, Ian (1995). *Law and Literature: Possibilities and Perspectives*. Cambridge University Press.

　　(1996). 'The Political Context of Shakespeare's Constitutionalism', in *Shakespeare Yearbook 7*. Ed. Holger Klein, Peter Davidhazi, and B. J. Sokol. 275–90. Lewistown, NY: Edwin Mellen Press.

　　(1999). *Shakespeare and the Legal Imagination*. London: Butterworth.

Ward, Jennifer (1995). *Women of the English Nobility and Gentry, 1066–1500*. Manchester University Press.

Webster, John (1927). *The Complete Works*. Ed. F. L. Lucas. 4 vols. London: Chatto and Windus.

　　(1974). *The Duchess of Malfi*. Ed. John Russell Brown. Manchester University Press.

　　(1975). *The Devil's Law-Case*. Ed. Elizabeth M. Brennan. London: Ernest Benn.

Welsh, Alexander (1978). 'The Loss of Men and Getting of Children: *All's Well That Ends Well* and *Measure for Measure*', *The Modern Language Review* 73: 17–28.

Wentersdorf, Karl P. (1979). 'The Marriage Contracts in *Measure for Measure*: a Reconsideration', *Shakespeare Survey* 32: 129–44.

　　(1985). 'The Time Problem in Othello: a Reconsideration', *Shakespeare-Jahrbuch (Bochum)*: 63–77.

Whately, William (1619). *A Bride-Bush: or a Direction for Married Persons, Plainely Describing the Duties common to both, and peculiar to each of them*. London.

Whittick, Christopher (1984). 'The Role of the Criminal Appeal in the Fifteenth Century', in *Law and Social Change in British History*. Ed. J. A. Guy and H. G. Beale. 55–72. London: Royal Historical Society.

Wickham, Glynne (1980). '*The Two Noble Kinsmen* or *A Midsummer Night's Dream*, Part II?', in *The Elizabethan Theatre VII. Papers Given at the Seventh International Conference on Elizabethan Theatre Held at the University of Waterloo, Ontario, in July 1977*. Ed. G. R. Hibbard. 167–96. Hamden, CT: Archon Books.

Widmayer, Martha (1995). 'Mistress Overdone's House', in *Subjects on the World Stage: Essays on British Literature of the Middle Ages and the Renaissance*. Ed. David G. Allen and Robert A. White. 181–99. Newark: University of Delaware Press.

Wilkins, George (1964). *The Miseries of Enforced Marriage*. 1607. London: Malone Society Reprints.

Williamson, Marilyn L. (1986). *The Patriarchy of Shakespeare's Comedies*. Detroit: Wayne State University Press.

Wrightson, Keith (1980). 'The Nadir of English Illegitimacy in the Seventeenth Century', in *Bastardy and its Comparative History*. Ed. Peter Laslett, Karla Oosterveen, and Richard M. Smith. 176–91. London: Edward Arnold.

    (1982). *English Society 1500–1680*. London: Hutchinson.

    (1986). 'The Social Order of Early Modern England: Three Approaches', in *The World We Have Gained*. Ed. Lloyd Bonfield, Richard M. Smith, and Keith Wrightson. 179–202. Oxford: Basil Blackwell.

Young, Bruce W. (1988). 'Haste, Consent, and Age at Marriage: Some Implications of Social History for *Romeo and Juliet*', *Iowa State Journal of Research* 62: 459–74.

Index